REFLE

Wasyl Nimenko

Goalpath Books

REFLECTING

ISBN 978-1-908142-53-5

Published in Great Britain 2020

Copyright © Wasyl Nimenko 2020

Goalpath Books

Wasyl Nimenko was born in Ipswich, England. His mother was a staunch Catholic from the O'Dowd clan in the west of Ireland and his father was a staunch Atheist from Dnipropetrovsk in eastern Ukraine.

Wasyl studied medicine in London then psychotherapy with Anthony Storr and Ian Gordon-Brown. From 1982-1991 he worked with survivors of torture. He has worked independently, in the NHS and with the homeless.

Although Wasyl brings his experience from working in medicine and transpersonal psychology, the path he took is based on eastern spiritual disciplines and so the theme of his writing focuses on inner happiness. He began meditation in 1972 and is a frequent visitor to India.

ALSO BY WASYL NIMENKO

CONTENTS

OUR PLACE IN THE WORLD

OUR RESPONSE TO THE WORLD

TURNING INWARDS

REFLECTING

OUR PLACE IN THE WORLD

1. ANIMALS

Rescue Cat Trust Restored

She was thrown out and abandoned on the street with her five kittens who were rescued immediately from the cat rescue home. She was there for eighteen months, rejected, not wanted, passed by every day by everyone who wanted a cat.

Then we saw her. Her attitude was unfriendly, maybe even bitter and resentful, probably wounded by beatings, but shining through she was still her own self, with dignity.

One year after hiding everywhere, always hyper-vigilant, she suddenly refused to be alone. Everywhere you went inside or outside she was there for company, affection, her hyper-vigilance gone. She sits curled up anywhere, right now on a chair. A small bowl of water, milk in the mornings then out for mice. In the evening back in for company and purring.

Cats and Dogs

It is not that I don't socialise so much with humans, it's just that birds have a sweeter song. A dog unconditionally turns up to be stroked. A cat is honest about purring.

A cat will be with you; a dog will stay with you. They both miss you and they welcome you back.

Comparative Consciousness

When cats are still with their eyes open and awake are they just being still?

I ask because they seem to be and they seem to be able to be still better than us.

Peacocks

Some men and women think they are amazing to women and men. It's amusing to see them making a display like a peacock in keeping with the origin or the species.

Love and Affection Now

Cats and dogs help us mostly in one single simple way as they help us stay in the present moment.

They don't live in the past. They don't live in the future. They don't want to save up. They want things now. They don't delay affection. They show it immediately. They show their fear, their anger. Their love is on their face and tail.

Perhaps

It cannot be disputed that it is a lonely life not just for us but for animals too. It cannot be disputed that everything is moving and is part of life in some way. It cannot be disputed that animals may also think about this.

Present But Hidden

Cats don't seem happy or sad as they seem comfortable or looking for comfort. They don't like discomfort and leave to seek it elsewhere.

We too desire our happiness and we look for comfort too. But how many of us look for and find happiness, not knowing it is already here.

Wild Animal's Wisdom

Adaptive to everything seems to be the main quality of human thinking. Most of all, man respects wisdom to do the right thing and protect his own. Some endure pain until death for an ideal or a friend.

But others enjoy committing genocide or torturing to make an impression. Despite final warnings of our lethal intake of food, drugs or alcohol we can't override our own intelligence even until death.

How can this intelligence be so desirable when it is our worst quality not serving our interests as social animals?

When wild animals learn what we do they shy away from us and hide. We may be wise to follow.

Our Neurosis

Our neurotic traits, like the animals we force them on, are due to living like the animals we cage.

Education

I've learnt more from homeless people about people than I have from scholars, professors, doctors, teachers, bankers and lawyers.

I've learnt more about people from straight forward simple people than I have from scholars, professors, doctors, teachers, bankers and lawyers.

I have learnt more from animals about people than I have from scholars, professors, doctors, teachers, bankers and lawyers.

We are Not the Only Consciousness

We are not the only form of consciousness responding to stimuli which can mean life or consciousness. Flowers and animals don't want to die. Flowers and animals may worry about when they will die. The planet may also worry about when we will die.

Specialised

Flying, swimming and hibernating are for the eagle, shark and bear whilst our speciality is to think, but what is it for?

Not just to compete, survive or just to stay alive. Not to build and create so perhaps it is for consciousness of happiness of being.

The Mouse

When you think you have heard a mouse, everything else is put on hold, thoughts, feelings, everything in life for a mouse.

Why

The question animals do not ask is why? Maybe they see it as forbidden. They do know that they don't ask because sometimes they seem to know without asking.

How Very Dull We Are

If you have not written about your cat, perhaps your cat is not interesting apart from its desire for food. But look here at us, pretty much the same, our basic desires often changing the course of lives forever.

Not many cats have that degree of influence perhaps because they are only regarded as pets. We do have influence but only because we are regarded as human.

How very dull we are to make ourselves seem so much more important when compared with our cats who actually know they are superior.

2. EQUALITY

We Don't Know

We can never know what goes on inside another person's head. We don't even know what our next thought will be. With little humility, we speak as though we know others and ourselves.

Occasionally, an honest person who admits they don't know, makes us see most of what we say is based on our imaginings.

Others don't know any more than us, cannot predict their own behaviour or the weather. How much happier just to know you don't know.

Goalpaths

The path is none other than the goal; the goal is none other than the path, so you are at exactly where you are supposed to be.

Anywhere you try and go leads you back to right here on the path and at the goal. They are not in different times in different places.

Knowing truth is seeing you cannot gain what you already have.

Equal

Very careful not to get anything wrong to offend anyone's anxious traits in case they feel angry, in case they don't like me.

Hey, you know, so what. Can I do this for everyone my whole life? Do they and I need to grow up? Do we need to move on?

Manners are essential but I am not their servant, therapist or hired hand or stuck in any permanent role, I am equal.

A Bit Crazy

Sometimes I have to change where I sit just to see if I am seeing things right or to see if moving will magically change them.

Perhaps this is when things need changing and I can't see this yet, but I sense that something is peculiar.

Maybe this is intuition trying to bring itself to my attention.

All I can do is follow my feet and move to see a different position.

When I doubt this I think I'm a bit crazy but then If I was, I'd be the last to know.

So doubt is my close friend who can also seem strange.

The Nameless One

When we meet someone why do we feel compelled to give them a name? Why not have someone who is nameless whom we have no words to describe?

Do other creatures have names which fit things or do their instincts of danger, food, comfort and shelter guide them like they guide us?

Does the layer of words we see as our intelligence cover up our instincts so we can pretend not to be like other creatures? The naked truth is we are the same?

Equally we are what we are

As conscious as we can be in this world is the same for all but uniquely different for each of us. There are different levels which we can reach but we are all stopped by ourselves, others or events.

Comparisons

What they have done is a full and balanced life, whilst what I have done seems more chaotic, blown by a different wind. Taken far away and then back to where we all started, we didn't compare notes but we do compare now we are home.

The Thinking Altruistic Savage

Despite our good deeds or kindness you and I are still savages with a choice. A crafty predator with no sorrow for damage, destruction of life, families or communities.

Inconvenience is seen in the trails of our footprints after activities to encourage desires in others for our benefit.

Indifference, denial and arrogance, happily displaying anything obtained by deception, theft or force but especially thoughts.

The Same Minds but Different

Remembering Indonesian, Chinese, Indian, Brazilian saints, whether Hindu Christian Jewish Islamic or Buddhist shows respect for the lineage of what we see.

But what all of these uncover for us to see is we see the same. We have the same body and although we want to be special in who we are, we act the same in all our behaviours, each wishing for happiness. Like our fingerprints, our minds have different patterns but we are the same.

No Potential Future

The future is an illusion. It never existed. It will never exist just like the past, the future cannot exist. We have the potential to guess the future only if we use the ability to see what is already here, but we can never see the future.

Tigers

Why should we be so conscious and fulfilled that we will want to leave this body but tigers don't? Why should we need to have a reason to live but tigers don't?

Why should we be so attached to everything but tigers aren't?

Why is it we seem to have lost our minds whilst tigers haven't?

Inner Governor

You know where to find me. Well most of the time, even sometimes when you looked like you might lose it.

Something seems to catch you just before you can't be caught. Is this precision skill or an inner or outer guardian?

Not knowing, not believing and having no outer control, how can anything be managed except from inside.

3. KNOWING OUR PLACE

Being True to Our Self

When we are jealous that someone may take our position, perhaps we can be generous with that person. If they betray us, it was meant to be that we were true to our self rather that the need for position.

Meeting Again

On my way to a meeting I was asked why I was going. I said it was because I knew about torture. The person turned and walked away from me because I was not an academic.

I was talking with someone I was at college with, now a Knighted Professor. When I asked his Lady wife, "Are you a doctor too?" She turned on her heels in a huff and walked off as I had forgotten she had trained with us too.

Criticism

We can think and then actually believe that we are clever to criticise rather than look for the good. Criticising inflates our egos full of hot air whereas looking for the good shows us what we are.

Permanent Stillness

Since seventeen, when for the first time I was able to be
conscious in the peace and bliss or stillness, nothing has
changed.

The world with its people, buildings and landscapes looks
different on the outside but on the inside, everything is
exactly the same in stillness. It is good to know my place.

Non-Reunion

I nearly didn't recognise him at first because the epaulettes
fooled me into thinking it couldn't be him but it was.

'Hey old friend,' I called.
'I can't talk now,' he quickly replied. 'Later after I've finished
with these people,'

As he acknowledged the pearls on the civilian woman, he
thanked her for coming to lunch in the officer's mess.

A year later we met at a college reunion evening and he said,
'I'll be in touch when I start my new retirement post with a
charity.'

I emailed him a year later but my email wasn't replied
to after the London Gazette's announcement of his
Knighthood.

How happy it is to be simply happy with yourself.

Unstoppable Stillness

Up in the cool slopes of the hills and down on the sweltering plane the unshifting sense inside is the same.

Unmoved but connected, detached but moved, the heart is still beating with unstoppable stillness.

I am touched

I am touched by you asking when others would not penetrate, when others would not ask, when others would not express the sensitivity.

4. PRESENCE

The Presence

There is a sense of being in the presence like in a temple or on a mountain. When I peer at our mortality I can see us coming and going through this life, walking but still, passed through in a flash and all this will be gone. The landscape similar, just with new batches of us already coming and going.

Vigilant Presence

Stillness keeps up its permanent vigilant presence even when we sleep.

Happiness is Inside

Are there sacred places which you can experience to make you more yourself?

Where do you go when you want to hear someone to inspire you to go inwards to help make you see. Who do you go to?

When you want to be somewhere sacred to make you feel in the presence of something greater, where do you go?

When you want to experience something to make you more conscious, where do you go?

Presence of Ancestral strength

Whenever you go away, even to distant lands, it is only an apparent distance and time away from this heart and these hands. The illusion of time, letting you see with different eyes because you are somewhere different, drops away when difficulties arise. What has been relied on is tried and when the strength from ancestors is summoned, inner decisions are resolved.

Presence

There is an awareness of the intangible by our Inner self. There is an awareness of the same intangible, a presence in everything around us by our inner self. This is presence.

Present

For a while we are like a flower in bloom, full of our own colourful character with our own singular marks of identification. Our presence, briefly proud and unreproducible. Then gone but forever present.

Guesswork

How can you understand a presence when you walk into a room? Someone is just there. Words cannot describe our consciousness. Conscious of someone different, we can only see what their consciousness does to our consciousness.

The Power of Presence

Presence communicated effectively is more eloquent than words.
Presence is older than thoughts, older than words and lasts longer than words.
Thoughts captured just before they grow, recede and will go and let the self show.
Presence, a look, a glance, a sign, a pause or a moment is more than any word.

Absence

The brightest mind is not the person you relate to. The strongest hand the most beautiful face are not the person you relate to. The most deeply felt characteristic of someone is not what you see, what you hear or what you feel but their presence.

Dull Dull Dull

Dull we may look. Dull we may act. Dull we may seem but our dull thoughts only reflect our ego, not the presence of the shining brilliance of the inner light of the self.

Waking Up Happy

The presence of happiness at the start of a day cannot be compared. Nothing matches it, seems like it or feels like it. It can't get better but can carry on like the sun brightening everything.

Spark of Fire

Fire as a spark of light, like realisation, the fulfilment of consciousness, is the one wishing being the many.

Fire as a spark of light is the energy behind the passions of love and anger behind creation and destruction.

Fire is the nature of our heart, of what never ends and never starts.

Just Presence

What if I don't live? What if I don't get a chance to see this? Maybe it is just a presence I feel I wont see.

Maybe

I write in hope that you can look back at all of this and find something of value in these words because these words are traces of what is seen inside. They are a record that something of value went on and can go on in you too.

Love Itself

Fondness is from our heart only for certain people, whose love is precious, whose face is love itself.

Most Talk

All talk ends in silence so why do we indulge so much in talk? Is it a simple compulsion?

Perhaps we don't keep more quiet, thinking that talking is better than silence because talk is a release of nervousness.

In silence there is no nervousness, only the calmness of a mind disengaged.

In talk there is fear, friction, worry and many arguments but there is great peace in silence.

Endless talking can avoid being here in silent presence. In talk only words can be spoken but in silence volumes can be communicated.

Words cannot express the power of presence spoken through silence. All talk and words end in the stillness of silent consciousness.

Still Living in Hope

Someone with any sense would tell us all to shut up to keep quiet and be silent and be at peace with everyone.

Remnants

Little things remain of us, mementos of our hearts. They are not taken or left. They are just like we were.

Where Is It?

When the statues have all gone, all images put away, where is what is left of all that was our way.

It is not with the images which have all gone or the thoughts which imagined them but the self before the thoughts.

Our Presence

Perhaps all we can be is our presence. Perhaps all we give and leave is our presence, not our words or deeds. Perhaps all we can be is our presence.

5. MIRRORS

Relationships

A good relationship is more than a mirror of yourself. It is a mirror which not only talks back to you, it kicks you hard and steps hard on your foot.

If you are unhappy without a relationship having one won't always make you happy because you have to be happy to have one with yourself or a relationship will leave you.

To work, good enough relationships are like having a part time job as they always need regular focused attention and effort.

Mirror

Identifying with the sacredness of saint's faces and with the spirit of sacred spaces is a mirror.

When we stop looking at personalities and adornment our eyes are opening.

When all we see in the mirrors is our self, what we see is naked and at last we are awake.

Psychological Mirror

It is a surprise to suddenly see you've been trying to appear like a different person, not who you are.

It is a surprise to suddenly see you've been trying to appear like a smarter person, not who you are.

It is a surprise to suddenly see you've been trying to appear like a helpful person, not who you are.

It is a surprise to suddenly see you've been trying to appear like an honest person, not who you are.

It is a surprise to suddenly see you've been trying to appear like a sorted out person not who you are.

It is a surprise to suddenly see you've been trying to appear like someone else, not who you are.

Rear View Mirror

When you become the person you criticised. When you think the way they do, the person you thought you were has gone.

You can only accept yourself or change, you can turn your back on what you became, stand up, walk away and move on.

There is finding the centre again, finding what you really are with not too much rear view mirror gazing.

In the Mirror of the Self

You kept on trying to fool me in so many different ways and you nearly fooled me as the distractions were never ending.

But your game had to have an ending. It couldn't be kept up. It wasn't me I saw in the mirror because the collection of thoughts pretending to be me is not who I am.

6. ILLUSION OF THE EGO

AI

If you write down two thousand thoughts over a year or two, you see your ego has an endless appetite for taking up time and for seeming important when it is only an electrical circuit on autopilot.

It is artificial intelligence because it is not real. Real intelligence is consciousness without all the thinking.

No Rest Until the End

Finding the self and being the self has no end whilst the body is alive. The body's functions fool us into thinking we are just the body. Intelligently and with commitment it does its job.

There is a limitation as it cannot get behind what it thinks it is because thinking is limited by thinking. Being conscious is not thinking.

Inner and Outer Journeys

Getting on with people who you have to journey with until you decide to get off is choosing. We choose how much of our time we are in the world or in solitude, detached from things of the world.

Our Life

What our life looks like to me is being human but heavily
programmed by everyone to think we are the ego, the
collection of thoughts instead of the beautiful happiness
inside.

Humility and Modesty

Deceived by our own creation the ego, an illusion just
composed of thoughts we make a case for it and justify its
importance rather than be humble and modest.

Challenging

I look at what I have tried to do. Most of it has been
passionate challenging of inconvenient truths, sometimes
arguing with the home office on the phone. Sometimes
challenging psychiatrists, challenging fraud, challenging
thinking, but mostly challenging and accepting myself.

Painless

Thoughts are painful. They are not what we are told they
are. Without them we are happy, our true self.

There is

There isn't nothing

Putting on the Mask

Monday mornings are blank until I get in the car, then the scary part begins. I look at what I could face today and I have to let it happen. The adrenaline kicks in when I find my doctor persona. Then I find my doctor voice and I detach and watch.

Ignorance Gone

When there is nothing more to break down, there cannot be further suffering because there is no one to suffer. There is no fear of death as everything has been relinquished.

Happiness is Nothing

To be happy you need nothing. To be happier you need less. To be happiest you need the least. To be happy you need nothing.

Awards

Awards should decorate someone's life. Awards should punctuate their efforts. Awards should encourage others. If there were none perhaps these aims would work.

Awards and medals do not decorate the fallen or the workers but the privileged. Those who keep us sane don't need medals to keep going because they keep going by being true.

For Certain

There is no desire for happiness without suffering first. There is no desire for inner happiness without repeated suffering. Just when you think you have turned inside because you have suffered enough, you may begin suffering four times more.

This is only the beginning of turning inwards which repeats itself every day, seeming to get unbelievably worse to make sure there is nothing to turn outwards for.

There is no price for happiness. Everything has to go. What you thought was you is devoured. Everything has gone except happiness.

Brain Hard Drive

I say I am anxious about later today but what actually is the I that is anxious?

Is it the collection of thoughts and memories like information in a folder on a hard drive called Ego?

The thoughts are collected in electrical circuits in binary form electronically or chemically and electrically in our brain.

Who identifies them or denies them? That observer is the self.

Un-negotiable

You cannot negotiate with the Self as you cannot negotiate with God.

Suburbia

I am not a suburban animal with walls to threaten me, to tick boxes for my food. I would rather be in the wild foraging or begging for my food, which is what the world is.

7. INFLUENCE

What You Do

I don't miss the life I used to have. I don't miss the well known people but I do miss the honesty I saw in hearts when I saw what they could secretly do to help.

No Change

Money cannot change what you are but it can shine a light on you which can darken what is seen.

Please Object

I don't object to what I've said or done but I hope you object because that challenges it, maybe improving it.

Changing The Wind

All the effort trying to change people is like changing the wind. It cant be done. Only the wind changes itself.

We Can Show Only By Example

There is nothing better we can say or do than living by being an example.

Tunnel of Light

Sometimes we go to the wrong end of the tunnel to look for light which is always at one end. We can think we are looking for it but we cant see we are searching out the dark.

Amplify the Positive

The more you work towards the positive, the more detached you become from the nature of negativity.

Eventually you get so detached from negativity that it is impossible to be in the same place.

Not For Me

I could spend much time looking at the images of all the people I love but for some reason I don't.

Maybe they were not taken for me but for others to look and see what I was trying to share, which is only what I see.

The Happiness of Ignorance

We don't know when our luck will run out, when we then say to ourselves, 'Rotten luck.' Knowing we don't know is a blessing as knowing would be a tragedy destroying our happiness.

All of Us

I saw a woman today who was like most men and women, uncomplicated, straight forward, friendly, kind and hard working.

Carrying On

The only way to carry on is to be polite. Calmness, patience and careful listening, especially silently, say more than words.

You Are Your Choice

If you mix with people you can become like them or they may become like you. You can choose to be with certain people but don't forget how you are influenced is your choice.

Where Happiness Is

Strive for nothing because in nothing is the fullness of stillness and in the fullness of stillness is happiness.

Leaving

We think our children are leaving us but feelings, attachment and memories reinforce that this is not true. Our children do not leave us. We are going our own way finding all the things we have reflected on as we leave them.

Inspiration

The most inspiring thing is not another person. It is not a
place I love. It's not a book or a film. The most inspiring
thing is not what someone said. It's not a poem of play. It's a
blank piece of paper, like the self.

Top Secret Gossip

If you have a conversation. If you see a doctor or a lawyer,
don't say anything important because there is no such thing
as confidentially in any of the worlds you see. The only
secure one is the one in you which doesn't gossip.

8. PLACES

There Too

There are places we don't remember but they remember us for others to imagine that they were there too.

The Rooms

The rooms are where you see people. Either they come to see you in your rooms or you meet in the rooms.

The room we are in doesn't matter. Are we in our own self? It is not the place that matters to be.

Yet

Places stay but we must go. Perhaps places let part of us stay in a consciousness we don't know yet.

Travel

We travel to find unknown lands, interesting people with stories but what we do is travel to find our self to find our own inner story.

Mountaineering

We don't climb to conquer mountains only to know our self. We shouldn't climb to conquer anything only to know our self.

9. SEARCHING FOR HAPPINESSS

Get Out of The Way

What we all want is the same, it's just how we get it that's different.

We all want to be able to make ourselves happy with no pain, to be happy about everything with no painful thoughts.

We get in our own way. We sometimes blame this on others but whichever way, it is our thoughts which get in our way, so find out how to get them out of the way.

Inspired Desire

What inspires me most is pain. Yes pain, then the desire to not have it. Pain makes me desire the happiness I know is inside, the most powerful inspired desire.

10. TURNING INSIDE

Eternal Internal

Externalisation of our thoughts, externalisation of our dreams, externalisation of our desires, externalisation of our happiness, externalisation of our self is in the opposite direction of happiness.

Turning Inside

Wherever you go in your mind you always come back to one thing, conscious of just being happy in stillness. Awareness of just this with no thoughts is your natural default but relentless conditioning as you grow up obscures and eventually hides it.

You can imagine or believe your happiness is outside you until enough suffering and pain brings you to your knees and your ignorance is removed leaving you only one place to turn, inside.

Turning Around

Just before I see anyone and am with them, I turn inwards and I try and turn off my thinking to let myself just be. I have to close my eyes or put my hands or feet together to help me turn inwards to be my self.

Selfish

Sometimes I only seem to have one interest which is being happy inside. Everything outside is only there to support this one thing which is about the self.

The self was there before my thinking, before I could see, hear or sense anything. It is this that I am all about, not the part of me that thinks. It is not selfish as it is to be shared.

Insomnia

Suffering makes your mind overwork and you cannot sleep for thinking. Only when you are exhausted sleep arrives but is short.

It feels like it is never ending. It is painful, strong even overwhelming but it is only the mind and body which are overwhelmed, untouched is the inner self.

Perfection

Every moment of consciousness, every thought and feeling, every movement and interaction are perfect as they are meant to be.

A Single Home

There is always a need to look in. We cant look out without looking in. There is no journey unless it starts within, so we should always be within.

Frequent Reminder To Be Still

The attitude to need to be in a special place for detachment, solitude and silence is to enquire, surrender and meditate to remove ignorance to be still in happiness and truth.

Be Still and know that I am God

Is not about the person who said it. The I is about you. It is about being still. It is about being conscious of one thing. It is about the stillness of who you are.

Impossibilities

Have you ever seen someone lift a happy cat up by its tail? Have you ever seen the best swordsman use his sword? Have you ever seen a happy rich man? Have you ever seen inside?

Only Being Now

Our Time is only now. We think it will be longer but it can only be now.

Our time is perceived sentimentally as what we have been and emotionally what we have left but it can only be now.

Our time becomes other people's time as we see we are handing over the baton in our relay but it can only be now.

Being Poor

If you try to live thinking that money can make you happy because money can let you have things, do things and be things, you may live long enough to see you are poor because all you have is money.

Being Conscious

How clear to see we are only our nature, what we say, write or do are only the results of our mind's activity. But our nature is just being conscious.

Inability to Stay Still

Returning to see you have been thinking and not being still is the return to consciousness from reduced consciousness.

Our inability to stay with being still is our greatest weakness, being still our greatest treasure.

Thinking subtlety loosens our grip and off we go on another tangent of thinking until we return again, seeing we have been thinking, not being thoughtless.

Being still is our permanent nature, thinking our temporary interrupter, just as dark appears necessary for light.

No One

I know what happens at the end but what is going to happen to me next?

Me is just a collection of thoughts. Me doesn't exist so who does what happen to?

Perhaps nothing happens to no one?

When It Doesn't Work

When you cannot write, usually life is showing you it is more important than writing and is what you may need to write about.

When you cannot draw, usually life is showing you it is more important than drawing and is what you may need to draw about.

When you cannot sing, usually life is showing you it is more important than singing and is what you may need to sing about.

When you cannot meditate, usually life is showing you it is more important than meditating and is what you may need to meditate about.

When you cannot be still, usually life is showing you it is more important than being still and is what you may need to be still about.

Shocked to Make the Effort

Too much pain and suffering eventually turn us inwards to find the special place where happiness is.

We align with our inner self using solitude, detachment and our attitude.

Through silence, meditation, enquiry and surrender we begin our aim.

Our aim is removal of ignorance to be happy in stillness which is already our truth.

Basically, shock changes us inside to make the effort so we can embrace inner happiness.

Always Already

You cannot arrive at where you already are unless you sleep and forget.

You cannot become what you already are unless your life gives you so much pain.

You cannot acquire what you already have unless your life gives you so much suffering.

Fear of Unhappiness and Turning Inwards Now

Fear can be of everything in the future. When we stay with what we are now, fear cannot exist in the present.

Desire can be for everything in the world. When we turn our desire for happiness inwards we are given everything.

Thinking Thief

What is behind us and in front of us stops us being where we are within. Why cant they say it in school? Why don't they tell us? Why aren't we taught the truth that happiness is within?

It's because of fear that we would be happy, fear that we would not be interested in the world, fear that we would be detached from the world and fear that we would have all we need

Just Being Still

We have not lost the ability to turn inwards to find our inner stillness. We have just been over programmed to think all the time, instead of just being still.

Just Being Stillness

Freedom is always ours to be what we are but we mistake what we could be for what we are, chasing our freedom further away.

From Suffering to Cure

Writing about what cannot be written or described in words
is vital to understand it.

What cannot be described properly adequately with words
has to have more help to be seen. Seeing it is understanding
so it can be experienced.

To experience something it has to be encountered but first
you have to know about it. You have to be looking because
you desire it.

To desire it you already know it exists. To get there you
could follow someone who has been there but they are so
difficult to find.

Some will have left a trail of words you can follow outlining
the path they took, only so that you can find your path
easier.

Fighting for Peace

My father would have loved the new country he was in.
A refuge, an escape from the lethality where he was born,
which I have heard from him and others from elsewhere but
not seen.

How do we keep safe from what will be repeated? How can
we? We can only keep safe if we become involved in it, being
part of the whole process of fighting it.

Complete Effort

Overwhelming suffering leads to complete release through complete surrender which gives us complete control.

Endless searching for happiness inside changes the outer world, unfolding it as a mirror of our inner happiness.

The Senses are not all we have

It seems like only when there is some kind of ending, even a death that we come to our senses and realise our senses may not be all we have.

The senses information processed through the past memory banks, then coupled with the imaginative future of our brain, let us see our self once again.

Sometimes we are in so much pain and distress that the suffering becomes too much. Overwhelmed, there is nothing left to hold on to.

Like a drowning person, we cling on to the only passing belief and we hope so much that we surrender to the belief. Our ego has gone but consciousness remains.

Rock n Roll

To love Rock and Roll you have to fall with the rolls then rise against the rocks. It shows you life, so you can have music, then the stillness which your own inner sacred mountain shows you.

Today

Today is the only day you will ever be with no reminders from the past, no thoughts or the future because you can only be conscious now.

All Else Second

What has influenced me is someone who tried to find themselves in the time they had with as much effort as a drowning person gives to breathe. All else second.

Unaffected

A thousand years back or forwards our brains like the rest of our bodies have been changed by use. The environment which we inhabit constrains or frees our mind's adaptation, our consciousness unaffected.

Idealism

The tenderness of words, forms or sounds we leave behind may not reflect what we are. They may reflect the opposite of what we are, only our idealistic thinking.

Other Than Being Itself

It can almost seem to drive us to the truth, trying to find out why we are here. What if any meaning does our consciousness have other than being itself, our self.

Freedom

The relief of not having to know anything. The relief of not
believing in not being good enough, allows happiness to
flourish within.

The satisfaction of seeing the rewards of suffering. The
practice of the presence of humility opens us to freedom
through surrender.

As We Are

Oh blank sheet of paper why has it become normal to try
and change you? Oh thoughtless mind, why can't I leave you
as you are? Where has this come from? Why can't we just be
as we are?

We can't be more important than we are. We can't be happier
than we are. We can't become anything. We can only be as
we are; nothing else.

Being Quiet and Still

One time you will see it is best to be quiet, to be silent and
not speak. One time you will see it is best to not think, to
have a quiet mind.

One day you will see silence is better for you, that when
everyone wants to be speak, silence makes you stronger.

One time you will see it is better to be still, then you will see
how things are.

Screen of Consciousness

Any words pollute this empty white screen of consciousness with darkness. Thoughts which form the words into writing can be stopped. There needs to be a desire to stop thought so the screen is blank. Only a non-thinking means will work and keep the screen of consciousness empty and white.

Last Words

The transient consciousness we have; the sense of consciousness we know is us, is the last aspect of us we have to let go of before its complete surrender.

We see by seeing what we are not

I have a body which is part of me but is not what I am. I have thoughts which are part of me but are not what I am. I have feelings which are part of me but are not what I am. All I can know I am is consciousness.

To Forever Hold

You have to get into the sound, into the moves, into the grooves and be there. Just feel what it's like to be there long enough to not to want to be there. To want to leave there to see the next place. He's fast, she's hot, she's cold. You know they won't last. They're not people you want to forever hold.

11. NATURE

Never

If you respect yourself, you can't disrespect anyone. Nature may make errors but is never indifferent.

If you are compassionate with yourself, you can't be cruel with anyone. Nature may make errors but is never cruel.

If you are simple with yourself, you can't be complicated with anyone. Nature may make errors but is never complicated.

If you are honest with yourself, you can't be dishonest with anyone. Nature may make errors but is never dishonest.

The Great Book

The Great book the greatest of all to read is the one that is in front of you, around you all the time to see. She shows you rather than tells you all you need to know from how things are formed and how things grow. She shows you death in all its ways. She shows you minerals, animals and plants and shows you how to the sun they dance. The greatest book is Nature herself, silent, roaring, weak and strong, teaching and showing us all lifelong.

Thread

There is a thread which we all have as the golden thread of life itself. It may connect to your partner, to an ancestor, a friend, to a memory or to hope.

The thread which connects everyone to make everything even the intangible real is the thread, the cord which is not cut at birth but woven as instructions deeper than our genes.

Not Knowing When to Stop

Nature does not always behave how we would expect. It can kill itself by destroying what it lives off.

It can be overgrowth not knowing when to stop.

It seems to have more feedback loops to encourage it to feed, to grow and to replicate than to stop, which includes us.

Copying nature

You cannot cheat nature. You cannot cheat life. It has its way of balancing because balance is its nature worth copying. The best art, the best architecture, the best relationships try and copy nature, being and looking the best.

Our Nature

We are given our share of what is nature. What we do with it is our nature.

So Just Be You

It's easy to be complex, difficult to be simple, to be natural, so be you. It's hard to be right and easy to be wrong but being right has more potential, so be you.

Too Early

We were told to start with, that life doesn't seem fair and that it is a full life. Every sense bursting with activity like a garden in full spring.

Soon the last days will arrive. Yes autumn is passing. We can all say this because it seems like a very long life at the beginning but then, we are surprised when we realise that it will be over soon and we will have to leave.

We carry on and start getting ready, realising there is nothing to be which we haven't been, nothing to do which has been left undone, nothing to say which hasn't been said, nothing to see which hasn't been seen.

Above All

Sometimes we don't know what has brought us to a place like this but we usually see it if we keep looking. Perhaps what has brought us here wants to show something inside us which is not just about thinking, and is what we trust above all else.

Above All Else

Trying to find resonance with someone reflects lack of stillness of oneself Returning to stillness is our origin and fate. Stillness is never early or late. Above all thinking at the end is inner stillness. Above all religion at the end is inner stillness. Don't listen to anyone. You have to listen to your self inside to find your inner stillness. Above all is your own inner stillness.

Invisible Cloud of Stillness

When there are no more words I am not dead. Senility has not arrived, a stroke has not occurred, but even if so there is peace.

It is nature taking its place, its time in its space, in stillness as others grow in my place.

There is no competition as nothing can be done. The invisible cloud of stillness silently takes over everything and everyone.

Our Natural State

Our nature is happiness so why can't we have it? It is unconditional happiness because it is always there but accessing it is conditional on being our self.

Our Natural Desire

We might have seen the happiness we expected from the outside world doesn't last and so we may have already started searching for the happiness we know is inside us.

Life for many of us may have been difficult, chaotic and so traumatic that we still suffer and turning inside is our only refuge. Happiness is our nature and finding it is our main desire.

Inwards

The aim of turning inwards is to find the happiness of inner stillness. When stillness is found it is our truth.

The tools we need to turn inwards are to be detached from the things of life with a quiet mind, whilst being fully in the middle of life.

What we need to do with the tools is to simply enquire into our nature and completely surrender to our nature by being still.

Flowers

Flowers are colourful messengers trumpeting and displaying that their fragility and short life are our shared state.

What We Are Given

There is no other, no next, only this which is what we are.

Precious

Am I precious about my inner state? It is precious to me? Maybe not to you or anyone else, so to me I can't be too precious.

No More Left

There is no more time available or wanted, no more opportunities; reality of truth suddenly becomes everything.

Not Precious

Not enough value is placed on the inner self. We encourage people to sacrifice it to industry, to society, to lack of stillness.

Unfocused

My head goes into a spin from too much driving around with no focus in sight. Eventually, my eyes become unfocused, then the inner balance needs trusting.

The God We Seek We Are

When we surrender to our nature we do a curious thing, as most of us surrender to God, but our nature is God.

When we conjure up an image of God, it is from inside our self, so it has to be an image of what is already there.

If it is an image of what is already there, what is already there inside us is God.

So when we surrender to our nature we surrender to our God, which is our self, name it what you want.

Bare Essentials

For all our technology the sun, wind and sea support life the most and are our essentials.

Chance

We have assumptions that our world is stable, that people are predictable and everyone is doing what they should do.

How wonderful it might be in such a pleasant state to see it like this.

Then accidents, chance meetings, fatigue, forgetting or remembering place us where we didn't expect to be and finally, we see.

Boring

Life is never boring but it may seem so if our mind is disturbed or perturbed. The most complete complex activity of our whole being is consciousness. Exploring it, being it is blissful but could not be boring unless you are disturbed or perturbed.

Stroke

Someone's thinking can turn from sensible to unintelligible noises in an instant. It's not that it could happen, it happens with a stroke.

It can change us into a dependent person who now needs total help but we only hear and see the fringes of what has to be done for someone like us.

Burdens which are not ours are not easy to even imagine just as not knowing them is a freedom some can remember as bliss.

Exercise and Sport

Exercise is natural and good for you but sport is manmade and can be dangerous. There is nothing wrong with exercise or sport but sport can injure you.

Exercise is a calming measured regulator but sport can be so competitive it can lose its way and become aggression.

The Best Pilot

In full flight ready to change, ready to stop, ready to
continue, keeping the main aim the main aim, the best pilots
are birds.

The Underground

There is always an underground group of heavies who use
muscle or psychological muscle, working for people at the
top of every organisation.

Countries, religions, farmers and shops. How else would
they get their dirty work done?

To Seek and Find

Plants expand to their limit everywhere they can go, not
stopping at blocks but repeatedly try to move.

We try and do things we can't and keep on trying
challenging and struggling to expand ourselves.

It is a quality of nature to do this persistently, to seek and
find without end, leaving all else behind.

What You Do and Are

If you say you don't like what you do, you put you down.
What you are during that time you put down you.

Troubles

Anything that moves is Trouble. Anything that doesn't move is trouble.

The Wake Up Call of Consciousness

Our consciousness is demoted to less importance than the transient happenings of daily life, so that we are hardly aware of our consciousness.

Our consciousness is almost always pushed into the background which it is mostly ignored and forgotten.

It only becomes present when dreadful things happen to us or others and our existence is threatened.

Bringing consciousness up to the surface so it is with us much more and more frequently is the beginning of inner work.

Too Straight

Sophistication is debasing nature and that is why nature has no straight lines. Forces form left and right making swerves and curves which may result in going in the same direction.

The straight line comes from man's sequential, logical thinking and wanting to achieve progress. Less progress is made with straight lines than with curves, swerves and circles, which is how all things grow.

A Thousand Nights

Just over a thousand days three years will be looked back on
like three weeks or months.

Memory is not of time but of people, places and things which
having changed.

Just over a thousand nights to emerge every morning
incredibly thankful to be conscious.

Respect for Nature

Just as we have some sense of the job we are doing, as we
begin bringing up our children we have about as much sense
that our own life is wearing out.

Being conscious of these is not usual because it is not part of
how we are programmed but comes sharply into focus the
nearer the parting comes.

Like a beautiful flower during a happy day, the cycle has its
nature which we respect.

Struggle of Fairness

Fairness strongly suggests something bound by rules
and standards but life in the outside world is not so well
organised. Animals are naturally wild, people steal, kill and
destroy the land they live on. A struggle against these is a
struggle against nature which cannot be won.

Blossoming Birthday

It's the first day of another year, a new year's day. Like daffodils and tulips trumpeting in spring, today trumpets in how young you are.

Like all the flowers we too as children of the Universe must age and in aging we blossom and give so much so others can see the beauty we are, which we never knew we were.

No More Praying

We don't pray anymore because we don't believe in god because we think we are god.

With praying gone that part of our self does not disappear and it still needs to be nourished. For being god to be true, we need to use that knowledge to be conscious and happy as only god can be.

Life's Peak

Completion of our biggest work is so satisfying because we achieve the best we can ever do. We reach the top of the highest mountain and we are radiant with happiness.

Why is there so much fear of completion when with every step nearer there should be even more joy? There should be increasing excitement knowing that we will achieve it then die.

Counting

Numbers must exist in nature. Nature must be able to count.
Not like we count by thinking but some other way.

How could nature be so accurate, without counting, without
computing, calculating? So nature can count.

If nature counts what else can it do? It seems it can make
things like you.

Standard Operating Procedures

Manufactured programmed thoughts and behaviours like
formal over-manicured gardens can leave you feeling as if
we are becoming unnatural. But perhaps it is just easier for
us to be this way in the world.

12. TECHNOLOGY

Progress?

Is man progressing, advancing and improving with a better quality of life? Are we as prosperous in that we are flourishing, thriving, happy, healthy and in a state of good fortune? We are more competitive and less co-operative, less sharing and we are more greedy, more focused on celebrity not equality.

Parents teachers and priests have lost their influence to psychology, technology and the New Age. We are in a crisis about our core values which define us as civilised human beings. We are over-immersed in virtual worlds, lacking authentic interaction with family, friends, nature but mostly ourselves. Binge use has substituted everyday experiences so we can no longer survive without specialist training.

We can't be kind or gentle, relate or relax without specialist training. We can't be fully conscious or even spiritual without specialist training. Have we improved and become higher, deeper people?

Just as all religions started at their peak and have always been in decline, we too are less flourishing, thriving, happy and healthy, so more down.

We are more materialistic, superficial, looking less inwards, and looking more outwards. We are becoming down and out.

Information Technology

Be careful not to have photographs of daffodils and not to have given them. Be careful not to have photographs of freesias and not to have inhaled their beauty. Be careful not to have photographs of friends but not to have hugged them. Be careful not to wish you had not wasted time wishing. Now you know this, be happy with what you have today.

Technology and Progress

Are we more happy? Do we have more time for our self? Are we more healthy? Are we more relaxed?

Currency

We have become obsessed by something which had value but is now valueless. How did we get rid of its value? It has replaced food, generosity, kindness, help and compassion. It is now digital, so completely valueless but it is still exchanged for time and for our life.

Without Method

The smile of eyes is not a method. The warmth of the heart is not a method. Listening to someone is not a method. Meditation is not a method. Praying is not a method. Survival is not a method. Death is not a method. Surrender is not a method Love is not a method. Science is a method.

Digital Masters

These thoughts, these words are just the first that come when I am waiting and are based around the first word which appears because I am not relaxing because of the screen where thoughts appear. The technology pulls me in, pulls me away from other things away from the room, the silence and from the walk in the field outside.

It has been days since I wrote the last line above this because I have been in the field walking. I have been walking, which is better than doing this. But this leaves a trace, a record of how you can get drawn in to anything when the task is to do what you came here for. It is a warning, a reminder.

The Latest Thing

Perhaps there are too many competing gas stations to speed up cars driven by fast drivers in a society which needs drugs to sedate them at night.

The green fields were exchanged for money which is now stored in the warehouses on the land. Those fields of green were consumed by farmers instead of growing food.

We invested in building more computers rather than planting bulbs to make future generations smile at the daffodils and be happy.

We invested in outer stimulation rather than turning back inside by exposure to singing, dancing, music, smells, exercise, chanting, and silence which turns people to go within.

Wallpaper

There are no books here because books are officially now wallpaper. What did they give? What will not be there? They formed the bundles of knowledge on calfskins first, then on paper. Then on scrolls, bound and also in Brail. What can be read on a stormy day? What can be seen and understood which never decays? Barehanded like Stone Age man under a naked sky, only those who have been taught to think then write will survive.

Virtual Reality and Sacred Spaces

Computers eight hours a day might be worse than being down a mine because where we look for happiness has changed, because what we think is happiness has changed.

Foolishly our sense of our self is formed by fishing for compliments in others opinions, by numbers of followers rather than looking at ourselves and our own self-worth.

We are not born unhappy but because the world makes us unhappy we look for happiness out there rather than inside, where it is hidden and can be uncovered.

Be a nerd be a geek, a loner, a recluse, an eccentric, a drop out who cares not a jot what others think about you because you are happy.

Be abnormal and visit the wonder of a sacred site. Go on a distant pilgrimage or a silent retreat. Be a freak and meditate or contemplate being a spiritual person.

On Board Computer

You have opened the front passenger window. This is causing increased air resistance. This is reducing the efficiency of your drive. It is increasing noise levels.

This may reduce the comfort of your drive which may distract your concentration and lead to unnecessary messages from the on board computer, negating the calming effect of fresh outside air on your face.

The on board computer is here to manage the environment, and judge that you can relax more, so you can concentrate more on driving and not suffer from any form of stress.

This is the second reminder you are not using this car at its maximum efficiency. You are ignoring advice which we have perfected because we think we know what you like.

You have not paid us for the upgrade memory chip which automatically opens the window according to your likes and which prevents messages like this from subjecting yourself to more chaos and stress. You can buy peace and calmness from us for money or this message will repeat itself.

Luddite

Do I want any more modernity to take me away from eternity? Do I need more devices to inject me with more information that doesn't protect me?

Reading Maps

When technology goes wrong and gives you the wrong directions, you realise what we have thrown away.

A person sitting beside you reading a map is a warm person not a tool of a voice presenting as help.

Technological Communications

Your computer mimics what people used to do, telling you important information, answering your questions which can be helpful.

Your computer can tell you how you could be feeling, how you should be feeling even how you would have been feeling.

But it can't tell you what you are feeling or what you are thinking, what your hopes are or your dreams. It can only guess.

It can't change your level of consciousness from remembering to wishing the future or being happy or just being alive in the present moment.

What people used to do also included their presence, a name with a history, opinions and attitude and their passion to be here alive.

Just Being

A group of men and women can achieve more than any machine, computer or technology by being consciously happy.

Warning, Ceaseless Technology

The essentials of daily living have become secondary to the never ending tidal waves of demands from interacting with technology. Technology has pushed aside, almost taken away my attention and perception of simple things which keep me nurtured cleaning, cooking and being still.

That distance from what I recognise can be manipulated by technology so it appears to be close when it is getting further away.

Perhaps I have to become so far away from what I remember or accept that warning bells ring to signal change must begin.

Collection of Thoughts

My secret wish in writing is to empty my mind, to drain it to permanent exhaustion so the hard drive will have nothing left in it that is worth accessing and thinking about.

But the quiet mind will try to restart the imagined collection of thoughts, the ego, which will tick over by itself imagining the world it thinks it is.

The Surrounding Skies

Shafts of bright light coming down from the sky through dark grey clouds and the Aurora Borealis in the early evening must have inspired stories of spirits in the sky. It still does.

The power of the skies changed when we started transmitting signals by radio, telephone, fax and the internet and launched aeroplanes, missiles, satellites and rockets.

We could not do much better than reclaiming the clean air of the skies, removing the pollution of signals and transport, so our hearts and minds are free from them and at peace.

13. STRANGE PEOPLE STRANGE PLACES

Foresters of Dean

They live isolated in the forest where the Romans settled for the coal and iron to make weapons.

Friendly but insular, single minded, sometimes chaotic, and possibly rebellious arms dealers extraordinaire. There are rumours their trademark was found on some of the Spanish cannons from the Spanish Armada. Today they are reluctant to travel, not even when ill. Hardy, resistant, their lives of secrets.

Arrivals

How you arrive is not important, it's what you arrive as. Did you have a good stay and arrive in your own happy way? Did you have happiness? Did you have pain? Did you pass anything on? Has everything you had gone? Are you happy to be here relieved all is done or did your life leave other people's lives undone?

As the graveyard keeper I let everyone in. I've seen many after a fulfilled happy life and the worst types from everywhere always want to arrive as the richest person in the graveyard.

Lizard Hand in a Crazy Land

The deep rhythms of the Aborigine digeridoo player in the
Sydney outdoor shopping mall vibrated in my heart. The
low note made the air vibrate and my chest wall shuddered
like it does with the deep note of a lion's roar or that same
note from a church organ.

Not sitting together but also on the bench, a white girl began
swaying. Then she fell sideways and then forwards. His deep
notes got louder as if to wake her from the needle's delivery.

Then she lost it and was falling to hit the concrete ground
face first, but between both was the lightening hand that had
just held the lizard carved on the side of his digeridoo.

Your Grave

Those rocks now lie behind the wall where we threw them
when all five of us dug your grave.

We moved them there after being here for thousands of
years. Slowly covered, drowned in the slowly forming peat
at one millimetre a year.

They were waiting for you ready to welcome you from a
baby, through being a small boy, a strong man to the death
which brought you here.

After thousands of years they now lie behind that wall in
the sun with you in their old resting place, both now settled
under the stars.

North Ronaldsy

The smallest of all the Orkney isles, you made me smile.

The birders and twitchers, the Kirk, the pub with no beer or food.

The doctor selling fags and booze to his patients and still the General Medical Council saying it's not unethical if he wants to.

Escapees

Orkney, the enigmatic isles of ancient things, I remember the wind with hardly any trees, many called Scot and many pure Vikings.

Land of the lights, the burial places, Tomb of the Eagles, the bones, the escapees.

The Royal Family

Freesias look special and the smell better than their strange elegant looks. The effects of inhaling their smell intoxicates.

The smell is difficult to compare except with perhaps honeysuckle, jasmine, or a rose, the rest of the royal family of all smells.

Signs

It is difficult to be aware of signs. The wrong ones always say, 'This Way.' The right ones don't say, 'Not This Way.'

Bookshop Armchairs

Do bookshops not have lounge chairs, arm chairs and sofas because standing up reading a book makes you want to sit and read it.

Maybe this option is deliberately removed so the only way you can sit and read further is to buy the book, leave the chairless rooms and go to a café or home.

14. OUR SECRET LIFE

The Secret Life

Reactive to reality and to fantasy trying to sometimes marry the two to find which way to go, we are this terrible beauty.

Unknown to most, spending more time in the spirit than the world or in the body, serving only that inner master answers everything.

Ignorance Removed

Life is experienced like watching a play with a curtain in the way. Vague movements can be seen and muffled sounds heard

Our perception and our reactions with the curtain are strained to guess what is happening behind the curtain and its effect on us.

Removing the curtain, all is understood, everyone appears silent and there is stillness when all is seen.

Nothingness

I'm not afraid of nothingness and I hope you are not because what could be more pointless than painful nothingness.

Self-Awareness

Being self-conscious we are self-contained self-confessed, self-disciplined. Being self-existent we become self-explained self-evident, self-induced. Being self-realised we become self-sacrifice, self-seeking.

Self-Respect

My occasional outbursts of disclosure twice a year are better than the self-harm of keeping my own feelings inside and not finding out how I am. My heart is not on my sleeve as much as it used to be. It is in my eyes.

Still Deceiving

Dreams of being in India still grab me every day. I've been in that dream, lived there but I still dream.

You still dream of someone, a love but only in your dream land. In the light of day you would still fall out.

Outgrown

When I look at the things I have kept and still keep from my daughter's childhood I feel slightly odd as I try to work out why. Some tiny shoes, small wellies, a coat and jacket as small as my jacket pocket. Dozens of her drawings from age four. I keep them because photographs are not as real.

Junctional Places

That divide on the shore between the earth and sea, the sea and sky, the sky and earth is where the mystery could be solved but is not permitted for its own sake.

On a boat the line between the boat and the sea, the sea and the sky, the sky and the boat is where the mystery could be solved but is not permitted for its own sake.

These seemingly ordinary lines, the meeting points of opposites keep us from the next level of the stars and beyond.

Everything and Nothing

Maybe there is only the spiritual. It is what we are here for. It is what we are. It is what we are doing. It is what we are being. It is where we are from, where we are and where we remain. It is how you are nothing and everything.

Glue-Force

The glue or force that holds all the billions of stars apart and together we know nothing about.

Words, maths and physics try to explain it but maybe the glue of force is beyond human comprehension.

If this is the case we are no less but it may be time to stop considering the consequences of this.

Desire

Desire can be anything but one thing it is which we are
not taught is that it is a duty. It is essential as food, shelter
warmth and love, the ability to enjoy our life.

The Spirit

There is nothing more important as it is everything about us,
what will be remembered about us, what we take with us
and leave behind.

Everyone is about it. Everything is about the spirit, our
world, all the billions of stars, the glue holding it all together
is our spirit.

Its Stillness

At first you can't see it and some never can but when you do
see it, it is all you can see. You say how could I have missed
it as it doesn't seem possible to miss.

The mountain in front of you means something but you can't
quite say what. It doesn't have a spirit. It is the spirit.

It doesn't move at all in its stillness, the same as our spirit
and that is why we find mountains are places of our spirit.

Solitary Lives

We don't live isolated lives only lives of solitude but we aren't told this. We have difficulty connecting to the things of the world because we think we are connected. We are more separate than we think or we are told.

15. EARLY MORNING

Hope (Early Moring meditation)

We wake each day in hope of what the day will bring. A still pool sits beside us to check the course we see. Then we jump, conscious, into the ever flowing river of life flowing right in front of us, in us, after we wake.

Star of Life

How can anything be so welcome as the early morning sun? How can you be more thankful than for the early morning sun? How can anything make you more alive than the early morning sun? How can anything make you more happy than the early morning sun?

To Wake

To wake and bake. To wake and meditate. To wake and write. To wake and be in the light. To wake to the day from night. To wake and be alright. Nothing is better.

Above All Thinking

Above all thinking at the end is inner stillness. Above all religion at the end is inner stillness. Don't listen to me or anyone as you have to listen to yourself inside to find your inner stillness Above all is your own inner stillness.

Have a Life

It's not where you end up, it's what you have done because we all end up the same.

It's the oceans of experience you have had in your heart, not the pension or property on your death bed.

Always Retreat

Whatever your senses present to you about the outer world, retreat into inner your stillness.

Whatever way your thoughts try and control you when they are not you, just retreat into inner your stillness.

Whatever your life seems to give you at the moment, retreat into your inner stillness.

Early Morning Sitting

It is now early morning. It looks a mixture of sunlight and cloud. Family and Friends are still asleep whist I sit.

Whilst they sleep, I sit in the same place. It's a sacred place and it's sacred time.

It is time of consciousness which is not cluttered by anything of the day or of anyone else.

Early morning Light

In a few moments the early morning golden light on the hedge will be gone. Now it is gone how do I carry on? Best not to think so much.

Early Morning

Here I am at another morning of my life, a day during which anything can happen.

Let's wait and see and I will write again after afternoon tea.

Our Origins

What do we learn when we see someone has been honest about being wrong? Could we have behaved that way then written it down?

Can we learn from stepping in the shoes of someone or have we forgotten what we once were, young, open, ignorant, happy go lucky, optimistic?

Impulsivity

I admit all my life I have done everything with one hundred percent energy. I just never thought of only giving half and saving the rest. I could have given less. I could have reflected more. I could have believed less. I could have planned. But I didn't and I don't regret what I was or what I still am.

Punctuating Reality

Between sips of tea, problems are raised and sometimes solved, if not they are just recorded. I've always functioned with tea punctuating problems, so why should I be in any way critical of Freud's use of cocaine. Perhaps we should stick to our own devices leaving others to their vices.

Light at the Ends of days

The early morning light is not valid any more than the early evening light, but we see less of it.

It's that I think differently at either end of the day and so I think the light should follow the same way. But it's only thinking, our unimaginable capacity to think and associate all our senses and try and find meaning in our thoughts.

All Things Done

One hour of nonstop writing, the first thing of the day. It doesn't seem to work any other way.

There is no one about, no sound, no obvious movement yet, only stirrings of these to come. Not yet wished, all things of the day will get done.

16. PROFESSIONALS

Emergency Doctor's Attitude

Believe nothing anyone tells you and only half of what you see.

Perils and Perks of the Job

At the end of a day, the gardener can't quite get the soil out of his hands, the banker the money from their mind, the doctor the suffering they have seen in another's heart.

As a student I was pulled out of the outpatients by the paediatrician who noticed my fear. 'When you stop being worried by children, it's time to stop being a doctor.'

Now children still scare me but because they carry knives after they have taken drugs their parents have paid for.

Only the sick need doctors. That's why I carry on, perhaps to meet that parent whose child has that knife that's next a gun.

To get them to look at how they think, to show them why they think they need what they want, instead of what they can have, to let them see what they are.

That Doctor

That doctor helps you stop being your unhealthy you. You are taken to another level, a new place which is also you, So what the doctor has shown you is that you can change, that you are different to what you thought.

Can you be shown other parts of you which you had not seen or thought of but might like to? There is a choice because first you have to want to hear, then you have to listen.

There is another choice because you have to want to take the medicine, then you have to choose to actually take it.

Specialist Advice

On my first day in accident and Emergency Trevor the consultant said, 'Believe nothing anyone tells you and only half of what you see.'

On my first day of Psychiatry Colin the consultant said, 'Don't worry there are only the mad, the bad and the sad.'

On my first day in paediatrics Hugh the consultant said, 'When you stop being scared of children you're dangerous.'

What would my advice be today? 'Your happiness trumps helping or healing others.'

Scenes

They really believe I've not heard this scene before, twenty to thirty times a year. It is what I see, but they are right, because I've not heard them speak this way before.

The familiarity doesn't leave me feeling contempt, only sadness with the frequent reminders that we treat each other with so little kindness.

I am disappointed that we don't improve with age or with generations of history.

The draining price of having to listen, the pain of empathic listening, then the addicts impact already showing on her baby's face always reminds me of the passion to help but of not being able to do anything.

The relief and joy of shutting the door on a difficult day's work, the decompressing meditation on the way home. There are many others whose day has tried them too, knowing the cycle must begin again at dawn, so we can all meaningfully live and truly feel alive.

Therapists

Too much therapy but no food in the cupboard. Too much therapy but no job. Too much therapy but no company. Too much therapy but no respect for anyone. Too much therapy but no inner happiness.

World Without Heart

Some want to understand as much as they can to change what they can. Some are happy with everything, knowing everything is as it should be.

Knowing is the path of the head, being is the path of the heart. Medical education without a heart cannot heal or teach.

Perils of Showtime

Many singers hate singing the same songs every night for decades. They leap at the chance to cancel performing to seek revenge on their choice. Some musicians are not interesting but have an extra fine focus on being able to interest and stir the masses with their skills.

Some comedians try to be cheerful despite frequently being depressed. They fight a cruel battle of having insight that their jokes will never let them win.

Some actors can never be beautiful enough because it would threaten their belief and world of competitive Narcissism.

Off Duty but On Call

Maybe this is just left over from the nature of what I do. Perhaps it is me not being the professional but relaxed off duty in the world on call to within.

The Farmer and the Fisherman

The farmers land is his to rule with a cold heart and a hard hand. Everyone and everything, a slave to money with no visitors or guests, unless they pay and all dogs shot if they stray.

The fisherman risks his life at sea, a servant to its weather, thankful for a lucky day. Always sharing what belongs to no one, helping with no fee, all who pass.

The animals fed sludge in cages, no grass beneath their feet, sun or touching hand. Only before their sale for slaughter to clear their ringworm are they put out in the sunshine.

The fish have swum the seas for years and freedom has been their lot. Most will escape the net, only a few are predestined for the pot.

No More Work

No more work I said, I don't have to work anymore but what I do now is work only on a different level. On this other level I now have to be to others what my elders were to me. Just one more step, as always one more seems to fuel the illusion that work will go sometime. But work is only a word which before was just life. How did we get to the illusion that ending it would be good?

Elite

The best swordsman never uses his sword. The best therapist never says a word. The best thinking is not to think. The best communication is silence. The best vision is with closed eyes. The best parent is the child. The best day is today. The best time is always now. The best king doesn't rule. The wisest thinker is the fool. The best chef is your stomach. The best doctor is you. The best friend is you. The best person to ask is you. The best person to change is you. The only person to change is you.

Conditional Work

It seems to be a condition that to be an accountant your own money is in a mess, if you are a doctor you are not well, if you are a dentist you have bad teeth, if you are a policeman, your hands are never clean, if you are a builder your house is falling apart, if you are a cook you are overweight, if you are a teacher you find it difficult to learn, if you are a psychotherapist your relationships are in a mess, if you are happy it's because you know suffering.

Professional Moral Gymnastics

How do you run a church, a school, a police force the armed forces or a country?

You ignore everything that is sacred. You ignore everything you know. You ignore everything that is right. You attack all opposition for resources.

Not Gobby

What a gossipy life this can be, but not in medicine as you
can only anonymously tell stories to guide but not amuse
others. Respect, compassion, trust, confidentiality
make many doctors quiet, so they are not gobby.

Professional Unprofessionals

Doctors are perfectionists who like the perfect death,
whether by nature or by their hand of intervention. Even
killing in combat has to be perfect for the death reports so
less time is spent treating casualties.

They can have indifference to supervising someone's torture
so that it can carry on being used to inflict pain and display
the naked reality of humanity

Only doctors and psychologists still supervise torture to say
if the person can have more so that it can carry on being used
as a calling card instead of banned forever.

Healing

What is this healing time that the physician knows of six
weeks? What takes place in the biblical forty days and
nights?

The Doctors Office

Industrialised medicine delivers doctors nurses and
receptionists who are unconcerned beyond being at fault,
unconcerned with your inner dialogue or outcome.

It would make no difference to them whatever you were
requesting, whether at a shop or a machine servicing centre.
It's a job which pays. You do not affect them.

But you ask only for acknowledgment to get help,
orientation so you can find a direction pointing to help, to
find hope for some change in how you are.

Sacred Oaths

Doctors used to be the only trainers of the martial arts
because they knew how to heal and harm. Now it seems they
supervise torture because they know how to cause exquisite
extreme pain.

Their healing light was partly their ability to cheer, balanced
by knowing how to remove fear but their art is changing into
numbers needed to treat.

I count myself lucky or blessed or perhaps both when my
doctor smiles and asks me about my inner dialogue. He is
the only person interested in what goes on in me, a man true
to the sacred oath.

Good news

What wonderful news to hear you are not going to be a scientist, a one hemispheric binary thinking cog in a machine, a doctor. Instead your world is ready to be drawn and painted by you in forms and colours which have no words. Books are now wallpaper, money is digital communication which has taken over respect for what is within. Nothing can create from inside except us.

17. WORDS

The Weakness of Words

I feel like confronting the establishment of thoughts and words. We use words which define us and don't use words because of fear when they could change us.

We are too scared to use words which do no harm but raise questions for which someone is willing to break our arms.

Where is the courage to speak with words which change how we are seen if it changes one thing?

Actions by sticks and stones still rule over words by the impact of breaking our bones.

Silence

The long words which you have to kook up first, the words which are foreign, the unnecessary ones are bad but worst are too many words or even just any words.

Most Loved

The short and simple words are usually the best meant and the most loved.

Gratitude for Words

Just this once, I want to say thank you to words for letting us expand our expressive capabilities, for showing us how limited our minds are and by their absence, what the self is.

The Sun

If there is time for a word, I am thankful for the sun and this beautiful life it nurtures.

Thoughtless

What is the use of sacred books when the only place where truth exists is inside your self? They can only turn us further inwards where words are not relevant, only experience. Words have to be abandoned for the state of consciousness without thought.

A Live Birth

What is it about words that have to be written? Being thought they have conception, written they are recorded and are in labour with influence unknown

Spoken they are alive, born in a new present. Heard on the drum of the ear they are meant for you, now changing your heart.

Writing it Down

We write what we might forget; evidence of what we know so others can see what we knew; that they may know too.

Write

How to write? Just do it. You can't learn how to write what you are meant to write. It is already there and will be written and whether you know it or not, it or not it will still be written.

Avoiding Arguing

Perhaps the reason for this outpouring of thoughts which can be discussed but which I want to avoid is that I don't want to get bogged down in my own trivial thoughts or argue about opinions. It is only clarification of thoughts.

Reading

What you read and comment on is not the writer. It is you; the effect on you is what you read.

The effect on you and how you think and how you feel helps to reinforce what is you and not you.

To Understand and be Understood

We write to understand and to be understood but also so others can turn inwards and understand.

Its own Self

Each time has no more than it would like each patient; occasionally there is a complex one who needs more.

The time it takes to write it is the time it takes to write it down, there is no thought.

Each time it is. There no hesitancy. It has its own self.

Inexpressible Healing

If words were great healers, we could go to libraries to find solutions to problems but words have no substance compared with turning inwards seeking inner change.

Inexpressible, the stillness of healing inside can only exist in consciousness, not in words.

Words

Have words helped man be compassionate, happier? Have words helped man relate better than his actions? Have words assisted man to help the planet and those coming after him? Have words stopped man killing, stealing or abusing since he formulated them?

Persistence

Persistent thoughts which demand expression in writing seem to have me in their grip. It's been seven months now since they showed up like this. Did I invite them or do they just need to be here?

As soon as I sit down or try to sleep, they are crystal clear compared with other thoughts. As long as they seem to say something which lets me see something about me, I don't mind listening and writing to see.

Giving up words

Words are dangerous things to play with. They can explode backfire and maim. They are weapons of mass destruction or construction of volumes of anything.

They are to be respected, restrained, understood, then given up for silence where stillness is found, experienced without words.

Writing

Writing our way to normality is an impossible task because writing comes after other things. It comes after awareness, then after thought and then there is writing it down. Normality can only be hoped for by starting with awareness.

No Choice but to Write

My nights of sleep are interrupted right in the middle by the need to write something. It's usually three o'clock and I can't even think of sleep until it's done.

No dreamy states of reverie, no warm soothing drink to melt away the need to write what has appeared on my path, regardless of the time or place.

Respect for this has been learnt or else the choice is endless sleepy yawning attempts to go back to sleep or hopeless attempts to enjoy the things of the world after the sun is seen.

In Full View

Soon I won't have to write anymore because I have asked myself, why keep on writing the same thing in different ways just because it can't be written. There are only so many times you can circle something to get a full three dimensional view so it can be understood. When something has no words, it keeps on trying to express itself so it can be understood and it can be shared.

Unspoken

Our spoken words fade and are forgotten, the written word lasts longer but the unspoken silence is eternal remaining as it is always.

Eloquence and Simplicity

Eloquence with words can simplify, clarify are but not
reality.

The Activities of Words

Writing words for different themes seems to bring the
themes to life and change them by expanding them so
they seem like something more when they are just words.
Different metaphors for the same thing, unusual ones seem
to almost colour something but it doesn't change what it is.

This Peace

This peace can only last so long, then something has to break
it. A crisis, death, an accident or even a row but it will be
remembered maybe just in words.

Wordless

If this writing about what seems important is kept up, it will
be seen there is nothing to write about.

Best here

There is nowhere better to write today than here. Nothing
can make me more happy than I am now. Wishes take us
further from what we are always.

Relay

There is always a writer, a poet, a healer, a singer and a rebel for each time and place.

Who We Are

After all this is more of this. This and that are the same when you see you are that.

Mistakes

Mistakes allow us to tolerate the imperfect in ourselves so we can be human.

From the Heart

When you trust and come from the heart of your inner self, you touch and light up the heart in others, allowing them to heal and be happier in their stillness.

The Greatest Struggle

The greatest Struggle is not with others or with the world but with our inner self.

Amusement

I'm not using you to make you use me to amuse you too.

Poetry

Poems used to be about beauty, love and happiness, now they are about the absence of beauty, love and happiness, our grief, sorrow, our regret and our astonishing stupidity. Poems used to be so positive and full of hope now they try desperately to see the positive in the negative. If that stops, poetry is over.

Civilised Rebel

Writing in verses allows expression without having to be too ordered. There is a free flow almost like the garbage that you imagine arising on analyst's couches. But with this, I feel good about it because it is being civilised. Being civilised is part of me but so is being passionately anti-establishment which has got me into trouble but not enough yet.

Censorship

Who said that poetry should not be about the unpleasant in man? Who made the rules it should not be about the ugly in man?

Perhaps poetry is so very unpopular because it seems only for the privileged who decide what is not acceptable.

All establishments are corrupt and those who censor the magnificent power of words are the guiltiest of hiding the truth from us about what we do and the demise of poetry.

Tell Don't Show

If it were not for screens, the movies and computers what would have happened to man?

What would have happened to his story telling, to his myths, to his beliefs?

Would we still be telling stories with words from a mouth to an ear to a heart and a mind?

I was there, I heard and I saw what are now the myths and stories that the media can only show but we can no longer tell.

Who Remains?

Try and understand I am not writing this for you, this is for me. Try and understand when you read it, this is now only for you

The Mistakes

Well if no one else is going to write to me I will. It is good to get an unexpected letter especially from your own self because we think we know ourselves well. But perhaps we don't know our self and we are the worst people to see the truth about our self. That's when we need to re-read what we have written to our self to see the mistakes.

Staying Inside

Rather than going out to please, I would rather be here in my own world sharing in the celebration of that. Even though my dark side is present, the bright trying to shine through wins as it has more encouragement because I have more need for it to be present and influence.

The Main Aim

Some days are just not good days for anything especially writing as it is sensitive to the whims of thoughts. Blown about by feelings of moodiness, the weather, visitors, the date, age, illness, weight, other people's moods which can all dictate writing. So it reflects life but all must be put aside to remember and keep the main aim the main aim.

Whose Truth is it?

Will you be critical of this or silent because you think it is empty? Or is the truth you are critical because you need to show that you are cleverer than me, when in truth I am only writing to show you how clever you are.

Lines

The delicate beauty of flowers, unexpected treachery, the aching heart freely expressed in a line with or without structure or rhyme. What happened to it? Why is it left behind when all stories were stored and told in it? All the important things communicated through it?

Message to Me

I never said I would write verse. I never thought I would.
I never thought I could. I never thought I should but now
as I have been writing it down. It's as if I am compelled by
something inside me or outside me. So I have decided that I
will give myself permission to carry on until I reach the end
of this message to me.

Staying In

I have hit a block in my eagerness to write. It's not that I
don't want to share but that there is nothing to share that is
obviously bright. On a rainy English bank holiday weekend
with grey skies, grey people full of the woes of life have
the usual expectations of returning motorists, moaning and
groaning about having to return to work on Tuesday.

Mantra

There is only so much you can write until like a mantra you
start repeating yourself, isn't that right?

There is only so much you can write until like a mantra you
start repeating yourself, isn't that right?

There is only so much you can write until like a mantra you
start repeating yourself, isn't that right?

Intangibles

I'm not part of a community with shops, schools and amenities all struggling to be at peace when they compete for everything.

I am part of an imaginary small group of women and men, the intangibles around the world, who sit in stillness and also write and exist only in each other's hearts.

Unknown Inspiration

Is there any reason at all to do this? There is no inspiration I can identify with apart from a compulsion to write.

There doesn't seem to be any source or any particular subject, just whatever appears in its own way.

I'm not bothered as I'm not a writer and who knows why they write? If I don't know yet, well no one can and anyway it doesn't matter until I do.

Offers

I have said no to arguing about academia, no to appearing for thanks, no to going away with people for money but there are some things I've not been offered and these I may say yes to which are all to do with stillness.

Destruction Rationalised as Progress

Our mind looks for an explanation in its own terms of our purpose here. Without a reason, it has to conclude the reason has not yet been discovered or we are meaningless. Being meaningless or not is only an idea of our reasoning.

Without words, does meaningless exist? Would we be happier without words?

Would the planet be as threatened and in so much danger? Is our reasoning our most destructive quality? Is progress destruction rationalised as improvement?

Distillation of the Heart

Words are more than they seem. Steam coming from water is still water. Words from the heart are the heart.

Some words are written only to be read. Some written to be spoken but all are directions from the heart.

Not Ready

Whatever we are is a start and although the next thing is also what we are, what we are is ready.

Apparently Particularly Odd

All the tension is over, the evidence is crippling against them, so change has to happen along formal lines.

I can't remove my enemy only disable them, so they can't act against anyone or recruit anyone.

Sticking by the strategic plan of systematic disablement of their cunning dishonest thinking will leave them overwhelmed.

This is my only enemy, my thinking. Only non-thinking can be used to stop thinking, which is why I appear particularly odd.

Retail Therapy Religion

Shops are now not our front window selling homemade cakes and pies. They are not on streets anymore, they are in buildings bigger than cathedrals.

Churches used to arch to the sky; their walls adorned by pictures and statues of those respected monks, nuns and saints who we looked up to as heroes.

Shopping mall's screens show celebrities we are forced to identify with, wearing goods we don't need, promoted by advertisers luring us to pay for their salaries and shares.

Prompted to Action

All these words and I can't say what I want to say. I can't say what you want to hear. What we want to hear is from inside us and we only need a prompt from someone else. It's not what's said it's what happens as a result, the words purpose is the action that follows.

To Write About Writing

The less you write, the more you have to write about.

That Which We Cannot Understand

I admit it. I do not for a moment think I do this. If I did I would be very happy with me but it is not me who writes because it doesn't come from my thoughts. I don't start it because it has its own control. It is not mine to change. It comes from what is inside and is the only way for it to have a voice. It is not personal, not my voice but what others have said. It is that which we understand.

After the Day Job

Sometimes I burn when others relax. I do too but by turning up the inner heat trying to carry on something which others would leave. Trying to complete what can only be done at night in another reality because there is stillness. In solitude there is only the inner light which can shine in others the next day.

I Don't Know

I can't write readable things a lot of the time. Mostly I can't write at all. Just occasionally something means something to me, then I record it and I never know what for. Will I ever look at it, I never know.

Lost For Words

When we are lost for words. It can mean we have seen truth.

Lucky Dip

Always busy writing, relying on the chance that I might just see something which has meaning but which is unknown until it is finished.

I need This Space This Place

How would I cope without this outlet, the facility to outpour everything? Redemption, pain, suffering, learning, resentment, gratitude, love, fear, anger, self-knowledge, silence, solitude, stillness. They all need this space but mostly happiness.

Worthy or Not

Most of what I write is to help my memory of what I have considered, so I can look back to see and reflect why I thought it was worthwhile and if it still is.

Unsure What Will Be?

It is difficult to see what this is going to turn into, these three hundred verses? Kindling for a warm fire, a resource, wastepaper, wasted time? Maybe I'll see some time when I look back.

Because of the Day Job

Anyone who reads this will most likely think, 'Thank goodness he stuck to his day job and didn't have any more time to write more of this.' But then I can change that by writing.

Lost Words

If you were with all your old friends you never see now, but would like to, what would you say?

Its Own Way

There is no style. What is there has to be written as it comes up. There is no editing. It is there just as it is.

What is there has its own way to communicate. Its rhythm of words and silence seem to swim naturally like everything in the ocean.

Clearer Still

When words which reflect us are taken away, we are just here with no reflection.
Spoken words are therefore second to what they try to say.
Written words are third and less clear.

Words Can Reflect Us

When words are left to themselves without trying to focus them, they have a flow which is their own, different from other tools we could use.

Undirected, they are true to themselves and form themselves how they are and how they want to be.

In Paradise

I used to struggle to write a line. Getting to the end took lots of changes. Now it is left as it is when it arrives. Perhaps if we were left as we were when we arrived, not programmed by what others want us to be, we would not be strangers to ourselves and others in paradise.

What's The Point?

What's the point of words when you are happy? Why would you want to be educated if you are happy with what you know? Why would you drink if you are not thirsty, eat if you are not hungry?

Light of Amplified Internal Dialogue

When you have nowhere else to go, some will take a walk, some will take a drink, some will sing or get distracted in order not to think.

Freely writing down the inner dialogue, sometimes helps me give shape to something awkward, painful or inconvenient but necessary to see and deal with.

Peculiar Writing Style

I know after so much writing that I'm not really in control here of what comes up to write. Whatever comes up somehow has been chosen so without hesitation is written immediately, with respect.

There is no choice, no thinking, just copying what is in front of me, like copying words written on a screen only these are unseen.

Embellishment

The story is to the point and focuses the mind. It could be embellished and would certainly be longer but what does embellishment do to the mind?

Embellishment can soften, colour, disguise and hide the hard facts, persuading you to accept them as separate from truth but not part of everything.

Servant to the Server

Do you ever believe what you do on your computer, what you write about, what you think and feel on it, is more important than experiencing it in real life? Do you believe your computer will be a better storage device than you after you have gone?

If we believe this and practice this we are practicing having less of life's experiences

We have become programmed to believe technology is more important than us. We are the servant.

Consciousness Does Not Need Words

Without any words would we enquire about the stars and ourselves. Fifty thousand years ago how did we wonder at the stars and our self?

Healing Our self

The doctor sometimes cannot heal what only we can heal. The writer cannot communicate what we are like. We cannot communicate what we are, only be it.

So Near to Know

I don't wear the right words or say the best clothes. The writing tastes sweet not neat. The look is a step inwards so near to know.

Self and Truth

Reality or what is true is only our truth because everything is subjective. All the information we use to see it is put together by us from where we see it. If truth is only our truth, then if we are true to our self, we know truth which is reality.

Enough is Simply Enough

I've written about my travels, my family, my work. I've written about made up stuff. I've written a lot to show what I see we are, so no more writing might help.

18. WARRIORS

Feeling Warrior

Some can write or draw naturally but this can be too under control of the mind, so it's better to draw with your other hand to show how your heart feels. Others can't do these naturally. Anything will do to express how you feel but you can always do something else to express how you feel.

You can sing, paint, and dance, jump across puddles or in them. You can whistle to birds or just look up at the sky. You can hug and embrace playfulness, spontaneity, anyone, a cat or dog. You can just be simple and childlike to express yourself, a feeling warrior.

Unknown Soldier

I didn't choose this path I found myself on. It was my life but I did choose to protect the defenceless.

I didn't fight for gain but to defend the land friends and neighbours survive off.

I didn't fight for posthumous honours but to protect the heart which will keep a place for me.

Unknown to you I am always standing beside you, your family.

Worrier to Warrior

Will I suffer from the material world because I have not invested in it? Will it catch up with me when I have no protection? I've not saved or met brokers to invest in property and businesses. I spent the time and the money on inner happiness instead. I have moments of switching from being an inner warrior to a worrier and my confidence dips. Then I change back to a warrior which reminds me of the path I chose and I am happy again.

Trusted Security

Wally was the security that everyone knew they could always trust. Always had the same look. Always the same chat, 'How are you mate?' Was good at cards too.

He was always positive, even when his wife died. When he had cancer and knew he was next, he still remained the same.

The singers and musicians in every rock and roll band trusted him. He knew their faces each time they came round and he could tell if they were in trouble or if they needed a break.

Never left his post, always there, firm and present. Few knew he died but many noticed he wasn't there anymore. He is what they think of when they wonder if they are safe and now being guarded over from afar.

Two Thousand Years to MAD

Why have we not valued simplicity, humility and compassion, only valuing money, power and ego?

These gifts we have are wasted on competition instead of spent on cooperative mutual kindness.

It took 2000 years to get to Mutual Assured Destruction. How long will it take to get to Cooperative Compassionate Concern?

Body Handling

There is more than a taboo about handling the dead which is talking about what's in your head. You are supposed to recover rapidly to get on with the next task happily.

Crack on, you have to man up and not seem like a pathetic chap. No time to let your feelings be reflected and so they remain permanently neglected.

What if the next task is just an excuse not to deal with the current one properly and is avoidance of looking at feelings to just look like a balanced human being.

Then we are being incompetent with unfinished business and its consequences. We deal fully with our dead but not us after they get locked in our head.

Repatriations

Returning soldiers in body bags, recovered then repatriated by friends who can only guess how they died and how they look now. They always ask was it worth it and say 'It could have been me.'

The loadmaster of the plane waits with the coffins as the plane lands ready for them to re-unite the family. The wailing wives and mothers, the daughters and sons, the seven year old girl in a purple dress runs up the ramp of the plane asking the loadmaster, 'Where's my daddy?' The loadmaster was broken.

The youngest military people are ordered to do general duties at repatriations, holding the door, serving tea or coffee to bereaved relatives, mothers and fathers who always ask the most questions 'Did you know my son, have you been to the front line?' The young are broken.

Combining personal loss with the injustice of conflict is a potent mix which strips those serving tea to the core. No longer naïve but seeing what man does and how it wrecks the lives of those he or she loved and the life they tried to build, now gone.

Now vulnerable and questioning all beliefs, their view of the world changes forever. Their view of work, life, society, politics and religions make them different people, no longer seeing the same purpose they did before.

After doing a few repatriations there is fear of meeting the families, anger at having to do more and anxiety of losing control and crying. Too many and they become detached, as if it's just a drill. Some become preoccupied and others try to reconcile the death but there will forever be the sense it could have been me, even should have been me.

Catastrophic Repatriation

His energy was not just passionate. There was a force with it informing you that this is what he saw, experienced and knew at the time.

He survived being an orphan, Communism, famine in the Ukraine, escape from the Germans, being recaptured, fighting against the Russians, being a prisoner of the British for nearly five years in Italy and England until release in 1949.

His honest words landed him in a psychiatric ward where no one believed him when he said that friends had vanished into thin air, that there were spies in England. Emphatically he said his friends were being taken back to Russia and that they would never be seen again. The GPs and psychiatrists were ignorant of history so they could not understand. Worse they didn't try and consider his version which was right and theirs wrong.

He was right but it wasn't the KGB in the UK, it was the British. The British recruited Ukrainians they gave refuge to, then sent them back to Russia as spies. But what the British and Ukrainians didn't know was an Englishman told the Russians all. When the RAF dropped them in the USSR they were all tortured, killed or sent to Siberia never to be seen again or to meet their nemesis Kim Philby.

No-one Knows

I don't own where I live and I have the same problem my grandfather had in 1930. A landlord with power over him now over me. Are we worriers, or perhaps warriors?

Most Fearsome Warrior

Only strong people get attacked because it satisfies someone's need to look stronger. They attack using everything, whilst the best swordsman never uses his sword.

The attacker doesn't know and doesn't care about the outcome. Without compassion they have no restraint, whilst the best swordsman never uses his sword.

The dishonest person doesn't know himself and is not true to anyone especially to himself, so is never to be trusted, whilst the best swordsman never uses his sword.

The man who knows himself can only be humble, supporting and protecting the defenceless, whilst the best swordsman never uses his sword.

When Illusions are exposed, we see nothing is lost or gained as there is only what was to start with, whilst the best swordsman never uses his sword.

Group Captain

He was senior, in charge and presented a hard front. He said
his men should not wallow in the emotions of death but man
up, crack on and get on with the next task.

Yet he nearly broke down and cried years after talking about
having wanted to drop his salute at the coffin of the man
with five daughters and instead just give the daughters a
hug, but he could not. He said he was a father too.

He told me he wouldn't help to change things unless he saw
the evidence, that looking at feelings after bringing back the
dead, added to the men's strength.

Obedient suppression of feelings in others by the very men
who lead heroes and not hearing or listening to their own
hearts will one day lead to a crisis of heroes being unable to
be heroes because the emotional risks will be too high.

Song for All Unknown Soldiers

I was only thirteen when they came to my school
I had no idea they were just looking for fools
I tried to see with wide open eyes
But what they wanted from me was heavily disguised.

The RAF, Army, Navy said they would pay
For all kinds of travel far far away
They promised me money, excitement and fun
All I had to do was simply carry a gun.

They could have had criminals, bullies or thugs
Not vulnerable children more interested in hugs
They promised us that they'd always be there
And what ever happened they'd really care.

When your last freedom's taken from you
That's when they tell you just what to do
I took orders but couldn't make requests
And my bullied mind never got any rest
Again and again, again and again.

Now when I think of what they got me to do
These people would force your children too
I was hit by a bullet that I couldn't see
It was memory of killing that impacted on me
Again and again, again and again.

Flashbacks by day, then nightmares in bed
I couldn't tell if they were real or just in my head
My innocence has gone but not the memories or pain
Of scenes of a war which was truly insane
Again and again, again and again.

On the crusade of the economy driven war
I soon realised these wars had all happened before
The deaths, the losses, keep on happening again
So the victories the medals are all just in vain
Again and again, again and again

If you fight for peace war will happen again
Without negotiation and tolerance
It'll happen again, again and again.

Political bunkers protect leaders from war
While innocent children are blown to the core
They give the orders to kill everyone
But won't speak the truth to anyone
Again and again, again and again

If you fight for peace war will happen again
Without negotiation and tolerance
It'll happen again, again and again.

Let girls just be girls and boys be boys
Let children be children and just give them toys
Stop our children standing on the front line
Use words not children now is the time
Again and again, again and again

If you fight for peace war will happen again
Without negotiation and tolerance
It'll happen again, again and again.

The Crusades, Vietnam, the World and Gulf wars
Northern Ireland, Afghanistan what are we fighting for?
It's time now to stop blowing others a part
Not be frightened to listen to their heads and their hearts
Again and again, again and again

If you fight for peace war will happen again
Without negotiation and tolerance
It'll happen again and again.

Song For the Effect of War

I took your life which then took mine
To pay it all back to you one day at a time
You child you left me all blown to bits
Invisibly and secretly you gave me this.

I sit and stare not at the past but into the air
There's no worry or pain just peace in this stare
My mind's gone and I'm quiet today
Now that there's nothing left to repay.

I can't be distracted from my stare ahead
Now there's no fear or screams in my head.
When my time comes to go I hope I have the stare that day
The smile of a person who knows the way.

My heroine I had to stop you because you came back again
Then I found myself doing it again and again
The memory of you is so much alive
Of you fighting, beautiful right by my side.

This can't be right we didn't do wrong
We're really friends singing the same song
It's not us that's the problem but those at the top
The politics the war games have to be stopped.

Killing was just a thought until I saw your eyes
Now it's a memory not a horrific surprise
Do I feel at peace? Yes and you do as well
We both saved each other from our future hell.

I know now we saved each other's lives
Only by what we saw in each other's eyes.
When I meet you again and look at your face
I will tell you then what I first saw was grace

Not Man Enough

The heads of the forces are not allowed to be man enough
to talk about emotions. Made to be too busy to have time to
look, too busy to just be how you want to be.

They are not their own person but what others want them to
be in exchange for promotion, pension and retirement. Put
them up against someone who has fought for what is his and
who passionately believes in this and the armed forces lose.

19. DREAMING

Living the Dreaming Life

I think I dreamt a dream but I'm not sure because when I lived it, I thought I had dreamt it all before. I dreamt this life before I woke and I wrote these words before I spoke.

Dreaming and Dreams

There is no evidence that dreams mean anything. When we are awake we wish for change. That is dreaming which we know is important but dreaming asleep is different.

When we awake from sleep there are no masters who have direct knowledge of what our dreams are for.

There are scholars of an imagined field of knowledge called dream analysis who claim they know what they are for.

Living Dreaming

When we wake and we have dreamt, are these the dreams we want to live? Do we want to dream of what others have or have our own dreams?

When we sleep and we dream of a world we are seeing, is that world any less real than the world we think is not a dream?

Living the Dream

A day with no issues could be a day to dream of but are you dreaming anyway and missing living the dream?

Still Dreaming

I have dreamt most of my life always dreaming for happiness in faraway places from here.

I dreamt of studying in India and studied so much, I ended up studying there.

I am still dreaming. It's my nature to escape reality to live dreams which still take me to India.

What I thought was a dream was an illusion. All along India was not a place. It was reality. It was all along and is my inner self.

Life and Dreams

Don't believe what therapists say about your dreams or nightmares because they are only guessing as no one knows and besides, you already know life is worse than dreams and life can be worse than nightmares. Why pay someone from the start to tell you about your truth, which only you can know.

Freedom in Dreaming Analysts

No one knows what dreams are for. Some may give warnings, others may unwind us. Some can remind us. They are ours to understand and not the dream analyst whose interest can be money, power and ego.

They can't take their meaning away from you but that's what they may want to do so they look better telling you they know better than you do.

Chance in Control

Dreams are what happen when chance is given control. All the most unusual things occur when chance and accidents are given the freedom, encouraged to have a voice and see what they can be.

Dreaming

Almost everything you hear and see was once a dream so dreamers are responsible for the world around you.

Where you live, your job, your transport, the food you eat, all started in dreams

Your leisure, your pleasure, the songs, music, pictures and stories were once a dream. If you read writing in your dreams or even add or subtract maybe your brain is telling you that maybe you are avoiding what is human.

20. TIME

Illusions of What Is

Thoughts to fill in time, words to fill in time. Speech to fill in time which cannot be filled. If time doesn't exist, perhaps the Romans are beside us and our ancestors are beside us as well as inside us.

If time is nothing, then the illusion of it may also make space an illusion of our condition.

Our condition may be temporary or permanent but not neither, so in what do we exist? Do we really exist just as we think we do or are we an illusion of the name and form of time and space?

Penultimate

Turns out the final is only the penultimate as there is almost always one more in us.

Final Time

The final time, the final process, the final draft, the final look the final book, the final sigh, the final cries, the final night, the final breath and then finally that look.

Time Zones

Working in different time zones is not working around the planet; it is the planet working you, the tail wagging the dog.

Infants School

I thought there would be nothing there, maybe just a carpark but there it was over fifty years later, the tiny playground, the three foot white circles on the red brick wall, we flicked cards at. The gateway where my mother said goodbye.

Shot

When I got up I knew I had been hit. At first it was a mystery as I thought maybe a horse or some unknown force had lifted me up and thrown me forwards flat on the ground on my face. I was hit only once and knocked into the ground by the sudden force.

I was shot. An ambulance man out shooting after dusk had fired, mistaking me for a rabbit. Thanks to an old thick second hand winter coat, the pellets didn't pierce my skin but there were sore areas where they nearly punctured me before I mysteriously flew through the air.

What Solitude Does

All this solitude what does it do? I've learnt about what I am, about how much other people mean to me.

No More Sitting Cross Legged

I was in denial until I realised no matter what, I could no longer sit cross legged on the floor and I had to sit on a chair at a table.

The hips, the back and knees couldn't take the strain without pain sitting where I had always sat, happily cross legged on the floor.

Denial for a week meant my feelings were being buffered whilst my body slowly let me know this is what happens when you begin to grow old.

Being There

My first abandonment was looking at my mother waving at me. She was leaving me at infant's school at five. She waited for me to realise I was being left. I gulped, sobbed tears and sucked in as if I was gasping for air. But I was drowning in the pain of being wrenched by being left there, of her leaving. It was just for the day not a term of months of painful abandonment, all the borders felt a couple of years later.

Day and Night Person

I'm not a morning person, an evening person or any part of the day person.
Consciousness of being comes and goes and although it seems impossible to be aware all the time, we are.

Some Days Are

Some days are just work, some days are just spiritual, some days are just family, some days are just history, some days are just forgetting, some days are just remembering, some days are just regretting, some days are just hoping, some days are just happiness, some days are just love, some days are just forgotten, some days are always remembered, some days are just being, some days are just solitude, some days are just silent, some are just still.

All Our Yesterdays

There are no new profound things to say or write as they all seem to have been said and recorded and mostly ignored by almost everyone. Perhaps there should be a ban on trying to come up with new things.

Coming up with new things could be banned until the old is known then the origin of any next step can be shown. No new wars, second marriages until the previous one is known.

Active reflection on our history, our thoughts, actions, friendships, enemies, stories and all our yesterdays, could be shown and known.

Natural Ease

At the wrong time nothing can happen. At the right time everything happens with natural ease.

Final Day Every day

Always use your favourite bath salts. Always wear your favourite shoes. Always wear your favourite clothes. Always wear your favourite aftershave or perfume. Always say what's in your heart. Don't ignore this, then reflect and say I regret and wish I saw this, now, with little time left. Write that letter, say that sentence, get that present for them or you.

The Final Phase

The surprises which you are told to expect when you get old are just like the surprises which you are told to expect when you are young. The difference is, even though they are expected, then they arrive, when you are old, they are more of a shock than a surprise.

Suddenly Apparent

Graveyards don't seem to have the same mystery I remember as a child because just five years ago the ground started to come up for me unexpectedly. It was not at first noticed but then it shocked me and only now graveyards have lost their mystery,

Sunday Night

Sunday night always has the feeling of all Sunday nights of something just about to end. Neither here nor there, there is the drawn out waiting for it all to end.

More Years

Getting older doesn't make you stronger as you've got a weaker body. You've got more bad memories, more traumatic events in your memory. The balance of losses and gains can't be assessed anymore because there are too many to make a noticeable difference. The inevitable feels appropriate for the first time as what could be done was. Who wishes for more years?

The Past

Nothing can change the past except I can accept it. I can see it as a time of growth. It was a necessary experience.

Early September

It's always an awkward feeling this time of year. Early September with the feeling of going back to the people at school, college or work after a break from the pressures of people in life. I want my solitude back. I want the happiness detached from the things of life.

Since childhood it's the same for most, the end of happiness in early September, conditioned by education, family or work to end happiness. I used to think one day it would come back but learnt it is only ever right here now to be seized in these days of perfect peace.

Not of Time

Where does time go? It doesn't go anywhere. It can't because it doesn't exist. Time is a thought of measuring what it has invented, which doesn't exist. Consciousness sees thoughts of time but consciousness is not subject to time as consciousness is not of time.

The Journey Tells Us the Way

The Journey tells you the way. There is no need to ask. Just wait for it to speak back to you.

Not Necessarily a Good Example

Would I show anyone else this way? Maybe if they stayed around or came back asking, again knocking on my door, asking for more.

The Dream

I want the dream to be over to show me the truth of reality as it is. Awake, sleeping or dreaming all are the same dream. I know I know this which is the dream explained.

Never both

You can be like everyone else or you can be yourself but never both.

With Family

I was worried for a while, perplexed is more accurate as I
thought all along I was wrong until I found my search. It
seemed I ignored the material and looked odd, took all the
wrong decisions. Seemed like I was going to end up with
nothing. All I am able to say is this is as good as happiness
gets.

What We Can't see Ahead

This wasn't what I thought would happen. It wasn't what
I thought I would do or where I would end up but I am
with my family, my wife and daughter. We are together in
happiness wherever we are. I am full of happiness. No more
full could I be. This is what I couldn't see. What we cannot
see when we are younger.

Sunday after Three

Why is it only just Sundays, when the afternoon is fading,
that the tasks waiting for the next day always fill my heart
with dread.

No other day or time brings this sense of wanting to avoid
what we know has to be done.

Is it the familiarity of the routine, the automatic behaviour,
instead of the freedom of walking away, we know we would
like to feel.

133

Obstructing Access

There is nothing wrong with man's body or brain only his thinking. He has too little to do with his heart. Consciousness of having a heart is overwhelmed by thoughts of anything else, eventually obstructing preventing access.

Personal Vehicles

Sitting in a German car dealership waiting for a cars tyres to be replaced, I sense our ever escalating wasteful use of resources should make us walk away forever from cars.

The car makers need us, we don't need them as we could be healthier and wealthier walking. The world would be less polluted. We would speak more, sharing everything home grown.

Heart's Servant

When thinking is not disciplined, you either become overwhelmed by thinking, which seems to have a mind of its own, or you reject it and find an alternative.

You can go to the heart and return there at every moment possible, leaving thinking only for its functions and your hearts servant.

You can observe thinking and see its nature. Thinking creates a cloudy picture of an ego which demands presence when it does not even exist.

21. BUSINESS

Seduction

We teach how to have everything material. We show by example we can have power and money and that these can give us everything. Resilience to not having these is not taught because not having them is discouraged as it seems no one wants us to be happy with our self. Then we see they want us to be happy as long as it depends on them and we pay them for making us think we are happy. They want us to maintain our delusion that the material world makes us happy by changing our sense and source of security. They control how we think we are happy by misleading advertising and seducing our sense of our ego's vanity.

Everything

To the man or woman who seems to have everything there is always one thing they do not have because it is unexpected but a rule.

The nature of our inner self is that it cannot have two things at the same time; everything and happiness.

Not Everyone

Not everyone is a traitor but people can so easily become traitors because they want the power, the money or the ego.

Sensitivity

Although we stand together, some of us are separated, divided by the desire for gain no matter what, even if the cost is other's pain, knowingly preventing them from being happy.

Dispassion

My automatic brotherly bonding ended decades age because of the pain I remember I once had to carry. The empathy I have for my brother's children is brightly clear but also detached as they too have had pain.

Projection

Does a blood relative mean more than we project onto someone we want to like and mean as little as the withdrawal when we don't.

From Business to Industry

Detached from the rest, stressful at its very best, the music industry, the medical industry, the drug and arms industries are what feed us more than food.

Different Paths

Advertising and promotion are not the way. Attraction is a steady path.

22. ADVERTISING

Bottom Line

Watching and listening to adverts and those trying to advertise always ends in a price.

Inadvertent Advertising

It seems so hard to be simple. It seems so hard to be clear. It seems so hard to be honest. It seems so hard to be kind. It seems we have lost what we are. Profoundly influenced by the subtle inadvertent advertising of satisfied customers who don't know what makes them happy.

Advertising Trick

Why can't we see what we have? What is our blind spot? Is it believing in others that we should have what they've got?

Is believing in others the root of unhappiness?

If we believe when others tell us that we are happy or not happy, then our happiness will depend on them. Perhaps we need to seriously ask ourselves what really makes us happy.

Advertising

It seems so hard to be simple. It seems so hard to be clear. It seems so hard to be honest.

We are programmed by subtle advertising to fear not being accepted if we do not have the latest of things.

We then accept we can be happier with something from outside us, when the truth is we already have all the happiness we need from inside us.

23. QUESTIONS

No Home Town

Back where I was born and raised I am not the wise stranger who says little and is asked lots of questions. I can't really speak. It is me who wants to ask how you have remained here when I have had to live away and be changed.

How have you not lived and mixed with strangers when I have spent all my time alone with them learning new ways to work with them? Why could I have not done this here with you? What was it about me that had to leave? I cannot come back as I need to let the wind curl my inner sail again.

Single Use Only

I don't wonder what others will conclude about my questions, about my answers about my purpose whilst I was here. They are questions and answers only determined by the nature of our consciousness, our single desire to find happiness.

Yes

Yes, is the answer to the question you have not yet asked yourself. The purpose of the answer is that now you can let go of asking questions.

Questioning

Why do some people not like us asking questions about ourselves? Perhaps they don't want to hear the answer.

Are these matters which don't interest them, don't concern them, don't bother them, or are we the people with the problem?

Mercifully there are occasionally people who don't just want to be entertained or use chemicals to alter their brains and there is always solitude.

End of Questions

We seem to search alone but many others are searching for the same as you and me. We search because it's our nature to question why we are conscious, what is consciousness and what is it for. What is our purpose, if there is any other than what it seems to be, maybe it is best accept it as just truth.

When We Stop Asking Questions

Are we part of a plan of something divine or a product of random meetings of the elements? Are we as special as we think? Are we the only beings who think? Do we exist beyond these dimensions? Are there other dimensions?

Perhaps we can stop being full of questions we can't answer. If we do we are happy in our self.

24. PASSION

Unity

Passionate about preserving, passionate about change, passionate about being armed, passionate about disarming.

Both sides have to be understood like light and dark then accepted as equal to be more than either as one.

Passions

On fire showing love quietly and on fire demonstrating against love noisily. Why are both so necessary for each to exist?

Passionate

How can I be passionate about silence yet have feelings in excess of most? Perhaps I am not in the presence of people I can relate to enough or perhaps I am out of touch. To be out of touch, out of reach, not able to communicate is probably normal. Just that I see it as not commonly expressed because we are too afraid of others, not of my passion.

Seeing Our Self in the Light

Whatever brings a ray of sunshine to your life treasure like yourself. Light is what lets us see our self fully.

Offending Truth

For every twelve good people there is one wolf in the group
who pretends to be the same but has no principals. They
read people well, are good actors and charmingly protest to
cover their tracks. They smile when they lie, cry when caught
to further themselves offending truth.

Protectors of the Defenceless

We all play the same, sometimes clean, sometimes not, me
included. Sometimes dirty, yes without exception, me too.
You will defend the defenceless, so will I even if it means
the assailant suffers the fate they intended their victim.
Protecting the defenceless is everyone's job who is defended.

The Rights to Air

You can only be truly passionate about rights which you
know are yours to protect. Others rights are no different
from yours because you both breath the same air.

Heart's

We only speak from our hearts with those we love and care
about. It may not be often but it always has more meaning
than anything else. It is these communications which are
always remembered not just by us but by those who notice
them and learn.

Soul Mate's One Request

Every day she talks to her dead husband and there is only one request from her to him. 'If you want me to be with you, come and get me tonight.'

Non Passionate Living

I didn't have any interest in non-passionate living until the passion went. Then I saw what a fantastic time I had and I was left with real memories not real estate.

Energy of Passion

Where does passion go for what we believe in? How fast does it go and why does it go? It doesn't return but the thoughts remain. Only the energy has gone.

Passion

Passion does not go for what we believe in. Energy for it reduces and does not return Consciousness remains, thoughts and the energy fade, but never the passion.

Imaginable

Isn't it magical that tomorrow will come. Isn't it magical that tomorrow will be another day. Isn't it magical that tomorrow can imaginably be as happy as today.

All Passions

I don't work with anyone young. We are all old but I am the eldest. No one is under forty. The men look smart but their hearts, boringly out of shape. None of the men care about how they look inside. None of the women are flirtatious inside. None of them talk or move that way. They have all gone so far beyond all that, all passions flattened and ironed out by life.

25. PSYCHOLOGIICAL ARCHITECTURE

Redemption

When the suburban sprawl has reached a critical point, there won't be enough land to grow anything on, not enough nutrients to grow humans on.

Perhaps with no more expansion of the ego, kindness will find roots and the spirit will flourish.

My Cell

We are allocated and directed to our sky scraper single cell apartments in the sky above the complex technological suburban sprawl.

Like bees from honeycomb cells, we have to escape from this sterility to be amongst the flowers to find nourishment for the soul.

The Apartment

A place where there is an exercise space but nothing to do. A library with books that can be seen but nothing worth reading. A place where you are left in neutral inside your head. There are millions of these places which are not alive, where not even a cockroach would want to survive. Is this where you want to end up?

26. REFLECTION

Note to Me

The last days, I want to be more gentle however many there are. I want to be more sensitive especially to me.

One Final Path

There is no single formula which works best for turning inside but whichever way we choose, the final path is always the same.

Knees

We rose from our knees over 70,000 years ago and walked out of Africa probably talking then too as we began to cover the earth like an infection.

When we walked, then talked, our thinking let us plan this journey but the thinking brought us down.

The meteor which wiped out the dinosaurs was a pimple compared with the millions of times more damage we have done since walking, talking and thinking.

It seems we can only wait for the final warnings of our extinction then we will be back on our knees, on all fours.

Being Here Now

We have been thinking like this since we walked out of
Africa thinking and dreaming we were going to arrive
somewhere.

We have arrived at the dreams we dreamt but the dreams
were not true. Like our thoughts now seem real, they were
just our dreams whilst we were in Africa.

What we were then did not threaten the survival of animals,
plants or the planet but now we are the executioner the
destroyer of everything we love.

Wallowing

The commanders ensure there is no wallowing in thoughts
and feelings about lost friends even if you carried your best
mate's coffin. You must crack on immediately with the next
task so all you can do is pray.

The Thread That Links Us

It is not how much time I have left, it is what is going to be
shown, what will I experience, what will I uncover, what is
in store for me, who will I see, who will they be, what have I
got left to do, to be so I can leave what I see to you?

You may pick it up to look at some place along your path,
then leave it to pass it on to someone else.

Experiencing

Time to get rid of all the stuff I have acquired, bought of bargained for. Time to leave no things around, nothing behind. Maybe just some words in the ether of the digital age or even some words in a folder on a page. Maybe only my experience not recorded anywhere just experienced then over.

Not Too late

I don't know how many days I have left or even if the next breath will come. I'm not aware anything at all is wrong; I'm just being clear and real about uncertainty.

I can't be thankful after the time has passed to be thankful. I can't say what I mean when the person can no longer hear me.

I only strive to be happy now in every one of my thoughts in the words I say or write to show you.

Two Types of Journey

Your body is under a death sentence. Your mind takes less distress with age. Traumatic memories accumulate with time. Enthusiasm once peaked never returns.

The whole experience of life can seem to have a rotten end unless the desire for happiness transforms it to a thankful spiritual journey.

The Only Way

The only thing that brings you to the spirit is knowing the spirit is here. Logic does not prove the spirit. The only proof of spirit is the union of experiencing it.

The only thing that brings you to love is loving. Logic does not prove love. The only proof of love is the union of experiencing it.

Companions walk with us

Not in time but of time you see what you are. There are no changes when the inside is seen.

Your heroines and heroes are mere companions walking with you.

We cannot yet see the oneness in our stillness.

Now I compare

When he came in the room you didn't seem to care. Now his body is gone you see him everywhere. You hated the sound of his old boots in your head, now you can't sleep if they are not by your bed.

The sound of him eating always put you in a mood, now you can't eat unless you hear yourself eating your food.

Funny how every sound is heard, every smile seen, how we just glance as if this is how we will always be.

Wonder

Wonder at the sky the moon and stars, wonder at the sun, wonder at the oceans. Wonder at courage, wonder at humility, wonder at compassion. Wonder at consciousness, wonder at the sense of wondering is exquisite wonder.

Eschatology

We do not live long enough to see the changes in the shape of a river, even if we did, would we notice them?

We now live long enough to see the repeating cycles of our own nature, even with this knowledge we do not change.

On the brink of catastrophe, when annihilation is the alternative, does our thinking accept that it is incorrect?

There is a selfish greedy recklessness, competing until death with effects on everyone, which even though some care about, can destroy us all.

Not Still Enough to Move

I haven't been bent over by the wind or walked and been soaked in the rain much lately. My sitting in stillness has been so disturbed I've not been able to be still enough to actually move into stillness.

Passing Something on

Most of our memories and reflections do not help but techniques of doing things are the best way to pass things on.

27. OUR DAILY BREAD

Company

Every day you have to be with this person. You have to have early morning refreshments with them. Who could his be? Whose company can you deal with no matter what, every day for the rest of your life? Who could this be?

Solitude's Company

Now the bread is baked and eaten what are we to engage in? Perhaps only in what makes us happy, the company of solitude.

Every Time

There is a rushed need to get to the oven. Not too late, not too early, just on time every time.

Conscious of Bread

Enough of this chatter about bread. Let's get it out, observe, judge and be thankful.

Nearly Done

The excitement is building up because the loaf is nearly ready. It will be ten more minutes, so I have to finish this.

Then the pleasure or disappointment will spread around the house from the smell of fresh bread when the oven is opened.

I can wake them up for breakfast of fresh soda bread, a white and brown loaf to make them both happy.

To Please

There is a loaf in the oven. It is how I remember to bake but I don't know how it will turn out. I never can.

It is not an industrial automatic process. It is made by my hands and because of my mood and distractions it could disappoint or please.

28. WORK

Working

Perhaps the young should learn work. The ones in the middle of life should research work. The old should teach work.

Work

I don't like my work but I love what I do it for. It's for my life and those in it.

Stop the Job

I don't like my day job. I only do it because it pays the best. I would prefer the free time whilst my health is good but my other work is me. I will only stop it when I drop. How can you not like yourself and what this produces?

We All Have to Act Our Part

I don't let my job take me to work. I act the part as impeccably as I can for a few hours, hoping all are convinced the act delivers. Then I ditch it as I close the door of the office.

Working Life

The ones in the middle of life should research work. The young should learn work The old should teach work. But there are also those others, equally important, those who should not work but need to lead contemplative lives for us.

Imposters

When after years of work the ego is no longer believed in because the self has taken command, others may say we have Coltard's delusional syndrome of believing we don't exist but that is not quite what it seems.

When after years of work we don't believe in other's egos because the inner self sees their egos as imposters, others may say we have Capgras's Syndrome of believing others don't exist but that is not quite what it seems.

Maybe their truth is only their truth because reality is subjective and others are delusional creations of imaginary egos supposed into existence by believing they are bundles of thoughts, which others condition them to agree about.

29. SECURITIES

Polarity

Security is leant through insecurity. Stability in leant through instability. Surrender is learnt through struggling and fighting. Detachment is learnt through attachment. Happiness is learnt from suffering.

Disguises

When I reflect on the opportunities I have turned down, the decisions left me materially insecure but more whole and richer inside and I am happier as a result.

When I reflect on betrayals which left me bruised they seemed like losses but were blessings in disguise. They left me more whole and richer inside and I am happier as a result.

It seems as if I am not allowed to be secure, no matter what but must stay permanently suffering insecurity. Perhaps it gives me a hunger, a passion to carry on surrendering.

Perhaps like a boxer going on too long, I don't know when to stop or I might be made just for this. I don't know.

Your Nature

Oh ever changing world of seduction, passing pleasures,
dreams of security, you are a clever illusion.

Oh ever changing world, always changing is your nature
because your nature is change. Mine is to be true to me too,
conscious of the need to be happy in stillness.

Securities

The material world not only doesn't seem to be my friend, it
is not. The people who aspire to this are also not, so who is
my friend.

I, most of all am what makes me happy but that is the inner
world.

I have tried to share others fear of the world but it is not my
business; it is theirs alone to deal with. Perhaps it is mine to
witness only, not comment on or guide.

I considered the evidence of being a witness to things which
may be an illusion, packed my inner bags and I am always as
still as possible on this short trip.

Alone we Relate

Seeing your thinking is wrong and you are not as connected
like society makes you think you are is a shock but
eventually this lets you relate to everyone as you are, not
with just your thoughts.

Securities and Happiness

When your loved one is struck down, exactly how will your securities make you happy? When your days are unexpectedly numbered how will your securities let you enjoy them in happiness? Ask yourself how your securities will let you be happier than happiness from within now.

Security

I have no security protecting me now or in the future from being vulnerable to landlord's whims and moods.

If I did, it could be taken, they could be taken, but the most important things could not be taken. I have myself, my attitude.

Ownership

Being attached to everything, you cannot be true to yourself. Having everything you want money can buy is being poor because all you have is money.

To let go of everything is to be at home everywhere because you are homeless.

To let go of everything you are the richest person because you have no attachments.

Investments and Securities

We can feel overshadowed, even a failure in comparison to someone who has been successful in the world. But that is only until we turn inwards and see the treasures we have inside, which they have declined.

Inevitability helps us accept

Life is on the whole mostly predictable because we follow or reject what we are given. We take risks or are conservative but most people follow what their parents taught them. The joys we experience are the same for almost everyone. Our suffering, our diseases and death are not predictable but are inevitable. We divide up into various groups for mutual support as our parents did.

Perhaps the most important thing is to be happy and have as much joy as is possible because of the inevitability of suffering, disease and death.

Perfect Security

The most elite of interesting company, fascinating conversations, adventures and descriptions revealing ideas are too painful to endure.

All invitations to encounters like this are avoided so successfully that I can say in total satisfaction of my happiness that I am now never invited.

Religion and Psychology

There are two things which I am not interested in; one is religion, the other is psychology. They have hierarchical authorities who mutually exclude others.

Most interesting of everything is the self which cannot be explained by psychology or religion because there is only one authority as no one else knows or is known.

30. OTHERS

Making It Up

You couldn't make it up because it is life. When you make it up, the lie loses the rawness of truth, like you always know when an actor is acting.

Discovering Being and Sharing

It is difficult to find out and accept, so we must know our self first before we can know someone else, but then we can just be. It is difficult to find out and accept, so we must be our self first before we can be with someone else but then we can just be.

It is difficult to find out and accept, so we must be kind to our self first before we can be kind anyone else, but then we can just be. It is difficult to find out and accept, so we must love our self first before we can love someone else, but then we can just be.

Usefulness

I accept that I am a worker for others and whether I choose or not someone will be profiting from me. It is the same for us all.

Just Being with One Person

Others amass more land, buildings, investments and I wonder if their dreams are free. Maybe they are more free because of these things. My dreams seem to reflect what I get deliberately get involved with. They are not about material things. Journeys, paths spooky silent places. Some seem to be in other worlds. Most are about being with just one other person.

Leaders

The world gets the leaders it needs. Their role is to restore the balance lost by those before them whichever way.

Looking In Each Other's Eyes Again

Man's habit of making everything easier by making them habits has led to everyone using things instead of themselves. From not walking to not talking with no eye contact and not playing to not physically taking part in life.

If man is brave enough to take some steps back we can learn to do, walk, talk, play, physically interact with the world and look each other in the eye again.

Gossip

Gossip is always full of energy but the wrong kind to make anyone feel good because it is about other people.

One Two Three or More at My Door

Having to deal with just our self is a battle of duality. Thoughts want to be uppermost in our mind as our ego but the peace of consciousness of being still was first. This is our condition, which we accept or restore.

I don't flourish in groups. I don't work in groups. I am solitary and prefer one to one company in all settings.

Listening to one person is complicated as there are so many voices present who can't speak who influences what the person says, so it is difficult to identify what the person wants. Listening to a group is different. They all speak not listening to each other, wanting to be heard as one voice when they and can only be fragments.

All Mixed Up

When you meet someone, it is not just a face with a body and a smile. There is an unmeasurable amount of influence going back decades.

There are important ancient family histories, stories, legends and facts, scandals and gossip mixed with truth and beauty and the result is what you see.

Stories

What we seem to others is the story we leave behind but the truth we live is what we are and is known only to us.

Differing Levels

Do you have to stay with those you don't like? Do you have to work with those you don't like? Do you have to eat with those you don't like or would you want to live off your own kind?

Renting

Renting something you own is renting part of you to someone else, whether a tool, a car, a house or even a body part like a uterus. It never makes you feel better about yourself.

Playing Our Parts

What is said about what someone, may have no relation to what they are like. Better to leave what you think about them as their work personality only.

What is said about what someone, may have no relation to what they do for work. Better to leave what you think about their work as their work only.

All Talk is Imagined

We don't have to imagine a conversation with anyone. It happens before we say everything because we imagine their responses and ours to theirs.

Our Small Talk

'So,' is the word to start every answer?

'You couldn't make it up,' is the current fashion in complimenting someone's talking.

Underneath and unspoken, the despair of emptiness is silenced by the egos current fashion of ego's to satisfy each other.

Of Our Kind

We all come from nobility. It is just what we do with our inheritance that determines if we are noble people or without dignity.

Treachery is always around to raise the status of the other person but so is humility to help us be accepted as of our own kind.

One Exception

I can't keep up with this obsession with numbers. One is the only one that is necessary. One is all there is. One being the exception the rest are made up and an illusion.

Labels

What we call someone sticks, like sticking a label on a jar. What labelling doesn't change is in the jar.

Thank You for Calling me Stupid

I am glad I was thought of then as being stupid because
otherwise now I could be seen as not having got anywhere
and still just being stupid.

The Village Shop

With all the knowledge at our disposal how come we don't
use it intelligently to spell out basics about ourselves so
that we can live more wisely, more happily to see the real
mechanisms behind how we relate, why we take too many
chemicals and food and drink, what they do to us, how only
a certain amount of work and wealth is good for us, what
different types of people we need and don't need, how we
can congregate together at times
and how we don't when we could to improve our own and
other people's lives.

The not for profit community shop staffed by volunteer's
two hour shifts watch, protect and gather in the lonely, the
vulnerable who need little else.

My wish

For today, I wish every day to have time to be with the ones I
choose, to withdraw from the world, to be thankful for being
conscious and for being happy.

31. REALITY

Nothing to Do With Reality

Reality has nothing to do with thinking, psychology or religion. Reality can only be seen if you are not distracted by thoughts. Reality is everything else when thought is not present.

Reality

Everything is as it appears to you. It is exactly as it seems to you. It is all there is and is a part of you.

All you actually have is you. Reality is that there is just you. Just you is all you can be, all you can know.

Strange Discovery

The discipline of happiness comes only from suffering.

What Appears the Same

There are different ways to turn inside, suffering is the beginning, meditation and solitude are the middle; stillness is the same at the beginning, middle and end.

Raw Energy of Stillness

When we step out of our shoes, new ways lie ahead for those to walk in our shoes with exactly the same energy we began with. There is a raw energy which encourages nature and life to simply be itself to the best it can be. This same energy waits inside us to show us what we are so we can show others too.

Stop to Reflect

Sometimes it is better to stop, maybe just to reflect, then carry on, which will happen anyway if it is correct.

No Truth

If it's not you it's not Truth. If it's not from inside you it's not truth.

Finding Truth

Truth is not at school, college or university. It is in you.

Where to Find Truth

Only listen to the person who looks inside for truth. It is the only place where you will find it. Only listen to the person who looks inside for truth inside you.

Where Truth Is

You will finally see after much searching, sometimes after several decades, the truth you look for, which you call reality, is only inside you.

One Way, the Only Way

You find out about you from you. Others can point the way. Books can point the way. Places can point the way but the way is turning inside.

What You Can Only Learn One Way

You can't find out about yourself in books. They can only confirm what you found by turning inwards into yourself.

Inside Only

Just as you stay inside to keep warm in winter, you can only find out about yourself by turning inwards and staying inwards.

Love and Affection Always

Our love and affection is from the heart always. Intangible affection, present always in everything, which is done or not done yet. Our love and affection is here and there always.

Still Good

The days new born baby checks are done, the expectant mothers are all seen, the seventy three year old with terminal cancer has died and the middle aged alcoholic is still in denial.

My room is a single cell where they all come and go, where I stay still, believing I am having a good day.

Most Full when Empty

I couldn't change to be concerned with only the material as it would be like me cutting my leg off or being good at maths. Why is this? What did this to me?
Was I born like this or did I become this?

I am most comfortable with no comforts. I am full of happiness with nothing to want. I am thankful for the worst things. I feel most connected to everyone in solitude.

Who is The Doer

At the end of struggling we have to give up control to whatever is our inner self, as it has us in its jaws. Whatever we do, it is not us who does it. It is the one who has us inside who does it, who is none other than our own self.

True to Our Own Self

If what we believe to be true is what our mind tells us because it has integrated all inputs from our senses and rationalised an answer as a conclusion, then everyone's truth is different.

Everyone's truth being different because it is relative means there is only our own truth. We can only be loyal to that one truth, our truth which is being true to our self.

Consciousness as a Temporary Resident

Maybe consciousness is not actually inside us and is not centred anywhere in space.

Perhaps it is something everywhere we can connect to or not depending on the strength of our signal.

Thought

I am not sure what to think or how to think or why to think any more when experience is so much better. We overuse this lofty apparatus and miss out on much that would make us happy.

States of Being

This life is a dream between two states. One is pre-birth the other is after-death. We know nothing about either or even who or what we are.

Not a Clue

We haven't got a clue about what we are doing as we only see when it is nearly over and too late, which applies to almost everything.

We Know

We are fortunate to be born and we don't know why. We are born into happiness and suffering and we don't know why.

It is an incredible experience and we don't know why.
It is full of beauty and ugliness and we don't know why.

We are conscious and we don't know why. We die with happiness and sadness and we don't know why.

The Same Unique Difference

I have gone off on a tangent on a path. I thought it was just me but when I asked, it seems like I'm not the only one.

We are so uniquely different that we are the same because each of us has so many differences.

Say it Can

When you are the only person who can do it, if you say it can't be done, you add to the likelihood that it can't be done. So just say it can.

About You

Enough of this from me because this is now about you, how you see it. It may take years to see this, even if it takes decades, it is all about you, which is what you need to pass on.

Then everything is seen

When you see that this is what it has all been about, what it will always be about, you can see your inner self.

Even Wrong is Right

What a colossal relief to know the path I took was right, that the people I have been following were right, that where I am now is right.

It could not be otherwise. How could it be? Even wrong is right as it is seen to change.

Confirmation of Truth

Although we think we know, we do know. When we see we are not the body at all but just using it for this journey, it is confirmation of what we are is truth.

What this truth is, is the stillness within which if patiently sought and stayed with is seen to be in everyone in everything.

What we Are

Truth cannot be argued with, only seen for what it is,
acknowledged for what it is, then accepted for what it is.

No Confirmation Needed

Truth doesn't need confirmation. It has it already. It has
everything.

Truth doesn't need to be acknowledged or written about. It is
complete.

It is us who need to see truth. It is us who need to
acknowledge it, to confirm it.

Then we have to follow it to be fully it which means
everything is secondary to it.

Finally

Finally we don't see with light but we see with inner light.
Finally we don't hear with sound but we hear with inner
silence. Finally we are not aware with the mind but we are
aware with inner stillness.

Freedom as a Chain

When you have detached, it is difficult to attach again
because there is no reason or desire, as false freedom has
been let go of.

Breaking Attachment

There is nothing more painful than seeing the one you love suffer at the hands of others. There is nothing more worrying than fearing what will happen to them. Letting go of them is impossible but necessary for you both to survive.

Thinking and Reality

It is so difficult to see what is going on now because we are so busy doing things, thinking things. It is so difficult to see where we are now from the distance of the future because that vision is so dim.

The ability to see perfectly is always here but almost always obstructed by what we are thinking and doing, instead of seeing what we really are. We usually only see what we are thinking or doing, not what we are.

What we are is obscured by thinking. Thinking is a thick fog stopping us from seeing reality. If we could see this, it could scare us so much we might get in denial about it because we couldn't deal with it.

As Close to Truth

Is it possible to separate reality from our thinking? What we think cannot be reality for everyone. What we interpret as reality is only our perspective from the input of our thoughts. But if we stop thoughts and stay with what is here, we see being conscious of existence is as close as we can be.

Seems Like Reality

The world we experience is the only what we choose but we are usually unaware that we choose. We then interpret our experiences so seek meaning, unaware we are only questioning our own choice. When we see the world is our creation interpreting it and trying to find meaning, stop. It is not what it seems like at all it is only our interpretation.

Most Powerful Desire of No Thought

So you now know you cannot trust anyone else and you have to trust yourself. But be just as careful not trusting your body even though you look after it and nurture it in every way because it can suddenly fail you with cancer and other fatal diseases. So you are left with only trusting yourself. Then you discover that thoughts won't stop and they keep you awake at night. Thoughts keep you worrying about the future, stopping you being happy now.

How do you slow, them stop them, and abandon them? Slowing and stopping them can last for a few seconds or minutes but this is only with help of tethering them to breathing or the sound of a mantra. But they always return trying to give them some shape in the form of the ego. Being identified as an entity called the ego gives them a reason to keep on forming. The ego can only be stopped by seeing this.

For this to happen you have to give up wanting any thoughts ever again. Not wanting any thoughts is the most important thing above all else. This means your ego has to go. Complete surrender is a possible alternative. Do you really want this?

32. LIFE FROM OUTER SPACE

Would They be like Us

Would Martians have cats and dogs as pets and friends
for company and exercise? Would they have stuffy
establishments to show they could endure financial wastage?
Would they gamble and eat out rather than in, sleep so
much, each so much? Would Martians be more like insects or
thin rather than obese like us?

Leave Us

When man discovers there is life on other planets
and eventually visits to see if there is any chance of a
relationship, could this be the result? 'We do not want you
to stay so please leave us now. We only want to be with
intelligent life forms who respect others and their ways of
life?'

The Visit

The visitor looked at us and said, 'What you do to your
weather, killing each other, eating your friendly faced
friends? No time for stillness, solitude, silence, self-
absorption, spirit nurturing. Drinking that false spirit, taking
those chemicals because you can't control your mind on your
own, I'm going home.'

33. US FROM INSIDE OUT

Marinated

We have to be soaked in suffering before we are ready to be soaked in the relief of surrender. Then we are ready to be marinated to see the uncovering of our happiness.

Damaged Isolation

Isolated by walls when there are many others on the other side of the walls just the same. Do we scare each other that much where ever we live? Are we socially so damaged and competitive, so socially isolated? Is that the reason for the walls?

Full of Thoughtless Stillness

I know so little, I don't know how people think and plan. I don't know how the earth works. I don't know how the future will unfold.

I have tried to know about my inner self, not through clever people, books or courses but by being with people who have sacrificed everything to be still.

We are only what we can be now, we are not our dreams, what we are is full of thoughtless stillness.

Isolation

I've said I don't know so many times more than giving an answer. Why do people continue to ask? perhaps they just want interaction. Maybe I am the only person they speak with all day; maybe I am the only person they speak to all week.

Resilient

There's not much further to go, just one last hurdle we tell ourselves all our life.

Living lives of increasing endurance, resilience eventually becomes the most valuable resource on the planet for survival.

Yes of No

It is important to check your mood and ask, 'Am I letting people in and are things impacting on me? How much am I responsible for where I am? Do I need to attend to myself?

Without Projections

We are each in our own private world in our own prison cell, the walls, floor and ceiling decorated with projections of our choice.

Without these we are still, conscious of our inner self. We are happy without all of these projections.

Masterly Inactivity

Walks can seem boring because they can seem to be just
about exercise but they are full of masterly surprises.

The best walks seem like the ones where you get inspiration
to write or do something when you get back.

But then there are walks when just before you get back
you realise you have not thought and you see it has been a
meditation of stillness.

Again and Again

Some of us do things the other way round from most.
It's not trying to be different but true to what we are.
Maybe it's because of less conditioning we go against the
grain. Perhaps it's not wanting to do and see the same thing
again and again.

Being Better Humans

We just go on and on for hundreds of thousands of years
wave after wave of parents, brothers and sisters. How much
have we changed, improved and become better at being
human?

Seeing Being

How good to see that we just couldn't see what we were
looking at was how happy it is to just be.

The Path is the Goal

How many times do I have to stop trying to get somewhere other than where I am? Why do we do this? Because we are conditioned to. We are programmed.

Unlike Pavlovian dogs we believe in delayed gratification, so we don't give up but carry on and on and on. When we are already where we want to be, we just don't seem to see the path is the goal.

The Best Time

There are times in the day which are best for being still, for writing, for everything. Sticking with these is discipline and is the way.

An Own Goal

What a massive relief to understand when we see that we are already where we want to get to, that we have always been where we want to be, realising it is the goal.

Always Home

It doesn't matter what others think and say. What matters is being on your path, doing it your way.

It will take you to unusual places, looking at many facets of everything, then you realise you have always been home.

The Only Way for You

When you have found your path, it is the only way as there are no other styles or any other ways.

One Goal

When you have found what you want. When you know your search is correct and on the right path, you give up all other searches. You give up reading. You give up entertainment. You give up all others, except those on the path.

Searching in Secret

Searching once started never stops. It is a secret search in solitude. There is only one goal. When it is found, it can't be named only experienced, its presence being sensed by others in them to find.

The Beginning of the Search

There was a brief flash but I saw it. I recognised it but I can't name it. It was something inside I wanted. It showed itself briefly to announce it exists. The search had begun.

Happiness Only

I gave up everything for happiness. I came here for this. There is nothing else. There is only happiness.

There is only happiness

In the acid bath of suffering there is no escape only disappearance. It's what I came here for, only for happiness.

Dissolved

Only this. How do I describe it? There is no one to describe it. It has devoured the person who started to look for it. The goal doesn't tell you that what makes you most happy is not having thoughts, which means you don't exist. You have dissolved.

Total Humility

Total humility is freedom from everything and binds you to everything forever.

Humility

If you have experienced humility and been to hell, you become spiritual. If you have not experienced humility, religion will keep you believing you can be greater than who you are.

That is All

Tomorrow may be a day of no thoughts, perhaps walking, eating, meditation, chores to enable these but that is all.

Just Being Now

Why can't we be in the same mood when we wake as when we went to sleep? Do our dreams make us that unhappy?

To Sleep and to Wake to Dreams

The last thing on our hearts and minds as we go to sleep are often not what we admit to. Hopes and dreams of luck and happiness would be great to wake up to as well as to fall asleep to.

Integration into Fantasy

Believe nothing anyone tells you and only half of what you see.

Believe nothing from any of you senses as they are not what they are made out to be.

You integrate the information and come to a decision which may seem sensible but is just your projection.

Saving You

How far away can you get from your inner self before it is too late? It is never too late because you can get there in the last breath which saves you from you.

On a Roll

We get on a roll with our preoccupations because we don't break up our activities with disciplining thoughts.

The Fullest of Times

There should be gaps in our life when we should be in solitude, avoiding people as much as possible to recharge.

Perhaps these gaps should occur several times a day not just during sleep, between ablutions and meals but in walking, drawing, writing and meditation so our time together can be full.

Bufferless

The buffers our parents could put in place could not protect us more than what we protect our self with by simply learning about our self.

Obscuring Us

Always there is what we are hidden behind, what we are busy with. Business is necessary for life but obscures us.

More is Less

The more you know, the less you are.

Less is more

The more we look for information, the less we know. The less we look for information, the more we know.

Self and Knowledge

The more we know of ourselves, the more we know of the world. The more we know of the world, the less we know of ourselves.

World View

People sometimes say what is going on for them.
It looks like it is them speaking about how they are but is only their world view.

The Brightest Lights

The majority who are not given the choice go about their life like sheep on the easy road. Only those who are able, look for their own path. These are the ones with courage and strength.

More than half die and most get badly injured managing to carry on in their suffering. A few go back to their original choice, finding late happiness which burns brightest.

How Most Roads are Formed

When you look back, your journey speaks back to you.
You chose your path from only two. Decadence to decay or
growth to happiness. Living the life of either chaotic messy
descent or the disciplined inner life of being consciously
happy in stillness.

But there are those who are not given the choice. They are
the majority. They don't ever see the choice is theirs. They
go about their life like sheep. The easiest path is how most of
our roads are formed, by sheep.

Red Flags

Each threat of ending of life brings us into the present far
away from where we were in the future.

Each threat silences thought more bringing us close to the
stillness we know we have to face.

Surrounded by Barbs of Sharp Thorns

With the filing down of the first barb, the branches holding
the barbs wither in the gentle winds of tenderness and the
heart within is seen and felt.

Balanced

Solitude is amazing but so is company, the freedom to
choose is balance.

Ideas

To read about the inner world and become an expert without practically knowing the territory is like the captain who has read all about sailing but has never gone to sea. Would you sail with him?

People with stories and theories like those who have never sailed a storm cannot show you an inner world where they have never been.

Importance of a View

Having a view to look at, to look out at, brings us into the world outside our selves.

Lone Wolf

If I could choose to be what I am and not be what I am not, I would have the world I know against me saying you can't do this, you can't do that.

They would persist until I agreed to change saying you must do this, you must say this, and you will be happy with us and we with you.

I'm not a yes person; I'm not a no person or a type in anyone's personality typography. I am a resilient lone wolf who likes to be alone and sometimes in a group.

My Turn

I do not come in to it. My memories and associations are not for display. Today is not about me it is your day.

But tomorrow is mine and all about me, to be spent any way which I almost have no choice about because it is only about being happy.

What We Are We Could Be

What we could be is happy in stillness which is our nature.

Today's Silent Stillness

The person I saw only needed to be listened to, even though she initially asked for pills.

She left without remembering she wanted them, having done all the healing work by talking.

Old Volcanos

All we have is our suffering and happiness. The inner transformation makes us like silent old volcanos at peace.

Suffering Becomes Strength

What you share about you is the most precious you have, showing your suffering turning to strength.

Through understanding them, through this sharing, others who listen and hear can begin to change their suffering and gather their strength.

Heartbeat

Who seems to sing the song best gets more applause but the creator has the heart, the rhythm of the tune, the beat of the drum. With the words are the heartbeat of the writer.

Flying South

Will I be happy today? I will search out happiness today by doing what must be done, like birds must fly south.

Flying North

What I must do may not seem to make me happy but it does because I am happy fulfilling my duty, like birds who must fly back up north.

Days of Happiness

When you are aware you have all the happiness you need for today, you cannot be happier. These are perfect days.

Detaching to Turn Inside

The recognisably famous for something eventually crave
the ordinariness of solitude, only found by detachment
from the things of the world. Only possible by surrender of
everything, few can detach and turn inside.

Foolishly Inside Out

How can we forget so easily the most important thing in our
life, that we are happy inside?

How did it happen? Why can't we see it because we want it
more than anything?

We have misplaced where to find it looking outside when it
is only ever inside.

Remembering we Forget

We forget so easily our nature is happiness. We forget that
we have all the happiness we need for today. We forget we
have everything we need for today. We can remember we
are happiness. We can remember we are fully happy. We can
remember we have everything we need.

34. SELF NURTURING

Realignment

Sometimes you have to step to the side to get out of someone's way.

Sometimes you have to get out of the light to let the light shine on someone.

When you need re-aligning get out of your own way. Get out of your light so your inner self can just be.

Stand in Your Way or Understand

Get over yourself and begin to see what is behind your ego. We are all given the same by nature but we choose what we become and want to stay as. Either get out of our own way or stand in your own way.

Just be

Empty blank surface we are obsessed with changing you. Just as it is difficult to leave you alone, so we struggle to just be our self without thoughts.

Un-mysterious Stillness

Thinking and religions want mystery. The Self wants the stillness of truth.

Un-mysterious

We become lost in the wanderings of the mind because the nature of the mind is inquisitiveness . . . to keep moving. The mind loves mystery because it loves to solve.

Mystery solving gives it its identity and reasons to survive. When there are no mysteries the mind begins to settle in simplicity and ignore complexities. Then serenity can settle like snow on dry land in stillness.

Mysteriousness

Don't be fooled by the mysterious. The mysterious is what they say you haven't got because it's just bait. A mysterious man and a mysterious truth are contradictions in terms which fool our mind.

We prefer the mysterious future rather than the plain present. Our minds prefer complications rather than simplicity.

Religions thrive on us being drawn to mystery, knowing the only mysterious thing is our ignorance of preferring mystery instead of truth.

So We May Be together

Yes, I feel odd, a stranger in my own country detached from
the things of life. Like a squirrel prefers to gather nuts, I
prefer to work on my own.

Yes, there will be a time when the fruit is shared. Until
then and after I will return to my gathering, getting things
together, so we may be together.

Humility and Compassion

If you are powerful, famous and rich and don't have
humility and compassion you can never be happy and happy
for others.

If you are poor and only have humility and compassion you
are happy for yourself and for others.

Uni

You took them all away in their youth. You seduced them
with your promises. You gave them food, warmth, shelter,
and thinking. Thinking is what fooled most except the wise
who you didn't outsmart. They just left you in your world of
thinking.

You still live in your thinking whilst those who left enjoy the
shared heart of being human before being intellectual.

Our Own Heart

We are just workers, our concerns not seen, our personal caring touch not valued because it has no price.

Perhaps our continued personal touch kept secret from the powers that seem to rule, lets us rule our own hearts.

Let the Good In

Good people are the only ones we should let into our life. Keep the others out as much as you can.

It is impossible to do this forever but the process must be maintained. Then the will is passed on and repeated time and again.

Principles

Time after time we return to the same few principles which keep us on track on our path.

There are few, silence, stillness, solitude, simplicity, humility and compassion.

Goodness Never Hides

People hide away when they know you have seen what they are like, unless they have goodness in their hearts which you would never hide away.

A Visit

Sometimes, someone dropping in changes your perspective.
Maybe it's their song that picks us up out from our
engrossed thoughts.

Difficult to See

Occasionally, only when another person comes across
someone you thought you knew, you find out what the
person thinks.

It is not deceit or dishonesty at work but that we can project
so much onto someone, that we seldom see them for real.

Freshening Up

I'm going to take a break from this routine of working at the
day job, walking and doing the main job.

All of it needs a change and a rest. I feel like a stale loaf
which is not fit for purpose.

But I can be refreshed if I give myself a chance, one more
chance, a double chance to freshen up.

Letting Life Be Itself

Whatever someone else is, they are being true to their self as
much as they can. Whatever we are, we are being true to our
self as much as we can.

Subtraction not Addition

No one sees in darkness but that's what we try and achieve to remove the darkness, so we can see clearly what is there.

It applies mostly to our inner self to try and understand what it there but the darkness only has to be removed.

Nothing needs to be added.

This is what can't be understood, that nothing new is needed.

Removing what is not needed is a subtraction not an addition.

Following Rules

There's no training apart from your experience of being a child. There are no rules because each child is different. All rules are to be ignored except one. Ignore all rules.

35. SMILE

Smile

A smile can change your whole day, more than words in a book, more than a week off.

Most Memorable Today

At least I made someone smile today: a five year old girl and a four year old boy, a woman with no money to pay for her pills and a man with not enough patience.

My Smile

A smile when passing someone who has no connection or interest in you, apart from giving you a smile, can't be bought.

A smile from a much older or younger person who you pass by, may be the best smile you ever get, that stranger's smile you can't forget.

Why is that particular smile so important? Maybe it's like a mirror reflecting an inner sedated part of us, we love but can't express.

Maybe that smile is our known but hidden potential inside. Us in full bloom, spread fully open like full consciousness.

A Smiling Life

As a boy I wanted to be spiritual, but not a priest performing rituals or giving blessings. I wanted the peace of a place where there was no fighting for peace, just peace.

I didn't want to be anything. I just wanted to be me happy with the serenity of the peace I saw in Franciscan monks. I wanted to do something which would bring a smile to others and me.

Decades have passed. The boy is the same and I now know what I did. I just smiled at people when we saw each other. Maybe it was easier than praying.

The Joy of Joy

I had enough after a short spell acting being an elder of the tribe, making seemingly important statements. I quickly reverted to my younger silent self watching for twinkles in the eyes, smiles. What joy there is in joy.

That Smile

We really are such a complex mess and not as straightforward as we would like, each carrying our ancestor's history around like a heavy load. Our history may be seriously heavy. Understanding it can be a long task and until it is worked through we hide behind a mask. No one is free of this as our past is inescapable like our fate and this is why, maybe we should smile more.

The End of Stories

The hospital discharge summary, which is how it works, was just bullet points: -

-Age 76
-Address Single room apartment
-Transport Walking
-Problems Frailty, Arthritis, Depression, High blood pressure

It missed: -

-War veteran with shrapnel in legs.
-Widowed.
-Dependants, looks after his disabled daughter, a dog and a cat.
-Looks after the neighbour's unemployed son.
-Anxiety about his untended vegetables in his allotment.

A man, who walked miles out in the cold to put flowers on his wife's grave, and then shared them with others. He is quiet and helps patients get through their ordeals. He didn't mention the friends he lost. He always gives you his smile for free.

What is Your Perfect Day?

Rain everywhere, windscreen wipers going with grey skies but fantastic views over the Severn Bridge. A perfect day, with my daughter who is at a party later. I see old friends later too but she's staying overnight to sleep tight to awake and smile at another perfect day.

Infectious

How good it is to be positive, to celebrate the positive, to seek out the positive and to smile with it whenever the opportunity appears.

How infectious it is to smile at someone else. They always reflect back how they are, sometimes giving back the gift of an unexpected beautiful smile, or just that they want to smile.

Be What You Are

Whether or not we admit it, we all live by a set of rules. To live well and be happy we need to ask if these are our own rules, or are they someone else's rules. I write my own rules down, check them and reflect to see if I still feel OK about them and if they need adjusting. Writing them down makes you clearer about you. Cringe-worthy though they may seem, here are my own rules.

To be happy, spend as much time as you can being still, as it will keep you on the path you are on. Call it anything, meditation, special time, and realise it is always with you. Be a weirdo, be odd, be abnormal, don't fit in, fit out. Be yourself, kind with compassion. Keep everything simple and smile at yourself. My rules sometimes work for me. Everyone else's sometimes work for them. Be firm and flexible and aim for happiness. Don't waste time wanting to get to some stage of your life faster as some things can't be controlled, especially when you are old.

Eat fewer root vegetables because they concentrate

chemicals. Eat just enough. Eat more fruit, nothing processed. Walk slowly, ride and drive slowly, think slowly and smile when you can. Go barefoot or have good shoes and don't forget to sleep in the open as well as in a good bed. You spend most time in both. Spend as much time outside as possible but don't sunbathe. Walking is the best exercise but don't do anything dangerous unless you have to. If you do, don't do it without crash landing gear and when it is over smile. Don't see sad films, read sad books or listen to sad music.

Treat others with the manners a servant would show to a King or Queen, then everyone is respected. Only see good friends, don't use them or pay them. Stick with positive people not negative people and return other people's smiles. Be as wrong as right but don't take daily matters into the night and give your smile whenever there is a chance. Thinking is not your master only your friend. Your master is not your ego which you see as yourself but instead it is your inner self. Happiness is the single aim of your life. Show your smile.

OUR RESPONSE TO
THE WORLD

36. FEAR

Thinking and Breathing Fear Away

Thinking starts fear and we then lose control of our breathing. But we can use our thinking to slowly get back control our breathing. Breathing is not only a barometer of fear but breath control is the best extinguisher of fear.

Fear of the Unreal

Sequential, logical thinking creates the concept of time by recalling memories and imagining the future. Thinking shows the past and future to be concepts, as our past and future are our thoughts.

Our whole life can be spent fighting against time whose inevitable consequences we try to avoid. It is better to have a still mind.

Why We Do and Don't

Fear is why we don't do most of the things we could or should do.

Happiness is why we do everything.

Being in Control

We keep old ways of thinking, thinking we can stay in control. We keep our old fears, thinking we can control our fear.

Old ways are chosen as the best because they are easy and comfortable but comfort to avoid change can blind us to what has changed.

We blame everything to avoid admitting we are not really in control and something else is.

We need to own up, give up the thinking that holds us back and give control back to whatever is in control.

A little less holding on, a little less control, a little less blame and we can let go.

Spreadsheet of fear

We don't know the day we will die. The date and time are all we can't be told yet.

The worry would begin the day of the news an announcement like an explosion changing all our moments from cherished ones to hopeless ones. If we knew, how many could cope or would care more? A new kind of fear with a date could appear instead of the old known fear. The scientist hasn't yet got the information to become our life's accountant with a spreadsheet of fear of our life and death. Let's hope and try to ensure they never do.

Propulsion

Fear is behind all our worst behaviours and our dream is a day without it. How can what appears to motivate us seem to be our worst enemy?

It keeps us alert and alive being aware of the consequences. Fear is a propellant into the future not staying in the present. Its enemy is the present. With a still mind fear is left behind.

Fear

Fear stops now from being felt. It blocks consciousness. It is our best friend and worst enemy. We don't seem to be able to live without it.

Fear is a response demanding attention as you can't just be when it is present.

Fear is a prison made of the mind and it is not often kind.

Fear takes your breath, it takes your body. It takes higher consciousness down to basic reactions of fight of flight then loss of consciousness.

Fear blocks and stops smiling and living. It raises a wall to keep it in. It is an isolating draining form of strain.

Fear can steer everything for all of our life or it can be seen and left alone with one single good breath.

Fear as Your Friend

Stop trying to be so reasonable and instead be unreasonable. Be absolutely certain about uncertainty. Look at what you are not looking for. Let fear of not being happy lead you.

Plug yourself into an energy supply of positive people. You will burn brighter and shine with their energy. They will help you turn fear into fuel and live off the dread of panic until even though you search it out, fear cannot be found.

Endlessness

Endless images inside, pressures to comply to provide outside. Pressures to conform, to obey rules not to be broken and not allowed to be a fool. Fear of failing, fear of fear, fear of sadness. I'll stick with myself and my happy madness.

Your Worst Fear

Let your worst fear happen to you in your mind. Imagine you fall over and that everyone sees your underwear. Let it happen several times and you will be laughing at what used to be your biggest fear.

Psychological Jail

Letting go of regrets, letting go of fear releases us into the present.

Letting go of Fear

Fear is the worst thing to carry around. Unpredictable it steals our happiness.

Fear of not liking ourselves, fear of not being liked, fear of not being approved, fear of abandonment.

Fear can be let go of like throwing a stone into a pond, don't hold on to the stone as you throw it, just let it go its own way. Do you think about where that stone landed after you threw it skimming the water?

Don't give thought to fear and fear won't give you thoughts about it.

Turning negative to Positive

Turning fear to fuel is not an easy change from avoiding it but if you try and do what makes you scared, you might get better about what is scaring you. So much so, you can't wait to feel fear and do what you are scared of because you know performing comes next. Then you see that the bigger the fear, the better the performance.

Calm Panic

Panic is a groove easy to fall into and a little more difficult to get out of because you get stuck. A gentle self reminder repeated endlessly to breathe slow until the message is home restores calm.

Confrontation for Progress

Fear of hesitating, fear of failing, fear of being overwhelmed. Avoiding fear of these ensures fear will get worse. If you don't deal with confrontation, it can deal with you without mercy. If you don't seize the opportunity to confront something, it is turned into a loss. If you give it a go, whatever the result, it can be built on next time, which is progress.

Normalising

Soldiers don't forget the fear that kept them alive. Sometimes it was right but not now in the middle of the night.

Letting go of conditioned fear is strange. Letting go of being afraid is new. Letting go of what might happen, takes practice and conditioning too.

Not being afraid in a safe place is normal but can take a lot of practice to feel normal, then be normal.

Letting Go of Approval

We are programmed and conditioned to want to be thought of highly by those above and below us, but needing approval can give control of us over to them.

Putting and leaving our self-esteem in other's hands is asking and waiting for trouble because disapproval is inevitable. Approval of what we are is only ours.

Overwhelmed

Being overwhelmed by fear, pain, loss, depression, someone, having no hope are all eclipsed by understanding.

What is it trying to teach us? What can we gain? What is it showing us, where our happiness is?

How do you cover yourself and sneak out dry from under a rainstorm? There is a way out to find. You have to find it in your mind.

Like Passing Clouds

Thoughts and feelings come then they go. They are not forever. They are replaced by others.

If we dislike a thought or feeling. If it produces fear or loathing, we can let it go, then think or feel a different one.

Thoughts and feelings are not compulsory. They persist or are freed by our choice and need.

Today is Now

So the day has arrived. Inner stillness has replaced fear. The time was here all along.

All it was trying to achieve was the calmness of being still, stopping thinking taking over.

No Surprises

Knowing yourself brings an honesty to all actions with no fear of surprises.

Don't Stick with Fear

By sticking with fear it sticks with you. If you move away just a little, turning around, distracted, it loses its grip and power.

Encouraged To Be Fearful

Why is it fear is around all the time and happiness isn't? Is fear more valuable to our survival, even if it means we are unhappy?

Is fear programmed in us from toddlers? If happiness is our nature then why are we encouraged to be fearful not happy most of the time? Why are we encouraged to be fearful, not our true self?

If past results show that we only get hurt some of the time, it is better to be happy most of the time than being fearful most of the time. Maybe we could try.

Primal Fear

Fear freezes us more than anything, even more than cold itself. Fear paralyses us so we can't do anything, as if we are numbed into inactivity.

Fear is such a primitive warning of things to come; we can never ignore fear unless it is the fear when we know nothing is going to happen, when we know it is imagined by us.

This fear we imagine, feels as real as the fear before something which is going to happen but when we know it won't, it wastes a lot of our life.

Above All Else in Life

When you have been through the shock of seeing a person you know taken, like a candle put out by the wind, then you have seen what life is like.

This does not go away but is an introduction to the events on their way, some generous giving joy and warmth, others threatening to take your life away.

This is when we turn inwards to what we know and trust the most because above all else in life, it does not let us down, as it is us.

Happiness, Fear and Thinking

Fear is why we don't do most of the things we could or we should. Thinking the right way is why we would do these things if only thinking could just stop producing fear.

Sunday in Two Minds Again

Sundays are part of my life but have never been my favourite day. Now, just as a child, it is the routine things that get to me. They suddenly remind me the routine of another week is close. Having a bath and getting things ready concretise it.

But where would I be without my Sundays? There are memories of church as a child, sharing the bathwater, looking to the exciting good things the week could bring.

Why We Should Look Up

We need to look up when we are walking to see where we are going in life. To check the ground is safe enough to see we are heading in the right direction.

We need to look up to say, 'Hello in there' to the homeless, to strangers, to children, to old people, to say hello to everyone, like and not alike us. Try it for five minutes one day once in your life.

Why We Look Down

Why do so many look down when they are walking? I can understand if its uneven ground, cracked or uneven pavements, and especially if it is because of dog or horse poo. But many of us look down when we are walking out of fear in case when we look up someone will mug us.

In America they teach you to tell your burglar or mugger, 'I haven't seen you so I can't identify you.' This lets burglars and criminals win and are how the world changes in their favour and perpetuates fear. Perhaps if we looked them in the eye they might change.

Dissolving Fear with Stillness

You speak about the fear you saw, fear you are scared of having again, how it ripped out all the joyful moments of those precious days as a child. You run like an athlete to avoid it but running and avoiding you never stop to look inside at stillness and this is what can dissolve your fear.

Happiness and Fear

Fear is experienced when you don't want it but conjure it up by thinking. Happiness cant be experienced when it is here all the time and we desire it.

Fear is why we don't do most of the things we could or should do. Thinking with all its reasoning doesn't seem to stop fear or help us be happy

Treachery

Even though most people are good there is always a wolf amongst the sheep. But the most dangerous situation is when there is sheep amongst the wolves. Then there is deception, manipulation playing games until everyone is fooled that everyone is the same, then everyone is betrayed by treachery.

37. DOUBT

Doubts

It is our nature to have doubts. Their effect is like friends who never stop reassuring us that we are serious about what we have chosen.

Doubtless

As night is understood and fades into dawn because the world turns, so doubt melts when confronted.

Normal is Difficult

Why can't I be normal like everyone else but I am told I am normal? Well if this is normal then it is pretty difficult being normal.

Normal is what I would call being subject to what happens outside me, as well as to what happens in others and also to what happens in me.

Worse is what I just sit here and imagine, fearful about the future with no place now to rest from this fearful, over thinking restless mind. Yes this is normal.

Double Doubts

How come doubts don't get weaker and why do they seem stronger with the passing of years, I kept on asking myself. Then I realised it is because my stronger certainty needs stronger doubt to counterbalance it.

Doubt is one of our strongest friends. Doubt arrives to check we are doing the right thing, then to reassure us that we are. It makes us stronger, more confident and more grounded. Doubt balances certainty.

Welcome the fear which doubt brings because it is only your inner self trying to alert to you. Treating doubt with the hospitality we would give to our most trusted friend lets doubt show us its message. Welcome doubt without fear and ask it what it has to teach you.

Thank doubt that doubt appears because it makes us more conscious and lets us know we are normal. You will be more confident if you make a good friend of doubt. Like having friends, it is our nature to have doubts. They never stop reassuring us we are serious.

38. ATTITUDE

Changing the Tyre

A bad attitude is like a flat tyre, you can't go anywhere until it is changed. It is not anyone else but you who needs to change.

Your attitude is your choice belonging to no one else. Your attitude may be your last freedom or even your last voice.

You can lose everything but not your attitude. You can only change it, so it is up to you how you want your final mood.

How you want to feel, what you want to say, what you choose to think, remember it is your attitude, your personal way.

Attitudes

What are my attitudes? Where did I get them? Do any need to change or be altered? Do they stop me being happy?

How do I look at certain people, activities, places and things I can be? How do they affect others and what do they do to me?

Do any need creating, adopting, cropping or dropping? If they do, I change too.

Respectful

I try to work out how to make a day positive whatever circumstances I find myself in because I know that my attitude influences the outcome.

I repeatedly realign my attitude and say to myself, 'I will be polite to everyone. My manners will be as good as I can make them.

When I am helping someone, I will be kind and I will be thankful that I am not the person I am trying to help.'

Being Within

Seeing what the inner world of our own self is like changes out attitude to the outer world. We become thankful that our inner happiness can change our attitude to everything.

Forgiving Our Self

Are we ever forgiven for what we have done? Do we ever forgive us? Can we change our attitude to what we did and why and wish us well that we learnt from it? Our attitude can change anything we want to.

Attitude

A happy heart carrying the weight of life. A happy song sung with a lightness of heart. A positive outlook about everything, especially most things are not luck but choices.

Shifting an Attitude

Not being thankful is a lesson not yet learnt because our attitude is frozen. When our attitude moves, thankfulness is felt.

When You Look Back

In your last days what will your conclusion be? Did you not care? Was everything about you? Was it just about fun? Did you have no principles?

Did you have a purpose? Who were you? Did you contribute to others? Were you kind? Did you help? Were you decent?

Instead of Revenge Imagine

Your display of power and assault were aimed to maim me, to cause pain and destroy me.

Instead the tenderness you could not destroy I want to give to you. I want my tenderness to help you realise you cannot imagine further assault on anyone.

Our Duty

Oceans are sometimes calm, sometimes rough and we too are an ever changing mix. Our attitude can be balanced or not and may need adjusting, so peaceful balance between opposites can be restored once again as a lifelong duty.

Mistaken Moments

There are moments when everything seems coloured with dark doom, but they are only moments.

There are moments when thinking makes us believe nothing will be ok but it is not all the time.

There are moments when we cannot see the worth in anything, even us, but only for a while.

There are moments when we cannot see light, when we think too much, but these are moments when we only see our ego, not our happy inner self which is always there.

Waiting for Tears

Why can some people cry so easy and I can't? What stops my tears? Is it denial because I am not ready yet? Fear of what would pump them out and down my face?

Blocked, stuck, not ready, fear, not enough support, no answer to them. Just being with my tears is what I want. Just being able to be with my tears is what I wait for.

39. NORMALLY ABNORMAL

Endless Types of Personality Types

Personality disorders are regarded as abnormal but may cause no trouble to others.

Psychiatric disorders are regarded as abnormal but may cause no trouble to others.

Personality types are regarded as normal but can be big trouble to others. They are all words to describe us when they are only words not us. They are the map, not the actual territory.

Only Two Races of People

The Second World War settled the different types of people forever. Viktor Frankl an inmate of Auschwitz frequently said that there are only two races of people, the "race" of the decent man and the "race" of the indecent man.

The Same Once in the Crowd

People sit in different places, postures, with different intentions, moods, problems, with different histories and different genes but we are basically the same.

Alright

I have difficulty not assessing things personally because that is how I see the world and this is what I have become from how I have experienced things.

I can't see things so impersonally, objectively like an informed judge. I'm a bit more jumbled up by life and sometimes I don't come out perfectly right.

I'm alright but I'm not always alright. I wasn't made perfectly but that too is sometimes alright.

Standing Back

Can you stand back not judging? Can you be quiet when you could speak? Can you just let things be? Could this sometimes be me?

Conscious Integration

Can you have different attitudes at the same time? Can you hold more than one view seeing things more than one way? Can you be objective and personal as well as be clear and imaginative? Can you read everything just visually and see everything in terms of words? Can you hear with your vision and listen with your eyes? Can you integrate different attitudes, perceptions and judgements, be conscious of them all, then that too with compassion?

What Turns Us Inside?

For all our logical thinking. For all our verbal processing and reasoning. For all our knowledge and technology, the absence of thought shows us our inner self.

If the World is Conscious

If everything is our best guess, then the world we think we see must be laughing at our thinking.

Anything Could be Real

There is no agreement about psychology about religion, the origins of the universe about physics or archaeology. We don't know what is normal. All perceptions and judgements are only our best guess.

Our Influence

Everything is as it is meant to be. If we change it, it is because it was meant to be changed, so perhaps we only imagine our influence.

Abandoning Abandonment

Giving up all attempts to be normal is freedom from other people's rules. Giving up norms is finding our own normality which is what we value above all else.

Great Peace

In days of great peace, nothing happens. In the stillness of days of great peace, there is just the peace of stillness.

Effortlessness

When the struggle is finished, like a dark distant storm, we know there is only temporary effortlessness.

Happiness is Inside

Those who tell you how happy they are, and tell you all the things you can have to be happy too, are not usually happy.

No Wants

Not wanting anything is the best barometer of happiness.

The Longest Book

In the quietest silence more can be processed and communicated than from the longest book.

Isn't It Strange How

Only through solitude you learn how to be with others,
Only through silence you learn how to communicate. Only
through stillness you learn how to move. Only through
being you know.

40. IMPORTANCE OF BEING WEIRD

Wiser

Next time you look at someone and see them as a fool, question how superior your thinking judgement is. Has the fool seen how thinking can be our greatest enemy and chosen to watch the stars instead?

Next time you look at someone and see them as a fool, ask why are they smiling and you are not. Ask why they are happy and you are not, then consider if they have chosen wisely and you not.

Eerie

Do you get a sense of eeriness more than others? Does it make you feel connected in ways we can't describe?

Does the sense of eeriness around you stay when you think it has gone? Is it with you at night when you sleep?

I thought it was just me but everyone seems to get this. Everyone I've asked thinks they would seem abnormal to others if they mentioned it. Perhaps being more open about it would normalise eeriness.

The Ones at the Back

Some people always seem to be standing back, not at the front, not eager to engage but watch from a distance.

They don't expend armies of energy participating in events of the world. They just run their own life of enjoying the present moment.

They are watchful, always seeming stationary, waiting for change, even though they don't move.

Brief Meeting

Unknown to you at first, a brief meeting with your inner self can lead to the point of your life.

Strange One

Do you often feel as if things are a bit vague, that you are in a strange state, different from others?

Do you feel as if you are different, moulded in different ways, in ways you cannot say?

Join me in being weird but happy in what we are.

One Offs

When some bulbs we plant are different and do not flower, when some trees are different and do not bear fruit, do we blame the sun?

When someone lets us down, when we behave badly, who should we not blame?

My Fantasy World

I can't watch drama on television. I can't watch most plays. I can't read complicated involved novels, because what people don't match up to are what I see every day.

Reading, theatre, television remind me of my job, so forgive me if the way I relax is to stay in a world of fantasy.

Weirdo

Whoever said it was not good to be weird doesn't know it is good to feel weird, to think weird, to see weird, to be weird.

Challenges

Some days I know I'm not doing enough for myself to just be me. I don't take enough chances with people. Yet walking by the river, just for me, I have to see what that shiny object on the ground is. I have to reach that far off gate and touch it before I turn around, not tomorrow, now.

Winking Dark Clouds

The past was shadowed like a dark cloud following me everywhere, darkening what could have been brighter moods, until I decided to use it.

I decided to look at it, to write about it then to sing inside me. 'It's going to get brighter. I'm gonna fight ya with happiness. I'm gonna fight ya with light.'

The Dark cloud now winks at me from a distance as it looks around for other victims. Perhaps it's just the singing!

Making Your Wish Come True

Identify and concentrate on your wish. Say what you want and how you want it assertively to yourself, then simply to others too. Only then is your wish possible.

The Good News

Today's good news is that I woke up, so did my wife and daughter and our cat. The good news is we talked on the way to school about unimportant things. The good news is I have the day off and I'm going shopping. The good news is I will take them to meditation. The good news is we return after meditation.

Normally Abnormal

What if this path doesn't go home but leads to other places including happiness, suffering and then dying alone?

Accepting what are not normal outcomes are what we are, open, not seeking, just being still with adventures warming the heart.

Imperfect

Taking risks, mistakes are not mines trying to destroy you but only there to annoy you and encourage progress.

Taking risks, leaving forgiveness behind, exploring what is not allowed, encourages further exploration. Perfection is the enemy of progress because it stifles looking further. Perfection halts all growth. Progress with imperfection is the growth process

Wondering

Wonder can be a blessing and a curse. To wonder about the stars can open the soul or stop the mind. Wondering about wonder is both.

Inner Peace

Inner peace is a blessing melting away the negative, the positive outlook reinforced. Anxious vigilance depletes efforts to be positive in outlook.

Inner Beauty

It is not the beauty in the light of a sunset, the contours of the mountains or in the rivers of the earth but in us where beauty is.

Beauty is inside behind the eye expressed with a smile and always inside.

Shared beauty takes us further inside to the light.

Divine Inspiration

Divine inspiration is supposed to be regarded as the only thing that logic cannot challenge or argue with. If you write from the heart of yourself and if you are an Advaitan, then your self is god, so your writing is divinely inspired.

In Christianity where the Kingdom of heaven is said to be within, then god is inside you, so if you write from your heart it can be divinely inspired.

I haven't got as far as looking at other religions because it seems if you can see it is true for one and you understand it is true, then the truth the divine is you.

Seeing and Listening

I value by sight but not above all else, not above consciousness. Sight is not consciousness, nor is hearing or doing. Consciousness is life.

Not Much to Ask

My own rules are, spend time being still every day, which should keep me on the path I am on.

Keep things simple. Treat others with the manners a king would expect from a servant, then everyone is respected.

Be as wrong as right but don't take daily matters into the night and leave happiness whenever there is a chance.

Odd One Out

Being the odd one out, you eventually see there are a lot of odd ones out, lots of us. So many that the only conclusion is the ones who are not odd are the odd ones. We are the sane ones because we are so crazy about life, crazy about love. It is for being and living, not about thinking about.

Anti-establishment Establishment

I started off being regarded as sensible by the establishment, then I refused to agree to conditions of living which to me were like killing myself, so I walked and walked until I was far away.

One day I was surprised when someone told me I was the establishment. Shocked I asked how did this happen. How did this happen?

I had walked so far away from the establishment that I could see without all the attachments, because I was detached.

Things Other Than Happiness

Do you fill in spare time with activities which make you happy because you are not happy? Do you do things you know are second rate to being happy because you know you are not happy? Maybe it would be better to look for what your happiness is inside you, not as an activity but being something else.

The Crazy One

They will always wonder about the crazy one because he or she is the one with the cutting edge, with the crazy unreasonable truths they are too scared to explore.

No Expert

When someone is treated like an expert, it is because what they know is a tiny bit more about less. There are usually many others who know so much more who could have been asked and done just as good a job.

It is good not to think or believe you are an expert even if you are treated like one because it makes you think harder and then you go deeper and further than experts.

Inside Out

I didn't want all the toys the others had. They didn't appeal to what was inside and I wasn't sure what did, until one day it arrived and found it was inside.

Redundant Thoughts

Perhaps I have let my thoughts run riot writing and now
they need to be reeled in so it stops. It has produced little of
importance, only confirmation it is redundant.

Now and Then

People I knew thirty years ago who knew me then would
not know me now and I would not know them. Why is this?
We know each other as well as we did then. It is just we are
doing other things which we don't know about.

Enemies as Friends

It is good to wander into your enemies' territory where you
are treated with respect and openness. Willing to learn what
they have to teach you about yourself, you can leave more
freely.

For You

Find your own instructions, even if you pinch some of these.
Yours are the only ones that you will see work for you. Mine
sometimes work for me. Everyone else's sometimes work for
them.

41. KEEPING OUR BALANCE

The Balance

Why are we so complicated, full of things that don't necessarily sit together easily? Let me speak for me first. I look for inner peace, yet at the same time I seem critical of injustice. I am detached from most but passionate about their loss of rights.

I will protect the defenceless even if it results in the offender suffering from seeing what they tried to impose on the defenceless.

Ships

A ship between two shores before a storm needs land. One shore let go, the other beckons with its hand. In some ways they are like us.

To sail at sea confirms the haven of land, which is not where ships should be. Ships are most themselves at sea.

Nightly they leave one port, then silently arrive at another before dawn, always giving their best, like us not knowing what is next.

Silence Sings On and On

The last time we saw Patrick he was saying goodbye from outside his ex-council house beside Glastonbury Tor. With the Tor he had found a mountain to live on the lower slopes of, so that he could be on an upward mountain path. His fatal condition brushed aside to show us how he finished inside, a person true to himself, a person who knew himself.

The last time I saw Patrick on my own, he was waiting for death to arrive, meditating upright in the middle of a hospital bed. I wanted to sing aloud to him the chant of the sacred mountain but without saying a single word, instead, we silently sung the same internal song. Old friend your body has gone, but I see we will not be forgotten for ignoring our thinking, because our silent stillness sings on and on.

A Thousand days of Chaos

A thousand times across the Severn Bridge. Two thousand meditations whilst seeing a thousand sunrises and a thousand sunsets. Two thousand days of chaos, pain and panic resolved. Fifty thousand patients. Fifty thousand moments of relief.

Full

Have you tried being full of emptiness so you are fully empty?

Mountain Paths

When you seem down and have fallen over, get up where
you fall, even if for half a step you have to crawl.

Mountains don't let you leap up their side; they give you a
choice to let you slowly grow inside.

Every wrong path you take, every mistake you seem to make
are all progress on the inner mountain path.

Whilst you camp on the inner mountain path, sometimes
clinging, sometimes singing, every pause, when there seems
to be no change, are growths of inner silent strength.

Clarity

When you know stillness, there is nothing to say about it.
Nothing can make it clearer than being still.

Fully Empty Room

What a sense of joy when no egos are in a crowded room.
Thoughts pushed away, compassion is to all and stillness
reigns.

Already There

Our growth is not what it seems. It is mainly within, unseen
because it is seeing what we already are.

That Within

No matter how long we live or where we live, we still have to surrender to that within.

Keeping Thoughts Away

Keeping thoughts away is not what we are used to doing. Saying no to thought is not what we are taught. But when we see thoughts cause most misery, we start keeping them away to make us happy.

Continued Presence

When you are home, there is nowhere to go on a pilgrimage to be happier. You can only continue to turn inwards to be happy at home.

Total Eclipse

How much can we talk of happiness? How much can there be? Always never ending is best as it continues to totally eclipse all misery.

To be Happy

Do not underestimate the skill required to ignore the negative in life to make you happy. It takes up most of your life.

With Just Today

To be happy is everyone's desire because it is what we spend all our time trying to be. We try so many different ways in all sorts of permutations. There are some who are lucky and realise they are happy just with what they have today and don't need anything else.

Monopoly

No one has a monopoly on anything apart the nature of their inner self.

Changing Attitude

Attitudes can be changed but sometimes until they are, we cannot move anywhere. Stuck we continue to wonder why. It is good to ask yourself, 'Do I need to change my attitude?'

Detaching but with others

Living attached to others, it can be impossible to be in solitude. Living detached you can be in solitude but be with all people if you choose.

Master or Servant

The inner territory can be guessed. We can have an opinion about it. We can read about it and think we know it or we can surrender, serve it and be it.

Triple Triad

We are known for our possession of things, our indifference to things, or our lack of things, especially money, power and ego, and most importantly, simplicity, humility and compassion.

Our Inner Room

It is our choice what we have. In the room we choose to live in, our responsibility is to change it if we want.

Neither One Nor the Other

Not everything that is wrong can be made right because they are the same; only on the other side.

Right and wrong like light and dark need each other to exist like men and women only exist because of the other.

No More

Eventually we know we can't be more happy or more thankful than we are.

Stick with What You Like

Only buy what you like, what you need, what you want. Don't buy to have something because of its value to others. It will only make you unhappy.

With Those

Being away, what is missed the most is not the surroundings or your things but the company of those you trust, those people.

The conversations which take you on a journey are only because everyone knows you for who you are. No one is trying to impress you and they only stick with you until they have to go.

It is where we all want to be again, back with those, back in that group, back on our own with them.

Exchange Clearly

When you are taking but in disguise of giving, don't try and make it look like someone doesn't want what you are offering. Be honest.

If you want something; ask for it. If you don't want something; say so. If you want to exchange; say it. If you are happy; share it.

The Basket

So many people stay together because of the basket. The basket is not worth anything on its own but it is what they have put in it. They only stay together because of what's in the basket. Sometimes the basket is more important than all the reasons they joined together.

Homemade Love

I remember a birthday meal I spent in a supermarket carpark in a car on my own, savouring delicious food. Today on the eve of my birthday I sat in another car park of that chain of supermarkets.

But I won't be there tomorrow because I will be at home, not in a car park of a strange town I once lived in, but where I live with homemade food and homemade love. My traveling work done.

Happiness and Harm

There is nothing wrong with desiring what is natural. Happiness is our natural state. No one can be criticised for being happy being their self, except if it harms them or others.

This is as Good as it Gets

Perhaps in just one of these moments I will be happy with my truth or perhaps I am already, but don't admit it.

Then, knowing I am, stops the search. Stopping the search ends any potential happiness of hope. Yes this is as good as it could ever be. There is no hope for anything better.

Stopping to Ponder the Wonder of Time

Today is a mystery now and it won't happen again. I don't yet know and it can never be repeated. I will remember it but it has not yet happened. How incredible is that?

Understanding

How can anything else apart from madness truly understand madness?

How can anything else apart from sadness truly explain sadness?

How can anything else apart from having lived truly understand life?

How can anything else apart from mourning truly understand mourning?

How can anything else apart from receiving truly understand giving?

How can anything else apart from being loved truly understand love?

42. HUMOUR

Guidance for my own week

I will try and keep my sense of humour which is so
important. It is one of our highest higher functions. I will try
and be detached. I will try and see everything as spiritually
connected in ways which include me but I don't yet
understand.

Nonsense

It is this time late on a Sunday night that I cant take anything
seriously. The week, and everyone's life going around in
circles. The sense it makes is nonsense.

43. ENOUGH PAIN

Stillness Is All We Are

We are always up against it, difficult people trying to get us in the ring, trying to engage us to spar with them, but it only disturbs your peace. So many times we find ourselves sparring and before we know it, we have been lured into the ring. Remember constantly your happiness and that stillness is all we are, then your guard is easier to keep up.

Anger and Honour

Anger can rapidly grow into violence because of lack of the experience, training and skill to express an alternative opinion in a more constructive way.

To reel the neck in may need sensitivity and education to allow overriding of provoked impulsive responses and instead, aligning with honour of our own kind.

Apologies

Forgiving and apologising are never forgetting. They mean always remembering so we don't make the same mistake.

Apologising often expects more understanding than may be possible. Accepting an apology often expects more understanding than may be possible.

Enough Pain

Our families sometimes they appear to make us look
smaller just so we might grow taller. Never passing you a
compliment.

When you really needed someone there, they made sure they
were there, always doing something, just giving you time.

You never give up on them as you know they exist for you.
Except for them you would not exist.

The one thing they teach you is to see what you are, where
you came from and no matter what, to respect this.

They showed you to stop anything when you've had enough
pain. No point in going back for more, again, again and
again.

Then you see that they showed you how to pass on what
you know and all you have to give: kindness, humility and
simplicity.

Pass By

If you play games, I may appear to behave peculiarly. I
won't answer your notes or return your calls. Making a game
out of how you get on is not ok. I can't waste today so I'll
detach, move to the side, stay inside and let you pass by.

Arguments

Don't get in the ring because there are some people best left alone especially people who want a fight.

A bun fight is always best over real cake instead of childish clever arguments which should embarrass them into being adults.

To reel the neck in by a small step back from the furnace of emotions is triggered by a simple thought which extinguishes all fire.

Don't Get in the Ring

Most people will get in the ring and have an argument with you, even if you don't know them. Because we fall for it so easily, we have to be more on our guard, so just don't get in the ring.

If you don't get in the ring you won't get psychologically mugged and you will begin to feel better, so don't get in the ring.

Start by saying to the other person, 'You are right.' then keep on saying, 'You are right, you are right,' just don't get in the ring.

R's to remember Instead of Roaring

Don't get in the Ring. Reel you neck in. Say to the other, you are Right, and keep saying you are Right.

Don't Step in the Ring

The problem with relationships is never the other person it is always us.

If you blame someone you are blaming, so talk or walk.

If you dislike someone and can't see love for them, fly or cry.

If you argue with someone you have chosen to get in the ring, so step back out or get knocked out.

If you resent someone you may think you want them to die but it is you who has taken the poison, so spit or smile.

When you can't get what you want, see what you actually have, then see it again.

Pain

How much more pain do I want? When will I stop saying yes to pain? When will I stop staying in this trance? With a threshold of no unnecessary pain how can I see them again? Detachment is the only way. No more to worry, to think or say.

Psychologically Mugged

I've got to stop this now as I've been hurt so many times.
I've had enough pain and I don't want more from them ever
again.

I've given them too many chances and every time I got
mugged. I didn't acknowledge the emotional pain but now
my feelings can't be mugged again.

This is being clear about me doing things, so I don't get hurt.
It is not about helping anyone else's pain. It is about me not
getting mugged again.

Being Selfish about Self Care

When will you say you have had enough pain, that you
don't just want to be the giver again?

When will you say they are not going to take off you again?
When will you think of you first and say no?

When will you say no they can't come and stay? When will
you say I've had enough, today is the day?

When will you wake up how you went to sleep and say
yesterday was the first day of me saying no? No becomes
the most positive word. It changes the uncomfortable feeling
inside into positive feelings of protecting yourself. You start
looking for times to say no just to feel better about saying yes
to you. Then you see why so many people do it all the time
and say no. It makes them feel good.

No Expectations

How much bad behaviour do we take before we say no?
How much pain do we have to endure before we say no?

Our thinking doesn't work fast enough to save us from
others because we have too much trust in our own
expectations.

Overwhelming Situation

The overwhelming pain of loss of a person you love has no
equal except if it happens again with another person you
love. Monstrously out of control feelings wash over fragile
circuits of thinking, then there is standstill.

Sometimes all that is needed is a rest from the machinery
trying to work out what can only be worked through.

With rest is some peace, some time for silence, so stillness
inside can be uncovered.

Natural Order

Avoidance of pain is our first response. Desiring happiness is
next.

After seeing the world, suffering is seen. What follows is
finding happiness inside.

Move On

When you've had enough discomfort, too much pain from being a punch bag, you see you can't do it again.

It could be after much change in a family or job. Seeing the things you can't change, the time has come for you to move on.

44. KINDNESS

The Three Important Things

What people are and what they do does not make as big an impression on us as how they make us feel.

One of the most popular quotes about kindness is attributed to the novelist Henry James: "Three things in human life are important: the first is to be kind; the second is to be kind; and the third is to be kind."

Authenticity

Kindness with simple disciplined good manners and respect make me feel better and civilised. I don't want a gold star experience of anything without authenticity.

Be a Donor of Kindness

Don't be a consumer be consumed by giving away Inner wealth. Be extravagant with humility, intoxicated with serenity. Be true, be still, be you. Be silent, be quiet, be self-reliant. Be kind, be strength.

Strength

Be true. Be still. Be you. Be silent. Be quiet. Be self-reliant. Be kind. Be silent strength.

The Smallest Things We Do

It's the smallest things we do which tell someone everything that needs to be known, confirming we mean what we are.

It can be the handmade card, the x for kiss or smiley face at the end, looking you straight in the eye tells you it's not a lie.

A cup of tea is enough, waving an extra goodbye on that day without a tear in the eye.

It's the smallest things that we do which tell someone everything like an early surprise with flowers.

Kindness Above all else

Gentleness and kindness are now not our first reactions to many people. Instead, defensive actions have become automatic thinking that they will save us from the wishes of aggressive people.

Kindness is always a better reaction but is faked by those who want to use us. They can leave us distrustful of genuineness, fearful of kindness itself.

Because kindness can be the most powerful thing which changes how we feel and how we see our world, we can't let other people take our kindness away, so we must never stop.

Being kind is the most important thing you can be.

A Secret Life

She kept to herself and none of the things which she quite liked in shops or magazines ever found their way into her life because her gratitude for being happy made her generous with her smile and with the warmth from her heart.

When it could be kept as a secret, she gave everything she could away. A life full of happiness, passed without incident, without a flicker of notice. She was here then gone but perhaps she is waiting to be found in you.

45. EXPECTATIONS

Expectation

Those who expect nothing remain disappointed. Those who have nothing can lose it when they get something. Better to expect getting something to lose.

Destiny

Immersion in the vast sea of our apparent interconnectedness in family or in work can easily drown us, so we are overwhelmed and can no longer be detached. We get drawn in, lured in and tempted. It is better to be a brief visitor like a holiday maker on vacation, detached from destinations but not destiny.

Letting Go of Expectations

What has gone? Our expectations, our hopes and dreams or our reluctance to let her be whatever she is no matter what.

We can only help her with the tools to do whatever she is going to do. Perhaps show her how to be still to give her the strength to endure it

Accomplishments

Being alive to what can be accomplished means not doing unnecessary things and focusing on what needs to be done, what possibly can be done, so that all we can possibly do is eventually done.

Trust

I trust me because I can't pretend I trust anyone because anyone can let you down, even if they don't intend to.

You can be set up to compete without knowing that you are competing or you can set yourself up. That is why I trust me even if I am wrong.

Entertainment

I am not an entertainer and I realised this when as a boy of twelve my magic tricks didn't work, so I decided there was no point in just being a fake.

That I can't entertain is due to lack of confidence because I am not amusing. I am not an amusement. I am happiest being my own self.

Our Expectations

They would understand what I have done but I don't know
if they would agree with me or if they would have done it
if they were me but they are not me. They gave me life but
I have to choose what to do with it as those after me will.
Inheritance is a mistake because its expectations pressurise
decisions. It is best to let someone be what they are.

Unconditional

When you don't live from your head, everything is
unconditional. Your self does not have conditions because
you are just you.

Unconditionality

When the last dependable person is not here, the only
unconditional person in life seems to be you but what you
think you are can let your self down or save you.

46. POSITIVITY

Dodging the Negative

You can keep drinking bitterness and keep chewing on
resentment, searching for hooks to hang them on, trying to
find a person to say you are right.

Or you can dodge the negative getting in your light, keeping
it to the side of you, so you can see your light. You don't
need to fish for compliments.

Some Days

Some days don't seem to be for happiness. Some days we
have to write. Some days we have to walk. Some days we
have to be silent but all of these let us be happy.

Divinely Inspired

What we do anywhere, no matter what it is, if it comes from
inside our self, it comes from what we see as the divine.

More Important to be Nice

You may be the best at a game, the best at the arts but
one day someone will emerge who is the same. The only
difference may be that they or you are nice.

Risk of Pain

Occasionally you have to let yourself feel bad for a while, without letting it last too long. Sometimes you have to feel how bad it has got and only then you decide to change it.

You don't want to look for pain but you also don't want to avoid the possibility of it because if you don't experience the possibility of pain you cannot experience the possibility of the alternative.

Listening Kindness

Listening to the inner self, keeping the ego in check in stillness, the inner person is heard. Listening to the inner self is the greatest kindness you can receive.

Not From the Head

You get a lot more peace when you live from the heart not the head, from the soul not the head, from the self not the head. The heart, soul or self or whatever you call you, does not have conditions.

My Contribution

What am I bringing to the table, to the relationship, to the problem to solve it, to life to make me happy? We can only bring our self.

From inside

Whichever way you can see it, it doesn't matter as seeing, hearing and feeling are only pointing back from where they came from, inside.

Bathed in Light

I remember, so can you, clear sunny days, everything bathed in sunlight, everyone bathed in sunlight. Is there any difference in anything, everyone or the sunlight or is it the way it is seen?

Silent Positivity

So many positive things can be erased with words. Careless words, cross words, humorous words, secret words or not enough words. Words can be dangerous things to play with. They can explode, backfire and maim. They are weapons of mass destruction. They are to be respected, restrained, retrained understood then . . . best given up for silence where stillness is experienced without words. Silence can be the most positive of all types of communication conveying everything words can't say. Being present, a look, a hug, a touch, a picture, a card, a flower can give more of you than words can.

Art World View

Our work and view of the world is like the artist and the canvas; the canvas should not paint the artist.

261

Positivity

It is possible to write about things other than happiness but why write about things which we don't want? It is better to write about what we want, what we can't see and how to get them rather than to look at what we don't want?

It is equally important to read, discuss and see what stops us being happy and what helps us be happy. There is no point in reading, discussing and seeing what makes us unhappy. It will only make us more unhappy.

Isn't it Great That

Isn't it great that darkness can be removed. Isn't it great that. Isn't it great that happiness follows suffering. Isn't it great that. Isn't it great that happiness is inside. Isn't it great that. Isn't it great that anyone can be happy. Isn't it great that. Isn't it great that it is free. Isn't it great that.

47. CREATIVITY

Stemming the Tide of Rationalism

Early experiences of distressing thoughts and feelings are
sometimes only healed later by correcting the errors through
drawing, painting, sculpting, singing, music, writing,
communicating our love, friendship and kindness.

Process Over

What you or I could communicate, which is little, has
already been and gone. The present has arrived and is here,
with time for peace, conscious of today and like all of them,
precious.

Artists and Their Material

Meeting artists is like meeting musicians as they are usually
not like anything which they present and why should they
be because they have taken a tortuous route to contort, not
resort to what we take for granted.

Spiritual Love

The best words worth reading, the best poems worth
writing, the best songs worth hearing are natural, those of
spiritual love.

Artists

Picasso showed where inside his true colours came from as his obsession with the female form pushing his genius to its end, his art slightly around the bend like us.

Gaudi's art's offspring everywhere in his buildings are asking you to speak, to respond to and rejoice in the artist's reflection of nature.

Creativity

Inspiration rarely comes from nowhere. Usually you think you might be able to do something better or just dare yourself to solve a problem or show it in a different way.

Then, falling asleep or engaged in something ordinary, you find yourself on a pathway which has just opened up in front of you. You are conscious you are on your own and feel alone with a hundred thousand pairs of eyes looking down on you, wanting to look up at you.

Being Shown

The person I knew has gone. They have been taken over, their holiday is now spent, compelled to sing, draw or write in silence whatever comes into the heart or into the mind. That which seems important has to be written sung or drawn. No sleep in to be lazy because it is life's work being shown.

Anti-perfection

Taking risks, the mistakes are not mines trying to destroy you but only there to encouraging progress. Taking risks leaving any forgiveness behind, exploring what is not explored, lets you expand your mind. Perfection is the enemy of progress because it stifles looking further halting all growth because progress with imperfection is the growth process. Imperfection is human which is your friend.

Pain of Art

We seem like such creatures of habit but only in some things, some times. We go for the same breakfasts, stay with the same people. Our minds are conditioned from the past that make the future secure, predictable, paradisiacal, comfortable with no inconvenience, discomfort or pain. Only artists are forced to experiment with themselves and their art. Some are already but some become what their art will show.

Comfort is stifling, so fear of discomfort is turned into fuel to go even further, to see what happens where they can go.

Some can sing the love. Some can paint the pain. Some can sculpt a hole so deep it seems like you'll never get out again.

But there are those who imagine what we can only dream and they directly show our eyes what our hearts have not yet seen.

Illusion of Songs

I used to believe in songs. I used to love anthems of our lives of our times. But these come and go like the people driven to write the lines who are simply part of our growing up and moving on too.

To have what the singer says you can find, you can't as they say 'keep on becoming.' You have to stop and be still.

Radiate

Silently radiate like a still eagle, like a small ray of light and influence is yours.

Failure

Failure is one of the best motivators and the best place to start from time and time again, as failure is always available.

Failure is begging for change, begging for improvement.

Failure has the greatest potential, more potential than success.

Happy Work

We become so fixated on what we decide to do, we can forget to enjoy the moments from the decision until we actually achieve it and the pleasure of work is gone.

Curves

The straight line is a curse and of all the lines is the worst. It has to be straight not bent or with an angle and not allowed to droop or dangle. It ruins the line of things which could be curved and better for the eye to observe. The body has got no straight lines. Nature is not sophisticated to be so poorly defined.

Turning Inwards

Hearing all the songs, all the music, all the poetry, all the stories in all the books, point the way to being our inner self, which is there all along. Perhaps they are mirrors.

The Best Light

It's not even breakfast yet and most of my day's work is done. All the thinking is gone. The day to enjoy is now here.

Artists know the early morning light is best because few people get out of bed to see it.

It looks more unusual, simply because the light comes from the other side.

The morning is best to see most things. The night brings shadows of fear, illusions which are only clear again in the morning light.

Art Is Us

All the best songs, poems and art are not about us. They are us. Songs sing only of our love for others in our self. Poems speak of our love of the world in our self. Art displays to others the love we could have for our self.

The Arts

The moodiness of the poet made me moody with you and you showed me how you have other sides too. I guess the poet seems like no hero but instead like a soldier, they try to show us things no one else can see.

It's not the paint or the brush that outlines the love; it's the stroke of the hand which weaves the story from the heart. It's only the presence of the heart we see in the stoke of the hand that draws or writes and the presence of the heart we hear on the lips that sing.

48. DIFFICULT PEOPLE

Dark Triad

When relating to someone is strained with lack of
agreeableness and conscientiousness, try and remember to
think of the triple personality the Dark Triad.

For success their Machiavellianism uses charm to
interpersonally manipulate everyone as they are
unprincipled masters of deception.

Their Narcissism makes them seem superior even grandiose
but they overdress to look good.

Their psychopathic coldness but impulsive love of danger
sees them take risks in leading.

The one in a hundred people with the Dark Triad personality
will exploit and take every opportunity to get what they
want no matter what. Watch out.

Passive Aggression

Telling someone they are stressed out, or they are angry are
none of your business if you are not going to help because
if you tell someone without offering help, you are making
them think about you, not them. You become the problem.

Keeping the Main Aim the Main Aim

A sustained attack of thoughts lasting one month can be so distracting; so consuming, it can take you to your limits of coping.

It can be any distraction from another person, someone challenging you or stealing from you who you can't formally stop, someone who plays a game.

Their game interferes with you by interfering in your control of your thoughts. Keeping a steady aim as things continue, your victory is more certain than you can see.

Keeping the outer aim steady, retreat inside to keep the inner aim as the main aim. Find inner stillness and silence and let this overwhelm all. Slowing the breath will eventually slow the thoughts, keeping the main aim the main aim.

Making Someone Look Stupid

Making someone feel stupid is a wounding that must not go unchallenged. Telling others doubles the wound and doubles the violence.

Making someone feel stupid is a wounding that must not go without discipline to understand their error in the use of authority.

Making someone feel stupid is a wounding that must not be repeated as no opportunity for a second chance should exist. Making someone feel stupid is a terminal event.

Compelled

A crook needs to be crooked to succeed. They are like this because they don't know how to be happy being straight.

They can create gossip and smokescreens to hide what they are really like. They can present as honestly doing good when it is all part of their acting.

If you don't play their game. If you don't play with them and you are not playful, they have to find another playmate because they are compelled by what they are.

Un-negotiate

You cannot negotiate to make meaningful progress with certain types of people because even inevitable, painful consequences may not move them. If they keep on coming back, they usually need to be firmly told.

Caution

People who use and abuse others approach them with friendliness, promises and kindness not hostility. Once fooled, because we are sensitive, we train to be defensive, cautious and guarded in how we respond as we can still be fooled, attacked and destroyed. We need strong unmovable defences.

Best Teacher

The most cunning, sadistic, greedy, selfish, dishonest, wealthy person with no principles taught me more than anyone about what I want.

Obituary

Why not give obituaries to people when they are alive, when it could have the most meaning, the most impact? Why wait until they are dead?

Perhaps it is a way of having power over them and their mistakes, a judgement which they do not hear. Perhaps obituaries are rude, cruel, vengeful and are having the last word.

Trusted

Not trusting is the most important thing to learn about everyone else. Not trusting is the most difficult thing because it is learnt only through pain received from trusting someone. Not trusting is vital for survival, vital for enthusiasm because you have to trust only you.

I don't want to spend an evening with

My teachers, my siblings, my customers at work, the prime minister, the King or Queen.

Intangible

We are refugees in a world which is still trying to get rid of us, a world which does not support the contemplative life, a world where there have to be results. The intangible is becoming the rarest of all. It needs protecting the most to pass on.

Protecting Dangerous Beauty

There is no rescue from life as being alive is dangerous and only we can protect our self. If we stop, the danger increases.

No one else can rescue us from life because we are meant to be here. We have been placed here by people to live this dangerous life.

Protecting our self from depending on other's protection and doing it our self brings peace to this dangerous beautiful life.

Mental Health and Personality Disorder

Realising a childhood friend you knew is not actually well is sad and at the same time a loss. Expectations are different as they can't travel the same distance and be with you the rest of your journey. Although you never stop loving them as a friend, the parting has already happened, the friendship changed.

Securities, Power and Ego

Whatever I have done or not but others say I have, is their thinking. It is known by me but thought by others.

Whatever I have been or not but others say I have, is their thinking. It is known by me but thought by others.

Other's investment in judging me may enrich their world of securities or may make it look like they overpower me or make their ego greater.

Inner happiness with our past overrides other's investments. It is legitimate permission to be happy now, harmonious, not striving for power, ego or securities.

Illusion

Perhaps we need to look again and make sure we are sensitive, not uneducated or inexperienced, just not willing or able to accept dishonest as honest or cruel as kind.

Perhaps we need to look again and make sure we are not willing or able to accept being smart as coming from the heart, religion as spirituality or duty as compassion.

Perhaps we need to look again and make sure we are not willing or able to accept hearing as listening or seeing as looking, thinking as understanding or doing as being.

Mindlessness

I told them not to be mindful, not to run mindfulness
courses, not to write mindfulness books but to be mindless.

They could only see their thoughts. They didn't try to
see without them. They couldn't see stillness, couldn't be
without their thoughts.

Now they have to cope with running corporate industrial
mindfulness courses, supporting the thinking which
produces the very reactions they were meant to help recover
from with mindfulness.

Religious Organisations and the Self

If you are part of an organisation, you have to be loyal to it
as you represent it. If you only have yourself, you have to be
loyal to you as you represent yourself.

Being loyal to an organisation means helping to maintain it
and may require concealment, collusion and coldness for the
greater good. Being loyal to honesty, simplicity and kindness
in yourself, there is nothing greater or better.

Justice

I don't believe scales balance sides. I don't believe blindfolds
objectively see. I don't believe the sword punishes. There is
no right side and there is no justice. They are only words.
There is however consciousness of deliberate intent to
destroy what is not theirs to even touch.

Passionate Nature to Injustice

My passionate reactive nature is from my parents and some people find it too much, but it doesn't worry me because it is only me trying to speak.

I have seen injustice and I have had injustice. It is incorrect to not act, to not speak, and if ignored, to not act and speak repeatedly.

I am frequently left a little disappointed others don't trust my over-passionate nature which is just like tuned up hearing.

Ignored

Being ignored means not being regarded with enough importance. Being ignored means not being taken seriously enough.

Being ignored means manners are not being heeded as a statement. Sometimes it is best to ignore being ignored, sometimes it is the end.

Blender

Maybe I need a blender, one that blends really well. I will jump in it and get blended.

Perhaps then I will get on with all sorts of people who at the moment I seem to have not really met.

Higher Ground

When you are troubled, stand back from the waves trying
to crash on you and take one step backwards up the shore
getting to higher ground. Keep on stepping backwards,
getting higher from the waves.

Finding yourself on higher ground, let go of everything
lower down. Look around you, seeing everything that makes
you happy.

Enjoy the happiness on higher ground, the silence, the
stillness. This is where you belong.

No Change Wanted

I'm so unchallenged today, I had to give up helping people
to change because they don't want to change.

I walked away from that because it made my batteries flat,
disappointed but not defeated, my calmness intact.

Courage is not on tap but comes from a challenge and we are
not ready until it passes this way.

Minding Yourself

I tend to stay away from people as they can cause
unimaginable trouble which you could not make up.

If you have not had enough trouble, mix in until you are in
too much trouble, perhaps then you will mind yourself.

My Opponent

Our opponents are our best teachers, so what did mine teach me? They showed me I am still passionate about what I do.

Through betrayal, dishonesty and gossip, an opponent can ignore responsibilities and abuse power, so it becomes a force against you, weakening you or correcting and strengthening your weaknesses.

It is good to be passionate about integrity, about being kind, about not being late, about respect.

It is good to be passionate about not lying, about being direct, open and honest, about simplicity, about hard work.

Your Opponent

Your opponent is always your best teacher, your best friend and often a hidden part of you.

Treat your opponent with more respect, above everyone else, as they can teach you more if you find out why they oppose you.

They may lay down their life to show you this. Even though you cannot see this, you cannot exist fully without them.

Leave Them Alone

Leave those alone who don't want your help as they will be looked after by their self or someone.

Professor Troubles

What you don't like, what troubles you, what makes you
upset, that is your best friend, your best teacher, your own
professor.

The best teacher is the reaction inside you, wanting you to
see you may need to change your attitude to the best expert
on you, and listen to your internal advisors.

Change or Leave

Yes it is correct, since stopping working for me, I've not been
able to stay in a job for long. Three months to two years
was the best of forty and if I worked the next forty, nothing
would change.

When I find out what's happening I cannot collude, so when
placed in a position where I change or speak, I have had to
speak and leave.

It has never been a problem for me to speak and walk away
and I have always been able to sleep at night, even now out
in the cold, I am warm inside.

Intolerability

Intolerable situations can be other people imposing aspects
of their lives on ours, so that our life is unhappy or not
fulfilling our self. Either we change and move or they do.

Stream of Jobs

My work has always been short term jobs. Eventually when I've seen my colleagues I've not been able to collude with them so I have always had to leave.

When I tried to oppose their conduct to protect the defenceless they had the reins of power, I had the path to the door.

I have my foolishness. Theirs was exchanged for pensions and comfortable retirement long ago. Integrity is not often comfort or being respected.

Refugee

Go to that place, the one you know as a refuge from outside, where you shine brightest in silence.

You will not let yourself down by having time and concentration until unity and happiness are uncovered once more.

Integrity

Usually in the thick of it we can't see what it was we started by what appeared like a small decision to stand our ground.

Complexity does not diminish our integrity. Secrecy and deception only highlight it.

Be Quiet

Unless you know something they don't, don't say it unless they ask and even if you do know something they don't, don't say it until they ask again.

Detaching from Overthinking

When we overthink, detachment is separating ourselves from others. Detachment is separating our processes from other people processes.

Detachment is separating our thoughts from other people's thoughts. Detachment is separating our feelings from other people's feelings.

Changing On Our Own

There are periods of deep inner change which may not yet be worked out in thoughts, so there is unrest, unhappiness, worry and we are often alone until it is processed.

Processing change can't be rushed even if it is instant change because accommodation to the change has to be met on every level, and has its own time.

On our own, our thoughts transform into words what we want to say. Only then, how we will live our days can be worked out.

Recovery of Your Own Life

Recovery of your own life may never occur but like a car crash, a crisis is usually the best thing to ever happen to get back what you lost and ditch the unnecessary.

Reclaiming and restoration of feelings, of clear thinking, of balance, of health can then be returned.

Reclaiming and restoration of friendship, of strength, of hope, of the spirit can then be returned.

Joy and Problems

The joy and problems we have with others, are a function of living with others and do not go. The joy and problems we have with our self, with being in the world do not go. Both joy and problems with others, our self and just being happy with our self are being vibrantly alive.

Complex Mankind

We are walking collections of interactive, integrated, complicated experiences ready and waiting to be explained simply.

We are happy to baby sit a lion cub. Happy to process information on computers. Happy to work for peace. Happy to help. Happy to love and happy to die.

Skip Once a Day

With everyone and everything, ask what is good. Life is a range of many different experiences. A smile, a child, a stranger waving to you on the road, daydreaming, making a new friend. Skip one step a day like a child.

Keep Busy

Everything comes with its own appointment. Answers come in their time, not ours.

We can't change allotted appointments because we want satisfactory answers. Just being occupied whilst waiting for the answer ensures we are ready for whatever it gives us.

People Problem Algorithm

People problems have a process. First there is a problem, then an awareness and then thinking about it as a problem.

Then there is acceptance, then the question of whose problem is it. Then there is who should deal with it, then letting them know. Then letting go.

Someone Special

Some days have almost everything you could have thought of to be perfect, then you are surprised because someone makes you happier.

Not Just a Piece of Kit

We are all pieces of kit and we perform various functions in different settings.

We move from one setting to the next and someone takes our place, like we took someone else's before.

We know our place and worth but sometimes not the timing of where we are supposed to be.

Sometimes we choose, sometimes others do but we are much more than what we do. We are a piece of kit for that setting, but we live and love in many settings.

Whose Stuff

When you leave your family it can be the right thing. You can continue to lovingly grow together seeing and being with each other.

Some families are dangerous company and you have to escape. Some are so distressed and incapable, they dump you somewhere.

Some families stop you getting on and won't let you leave, so when they keep on pulling you back, it may be time to talk or separate.

We have to find our own life, letting them continue theirs. Giving them their stuff and dealing with ours, gives us freedom to let all our lives blossom.

Be Direct and Clear

Always ask yourself what do you want from you today.
It is not what is usually asked but if it is not asked at the
beginning it will always have to be asked at the end.
Instead people mention in passing with a hint or a sigh that
you seem busy today and so it is not important.
Manipulation is a game only two can play so shooting first
asking questions later is the only way to play.

Mental Washing

Reprograming ourselves has to be done every day, if we let
ourselves be programmed by information from people, the
media, selling of everything by everyone.

Reprogramming ourselves every night, like washing our
faces of all the dirt we have accidently picked up, is essential
to keep us our authentic self.

Stereotypes

Stereotypes are more promoted than ever. They used to be
as straight forward as men seeming to want to be envied for
wanting a woman's beauty. Women seemed to want to be
envied for attracting the power of controlling a man's money

But the success of being attractive doesn't make either more
beautiful. With the increasing need to sustain the inevitable
loss of beauty, ugliness often replaces it and the potential for
a happy journey often ends stuck in shallow waters.

Ditch Stereotypes

The races, colours, religions we both share are conditioned learned thinking, so let's do some unlearning, un-thinking. All men want is just one thing sex. All women want is men's money. Black is bad, white is good. Cold is bad, warm is good. Stop these in their tracks from blocking you being free to relate to everyone

I'm Muslim get over it. I'm disabled get over it. I'm a foreigner get over it.

I'm gay get over it. I'm lesbian get over it. I'm LGBT get over it.

I'm black get over it. I'm old get over it. I'm in NA get over it. I'm left wing get over it. I'm right wing get over it. I'm Irish get over it.

I am Welsh get over it. I'm Scottish get over it. I don't have children get over it.

I'm British get over it. I'm Jewish get over it. I'm American get over it.

I'm a Hindu get over it. I'm Chinese get over it. I'm Russian get over it.

I'm a Christian get over it. I'm in AA, NA and GA, get over it.

I'm a loner get over it. I'm a weirdo get over it. I'm abnormal get over it.

Don't Give Your Happiness Away

Don't think about being happy. Just be happy. Don't analyse being happy. Just be happy. Don't give your happiness away by what others say. Don't let anyone take your happiness away by what they say.

Humanity

The quiet confidence of having the power of our teachers and ancestors and openly sharing with the young as equals is humanity.

Eclipsed

Big egos in the room, jostling for importance are totally eclipsed by one person's inner stillness.

Yourself

As knowing what it is to be a parent can only be known by being a parent, so truth can only be known by being true to yourself.

Mind Your Own Business

If it is none of your business, leave it alone. It is none of your busines what other people think about you, so just be you.

Guilt Anger Consequences

Someone behaving badly affects me, then they make me
feel awkward for telling them, so I feel guilty. They don't
change, but they try to turn my guilt into a problem, so that
I am the bad person. As it is not my issue, I leave them to the
consequences.

Only the Small Mistakes Count

Permitting a small mistake can cost us dearly because it is the
denial of small mistakes which matter because the big ones
are usually seen.

London Cabbies

'Can you phone a minicab to take me back home
please?' The patient asked me.
'Of course but you could get a cab on the street quicker.'
'They wont pick me up.'
'Why not?
'London Cabbies won't pick up black people.'

Since that time, I ask every London Cabbie the same question
and I always get exactly the same answer.
'Is it true that London Cabbies wont pick up black
people?'
"Well, you see, they all live south of the river. Can't get a
fare back Guv."

Asking this question is my small contribution to help change
this.

288

49. CHOICE AND OPPPORTUNITIES

Already Detached

'Where are you going?' Screamed the religious man three times.
'To play rugby for the school,' I said.

In front of the school of five hundred boys, the De La Salle catholic brother punched me four times so hard on the jaw with his fists, that each punch took me off my feet.

I didn't say or do anything because if I defended myself, my free place at school would have gone. Expelled instantly, my future place college would have gone. I stood still, upright, silent and detached. He had been the British Army Boxing Champion and now after the fourth punch, Brother Peter turned his back on me and he shouted at the whole school, 'That's for nothing, now try something.'

Fist Inspired Passion

When did the rising of passion begin? Was it from coping with the pain of the first sense of being alone? Or from the disappointment of my feeling of being ritually abused when that fist hit my face?

Self-preservation is escaping into a newly discovered inner land. Any defensive reaction to the first taste of abusive power is answered only by escalating pain and further diving inside to the inner land.

Four Reasons Why I Quit Psychiatry

The first doubt came when I heard that over half of the psychiatrists who were my teachers and role models had major addiction problems and few of the rest were considered mentally well.

Next was the treatment at St Bernard's in Ealing of a survivor of Auschwitz who had depression. When electroconvulsive therapy failed, it was suggested at the weekly meeting of all the psychiatrists that she should have a frontal lobotomy. My objection on the grounds that psychotherapy should be continued as she had had enough torture was ridiculed as was I. My connection with psychiatry was broken forever.

What made me quit my job at Oxford after just a few weeks, was the man who died of constipation on a long stay psychiatric ward, whom the Oxford coroner said was the worst case of medical neglect he had ever seen.

After I left I was reassured on hearing research evidence, that for people with severe psychiatric disorders, a six week stay in the Muthuswamy South Indian temple doing light duties produced the same improvement as a month of standard psychiatric treatment.

Alternative Path to Psychiatry

I wanted to be able to give what I could give, kindness and compassion, which had little to do with psychology. Wherever I was, I wanted most importantly to be with a sense of the inner self, the spirit within.

Do You Want a Brew?

'The new water heater is better than that old kettle,' the Psychotherapist said to the cleaner. 'Stays hot and saves me so much time. I can pour a cup any time and get more work done.

The cleaner looked her in the eye and saw the glint of self-importance. 'I prefer still using the old one, that's why I've kept it. I can ask someone if they want a brew. Then wait with them while it boils, spending that time together chatting or not breathlessly trying to save time. There's nothing wrong with the old kettle. No need to replace it. Waiting for it to boil lets me calm my thinking, so I'm not a servant to restlessness.'

Choiceless Paths

Even though I ended up on the opposite path, which was my second choice, my second choice was the best.

My first choice was the best, then my second choice was. They seemed different but now they are the same. They can only merge into one path.

The point of breakthrough was seeing and realising that the path I took was the right one all the time.

We can only see the road we are on not the one ahead.

The path we are on is the only one that can lead to the one ahead.

Predestination

Your thoughts are not original. They are not your own unique thoughts. They are common, quite usual thoughts which we have been having for thousands of years.

You think that your thoughts make you behave like you want to, but are you sure? Maybe you are going through the thinking motions which ensure what is supposed to happen will happen.

When we seem to choose, perhaps it was already so. It is a belief that choice indicates no predestination. But choice is not in truth optional. Truth is not a choice.

Only You

You only need to be true to you, only you. There is no one else you need to be true to. Not to the written word, neither to stories or books, nor to the world of comings and goings, only to you. Not to the teacher, preacher or doctor, neither to subjects, only you.

Inner rules

Get on with your own life, leaving others' lives and concerns alone. Love bearing no hatred seeing only the positive merits, overlooking other's faults. What you do for someone, you really do for you, so do it perfectly.

Choosing

We are distracted by being attracted to complexity not simplicity, to noise not silence, to movement not stillness, to resistance rather than acceptance, to desire not happiness.

We are attracted to thinking rather than being still, to importance not humility, to personality not principles, to gaining rather than sharing, to looking out not in.

We are attracted to the future not the present, to speech not the grace of silence, to style not content, to competitiveness not cooperation, to separateness not compassion.

We are attracted to distractions rather than non-attachment, to seeing parts not everything, to the many not the few, to the popular not the outsiders, to dividing rather than bringing together.

We are attracted to mystery not truth, to doing not being, to emotions not love, to power not friendliness.

In summary, we are attracted to complexity not simplicity, to thinking rather than being still, to the future not the present, to attachment rather than non-attachment, to mystery not truth.

The essence is 'Simply be still now non-attached true to the self.'

Involvement

Just because the majority supports a person, doesn't mean they are right. A whole country can support something and be wrong about it but be right about supporting each other.

Missionaries

Helping others only helps yourself to help others which is not wrong.

Helping doesn't help them help themselves; it keeps them where they are when their real need could have unfolded.

Helping can be a selfish act to further your own ends. Religion's missionaries know this best.

Forever Young

Brothers and sisters like to compete to find out and show you who they are and by joining in you find more about you as well.

But as adults, not leaving things like this behind, when there should be more serious things on their minds, is childish.

If the relationship is subtle combat and continues without development, eventually there is no choice but to leave and be with friends.

Going Our Own Way

Whichever way you go, all paths lead you to the same final path. Whichever way you go, it will be on your own path, nobody else's path. Your final path for you began so long ago and the choice never ends to leave behind your happiness, your nature and your smile.

The Outcome will Explain

However odd I may seem. However wrong in my choices, it is right just to be me. There is a strange intuition behind my choices I cannot explain, only the outcome can.

Choosing Happiness

We can sit around doing nothing or we can sit around trying to be happy by the only means we know.

An Unfortunate Man

The Russian or American billionaire on their yacht with their seventeen crew who can sail it to one of their mansions of coral bays, sand and surf and unhappiness are unfortunate.

No Trace

Would you rather leave no trace or something of importance? All traces will eventually go, so do you want to spend time leaving a trace.

Impact

Our pattern is not seen until we have nearly completed it,
our impact usually not until we have gone

Dropping Expectations

If we drop our expectations of someone, accepting them for
what they are and not trying to change them, we have less of
a problem.

Dropping expectations doesn't lesson us, but lets us grow
wiser branches for others to settle on.

Acceptance Our Friend

Maybe everything is just as it should be and we should stop
thinking how to change it.

Non-acceptance can be our greatest enemy, acceptance our
waiting friend.

If we accepted life we would have less to do, more time for
peace and more to just be.

Don't Miss Opportunities

Don't miss opportunities to be kind. Don't miss
opportunities to be with friends. Don't miss opportunities to
be your self. Don't miss opportunities to be happy.

You Choose

When you are young in your teens, you choose your nurturing, what you feed off and live on. You will remember this as it can be growth or decay.

To start with decay is only slight but all the slight choices of decay add up and as you start to feel unwell, others begin to notice. You isolate yourself with your choices until everyone has gone.

To start with growth is only slight but all the choices add up and as you start to feel happy, others begin to notice. Choosing solitude, your consciousness lets you be part of everything.

You choose your path from only two, decadence to decay or growth to happiness.

You can live the life of either chaotic messy descent or the disciplined inner life of being consciously happy in stillness.

Appearance

Why do we appear to choose unwisely? Are we copying someone, a parent, a hero a friend? Do we choose suffering because we can see the reward is happiness?

Choose Wisely

It is easy not to be happy, so easy to be sad. What persuades us is not worth more than us.

So You Think You Choose

Information you are given as a warning or guidance doesn't usually help, because it is your destiny that drives you, not your head. Whatever you do leads you there. Whatever you don't do leads you there, just the same.

Visitors

We think we have control over our world because we want to have control over our world. But we can also see our world has its own form, movement and intentions because it is not ours.

To Adjust During the Inevitable

My friend Narikutti had a guru, Yogaswami of Jaffna who used to say: 'All is truth. There is not even one wrong thing. We do not know. It was all accomplished long ago.'

We are more powerless than we want to admit, so surrendering helps us to be calm and composed producing an inner 'serenity of surrender.'

50. FATE

The Hands of Fate

Sometimes I ask, 'What is worth making a decision about when it was all decided long ago?' Either way it will turn out how it was meant to be, so a decision is made more easily.

Complete Surrender to Fate

Even though we know and even though we are told, even though we read about it and see it all the time, death slowly becomes more surprising and death acceptable as time goes by. Knowledge and health don't help accept it more. They can both make the thought of it worse. Perhaps only complete surrender to fate is the only way to keep it at bay.

Acceptance

Why should we be frightened of dying or death? It is nature and fate letting us fulfil our purpose? They cannot be changed from what they are letting us be; what we are.

Fate's Hand

When you are uninjured but others are not. When you survive and others do not, you cannot look at these incidents without fate having a hand.

Only Words

Past and future are words we use to describe thoughts of what is. Past and future are only words we use to understand fate. Past and future are only words for fate.

Your Journey

Eventually you see you have been following a scent. You have been listening for truth. You have been watching for it, waiting for it. It is the stillness here inside you.

Then you see your journey has taken care of you, the path leading to a place, a river, a plain, a sacred mountain, they are your stillness.

Fate

Fate is not anything like a power in control. It is not something that can be named. Everything is fate and fate is everything. Fate is what things are meant to be as they are.

Our Life as a Fateful Play

A long drawn out play with the characters people we know, playing their parts with us. Surprising us with their scripts and moves which seem written long before, because we already know the ending.

Compelling

Compelled to live, compelled to be happy, compelled to be and not to be is our fate.

Right on Time

Returning to stillness is our origin and fate. Stillness is never early or late.

Before In-between and After

Wave after wave of us fall and just like soldiers in denial who think, 'It wont be me,' we think the same just to buffer our acceptance.

There are never any exceptions to how fate is not just first and last but everything before, in-between and after.

51. MIND CONTROL

What We Eventually Find

You don't need a clever doctor. You don't need a psychologist or psychiatrist. You don't need anyone to tell you that you need to control your own mind. It is the simplest thing of all to miss that can leave us all in a mess, not seeing we are responsible for being in control of our mind.

Soul Mind

I am so happy I never valued thinking much and never gave it control as my mind would have taken over the direction of my heart.

Starting and Stopping

Just when I can't think of anything else and I feel that's the day done, something crops up and it finds its life on a page. How strange that consciousness lets thoughts form which search for words to become sentences which can be written spoken or forgotten. Stopping them is also its main job.

Most Powerful Medicine

Now is the time to be overwhelmed by a daily dose of my favourite drug, taken each night at the same time; my sleep.

The Drug of Drugs

There are no unwanted side effects. No one else is involved. You make a full recovery until you need more. It sedates you and lets you sleep. It gives you an altered state of consciousness, the most natural drug of tiredness.

Ignorance

In the West, what we don't know we call the unconscious, in the East, we call it the self. Neither is right nor wrong only names for our ignorance.

Without

With ignorance we are searching for happiness. Without ignorance the search is called off.

With ignorance our thoughts are in control. Without ignorance we are happy without them.

With ignorance we suffer in the outside world. Without ignorance we are happy inside.

With ignorance we have not surrendered. Without ignorance surrender is complete.

With ignorance we are busy in the world. Without ignorance we have detached.

Levels of Attainment

Some people seem to wake and change in their teens. Others in their twenties, thirties or in a late decade but when darkness is removed and they wake up, ignorance has started to go.

There are different levels of attainment, as some have only one eye slightly open. The lucky few have both eyes slightly open and most rare, someone who has one eye fully open. When limited sight is present for some there is only one purpose left, the desire to see completely, to have ignorance fully removed.

To Be Still in Happiness

You will have a certain attitude to want to be in a special place for detachment, solitude and silence. But to enquire, surrender and meditate, to remove ignorance and to be still in happiness, no special place is needed.

Light Comes to Us

There comes a time invited or not when you leave everything behind. It is merging with yourself, detachment from all else.

But unseen it is a merging with everything else. Because of the connections not seen, it is the final removal of darkness, so the light is seen everywhere.

More can be Less

The more you know, the more you know you don't know.
The more effort, the less effort is required until there is none.
The more you see, the more you see there is nothing to see.
The more you hear, the more you hear nothing to hear.

Great People

I have been in the presence of some good people, perhaps
some of them were great people. I have come across the
traces left by others who perhaps were great people.

Simplicity is often a sign there may be greatness. Humility is
another sign but compassion is the energy of the great whilst
getting on with their work.

Inner Self

I like people for their hearts, not for their thoughts. You can
call it the 'inner self,' anything you like but that is what I like.
Minds are like machines varied, sometimes impressive but
they cannot just be the inner self.

Unhappy Reason

How do I forget to remind myself to be happy, because I
forget to be happy all the time? There is no reason other than
reason getting in the way.

Bliss

I have moments sometimes lasting seconds or minutes,
rarely all morning or afternoon when everything in my life is
perfect, not a single thing is wrong.

These moments can sometimes be created if I want them by
not thinking, so I have to remind myself to choose them and
be in perfect inner happiness.

Days of Great Peace

On Saturday afternoons I always sensed the enjoyment
before Sunday's solemnity, the fun before the regrouping of
serious thoughts ready for the week of work.

In some places there are no weekends, no particular days to
the week no holidays, holy days on or off days, just days of
great peace.

52. OUR OWN WAY

Perfect

Why don't they tell us we are perfect, that we are better than machines ever can be? We can do much of what they do, only slower but they cannot be what we are; consciousness.

Why are we not told we are perfection as we need all of our mistakes and flaws to learn? Without them we would not have our polarity and be perfect.

Your Own Path

You have to go your own way, straying off paths from others; strong enough to be on your own, with enough fear to keep you alert.

Where is Happiness

I didn't follow the usual path of one job and a pension. I didn't invest in real estate, a holiday home or rentals. I didn't invest in collections or anything I could sell.

I tried to find happiness simply in myself even if it meant looking foolish. Switched off about the world and its affairs I found happiness is our nature but not in the world.

No Apology

Perhaps I could be criticised for having feelings which I show. Yes I sometimes wear my heart on my sleeve but usually when I choose to.

Maybe I could be criticised for looking inside to know my own self, being in solitude detached from the world to experience happiness there.

Psychoanalysis

The psychoanalyst said I had fear of abandonment. 'Who hasn't?' I thought.

My parent's past history was never enquired about, yet their history made me what I was, so I decided psychoanalysis was intellectual and not real.

I cancelled my appointments, but he kept on writing to me saying I could do well. I was well, I am well.

Oxford

I thought there would be some time for the spirit but there was none. It was all about thought, almost perfect thought.

Too much concern for the mind and none for the spirit, so I turned on my heels and looked for my own way.

Your Default

Your default should be set to be kind. Your default should be set to trust. Your default should be set to help. Your default may be misplaced, incorrect, fooled but your default is always the best option for you.

From Dreams

When you don't want to go the way of your father with the addiction or the way of your brother with dishonesty, you have to look somewhere else rather than up to people. Looking sideways or leapfrogging over things, even to another country can give you a sense of something else you could not see, which now you can change just from a dream.

Returning to Inside

In trying to return to the place inside where I am calm, I have to ask a question to try and rescue me. I have to ask 'Who am I, What am I?'

Only after I ask this inside, I find the place where I am calm, still, serene and see there are no words for being this.

Longing

Why do we create longing for happiness? Why do we dedicate most of our thinking longing for happiness which we already have today inside us. Why do we long for something which is already ours, which is inside?

Experience

I wish someone had left me notes. Notes about what to avoid. About being quiet and not broadcasting my thoughts. About being happy with what we have today. About being happy with what we hear and what we are rather than with what we say. If they had, would I have learnt this as well as broadcasting?

Notes

Why didn't people leave notes since they could write about what is most important in life. Why didn't they say how to be happy instead of commandments saying what we shouldn't do?

Why didn't they say the point of life is to live and be happy in yourself. Not to make others happy or to accumulate material things. Not to be thought of. Not to be thought of as clever. Why don't people leave notes saying how to be happy inside?

Inner Sight

Words are only words, an expression. Words do not describe decent people well enough. Words do not describe non decent people helpfully enough.

The eye sees, the heart sees and the body truthfully tries to tell us what words cannot.

Second Sight

Everyone thinks you have lost the plot by ignoring the masterplan they think you should be living by. Compared to their standing in the world you are not a threat.

Then the unexpected appears in their life so what was meaningless becomes the most important. From standing above you their only desire is to try and be happy kneeling or sitting with you.

Your room

Your room where you slept. Your room where you played. Your room where you studied. Your room where you were with friends. Your room where you now sleep. Your room where you work. Your room where you relax is only inside you.

Self Food

Knowledge feeds the brain but doesn't feed the self because the self cannot be nourished only be seen. It needs to be able to just be. It needs us to be still.

I Coulda, I Shoulda and I Woulda

There are so many things I could look up, so many people I should look up, so much I would look up but instead I keep looking inside to find out about myself.

Here

I was there when the fire nearly engulfed you forever. I was there when you left hospital. I was there.

I was there when you were in the accident. I was there when your friend died. I was there.

I was there when you realised your ignorance. I was there when you realised the truth. I was there.

I will be there when you die. I will be there after you die. I will be there.

Hope and Fear Light and Dark

I am not usually happy to see the sun set because a day has nearly gone, so there is always some fear of what the night may bring.

But I am always glad to see the sun rise because I am still here full of hopeful expectancy, a true morning person.

Here Now

Maybe we don't want things to be how they were. We only want to be how we are. Maybe we don't want things to be better in the future. We only want to be how we are.

For Me For You

This writing is for me and to give away but if you find it, you can have it and give it away too.

Congratulations You are in a Mess

Congratulations because the pain and suffering are almost over and you will be transformed. What a relief and time to be thankful.

Not Ok But Happy

How could I know I would turn out like this because years ago this is not what I expected my life to be like? Years ago I would not have seen me being happy with this but when I look back, I see that all along I have been the happiest I could have been.

Our Own Final Path

What leads you on your path may also lead another but for some it might be impossible. Others may take a path which would be impossible for you.

All along, all paths lead to the same final path which is the path of happiness found in stillness. Whether in solitude or with other, we find it on our own.

Happiness of Unhappiness

To be spiritually fit you need to be motivated either to be like someone in happiness of what they are, or to get away from how unhappy you are. Whatever way leads you is your own path.

Fitness

Keeping spiritually in touch is keeping spiritually fit. Fitness needs time, effort and practice. Spiritual fitness means being on the right spiritual diet, being with people on the same final path nurturing each other.

Being in the right place in our self is everything but because we have to live in the world packed with others who may need us, we need to be fit enough to move inwards all the time.

Inner Finishing School

Whilst we are still childish, we cannot deal with life. Whilst we are emotionally too sensitive, we cannot relate on all levels. Whilst we lack humility, we cannot learn. Whilst we are in denial, we cannot change.

Where Happiness Is Now

Always strive for nothing. In nothing is the fullness of stillness. In the fullness of stillness is everything.

Full Consciousness

As I write this time is running out. I am spending my time like this because it makes me happy to enjoy my own self.

Conscious of what I have got, why would I want to be doing anything which would distract me from happiness, unless it is sharing it?

How Long?

We have to sit on a mess until we get so fed up with it, we are so uncomfortable we have to move.

How Much?

How are we torn apart? How do we unfold? How do we unbox? How can we put us back together?

How Known?

How much can you know yourself? At what time in your life do you know yourself? How long does it take to know yourself? Is there an end to knowing yourself?

How We Look

We read to find out about a story but we are looking for our story. We don't know we are not reading but looking for a mirror.

Until The End

We don't understand some stories until before the end, just as our lives may not reveal our story until the end. A search for meaning may not be seen until then.

The Trace Left Behind

When you give up everything about something, eventually you see crystal clear why you held on to it, no matter what trace there is left behind to remind you of it.

On Our Own

We only find out we are on our own when we find our self on our own, without support from family or friends around.

Where we might have expected sadness, we see being on our own is being in control of our happiness. Purpose is where we may have not have seen one. On our own is being more connected to everyone.

53. ACCEPTANCE

Accepting Thankfully

We can think a lot about many things, of others and where we are but at some stage we see we have to embrace it, so we need to find acceptance.

Acceptance is not just taking what is offered but welcoming what is offered as a gift. The harder it is to accept, the more welcome it should be.

Acceptance is not about receiving anything but discovering inside us what we need to accept and being thankful about us.

Rehearsal

You don't often get the chance to rehearse how to respond to bad news. Just in case it is bad news, this is such an occasion.

Denial then nausea. Anger and disappointment. Acceptance, acceptance and more acceptance.

I Accept the Day

Whatever the day brings I accept it because it has been given and it has to be lived through, even if it has been given to reject.

My Deteriorating Mind

I know my memory is a little bit worse than two years ago.
Once or twice a week I can't remember some words but
because I am immersed and don't value them, I let them go.

Not having to build up any more, being able to let go,
accepting the state I have always been in is only present for
me now.

Alternatives to Truth

The true meaning even if spelt out and illustrated is not
accepted. Instead euphemisms, metaphors, mysteries and
stories are nearly always preferred to truth.

Grateful for Being Thankful

I am so grateful that I am thankful to difficulties. I don't have
to be ungrateful, resentful or envious. But being thankful
cures it of any negativity and helps accept difficult times.

Accept

There is always a way out of every situation. Even seeming
being blocked may be the only way out, which has to be
accepted.

Changing the Unchangeable

When we are in a painful place, sometimes it seems there is no way out. It seems there is no alternative but to wait and accept it.

In accepting that we can't change things, acceptance changes us. Only then do we see things differently.

Happy In Sunset

Just now the sun disappeared below the horizon but it is still very light and dusk will be here soon.

Acceptance of this inevitable darkness makes me turn up the light inside me.

With one sunset or a hundred years of them, are we wiser, happier fulfilled or are we the same as we were with the first one?

To Be Your Self

Suffering is not an option because it is handed to you on a plate which you have to eat. There is no choice about receiving it or about acceptance.

Suffering breaks a part of you down again if that part has been rebuilt since the last suffering. It is suffering's nature as is your nature to be yourself.

Near retirement

It is only now nearly at the end of my work that at last I think and feel able to do it. Unfortunately a tiredness has entered me simply from the wear and tear

Earlier on in youth there is no wear and tear so the journey of work seems easy and smooth but the wear and tear of age make it seem like more effort is needed to feel good about routine things.

The Old Hand

The amount you can do and you want to do reach a peak, then irreversible decline begins. There may be productive times with great effort but gone is the leisurely brush of the hand.

There is little time left, less willingness of the brain cells to work together. Everything of value has already been gathered in, so the hand is more desperate. But then it relaxes as we see it is the same hand.

Like a Flower

We think we will change. We think things will change and improve, not knowing, like a flower, which can't become anything but a flower, we also can't become anything other than what we are.

Acceptance is Happiness

Acceptance of today, as it is, as it changes develops and ends.
Acceptance of yourself as you are, as you change develops
and ends.
Acceptance of someone, as they are, as they change develops
and ends.
Acceptance of the world, as it is, as it changes develops and
ends.
Acceptance of today, yourself, someone and the world is all
there is.

My Triggers

My faulty triggers are so many only a few can be mentioned.
Like having a short fuse, being bad tempered, getting angry
and raising my voice, perfectionism, having expectations of
others and me, not liking criticism, not taking orders, other's
forgetfulness, not being reciprocal, being thick skinned,
frustration at being too soft, not able to reel my neck in,
being wrong, being sad, being sentimental and being too
self-critical.

Acceptance and Adjustment

We have to pick ourselves up and carry on in whatever
form we find we have become. We may not have the desired
resources but find we have more resolve.

Only Acceptance

We can't change what was given to us by nature but we can change how we nurture it. We can't change what has passed but we can change our attitude to it. We can't change another person only accept them.

Choiceless path

I can't stop the inner self. I obey its commands simply because I surrendered. Seeing what the world is like, there is no choice to remain there, surrendering is a choiceless path.

Heart of Me

Some get their excitement from the speed of things, others from being so relaxed. I've never been that way. I get my happiness from being inside.

Being on fire inside comes from nowhere. There is a need to express it in the stillness of meditation, sometimes in words. Either way it is the expression of the heart.

From the Heart Only

I gave up trying to fight writing as it is too strong for me so I obey its need to be expressed.

There is only one time I am able to stop it and completely ignore all writing, if it comes from the mind not the heart.

Dangerous Ferocious Beasts

The most dangerous ferocious animal ever to exist wasn't the T Rex. It wasn't the sabre toothed tiger. It has always been us.

We are a chaotic mess but there is some love in the mix and hate. You never know what you are going to get.

We can't stop

We can't work anything out. We can't stop our torture. We can't stop our violence. We can't stop our unfairness. We can't stop our unkindness. We can't stop our thinking. We can't stop what we can't stop

Treacherous

Treachery is something we have to be open to, otherwise we are closed. Like darkness is part of light, it comes with trust.

Variables

Some things take ten minutes, some less than one. Some can never be completed in words because they can't be thought or written, they can only be experienced.

Unseen Meaning

This commentary on the spending and passing of a life is not an attempt to give it any meaning, only to show what it doesn't mean. Then it might be easier for you to see your own meaning.

When half a dozen generations have come after us, our presence is no longer felt because no one has a living memory of us. It seems we are gone from other's life experience.

But we do not peak during life or after it in words, in pictures or anything we leave for others. What we give and leave to others is the thread of life itself for them to pass on.

Our Subjective True Life

Something you see from your position with your eyes only. It is what you see, not what others see, which is why we cannot in truth judge.

Truth is our truth only, everyone else has their truth too. We cannot know anyone else's truth, only ours.

Maintaining the Status Quo

Not accepting things in the past and still unshakable, we can survive without all the comforts offered. With our sight and hearts still, we can be unencumbered.

Accepted

We look for all sorts of reasons for why we are like this, our parents, our country, our school and our town, but it cannot be worked out. When we are limping and disabled we don't need to be worked out. We need support and help and to be accepted.

Mind Control

How can these thoughts be stopped? How can they stop bothering me so I can be in control? Mind control is the only answer because it cures most mental health problems, states of all kinds of distress. Suffering is stopped by stopping thoughts.

Honest Now

I will be patient and I will just be me for good now. No more dishonesty to me from me. I will try being simply clear, even with all the hesitation.

Our Best Teachers

Challenging to the last moment, abusers show us our weakest points so we can strengthen them for the next time. So paradoxically we should thank them; they are our best teachers of self respect.

Bigger Power

How do some grow without support and some need so much? What makes us so sensitive or hard? What needs to do this? Perhaps it is nothing to do with genetics or nurturing but the needs of something in us part of a bigger power.

Doubt

There comes a time where there is no doubt. When all else is given up, doubt is unknown.

Joyous Acceptance

Acceptance is the hardest choice to make. At first resistance reins but the alternative to resentment inevitability shows us we can have joy.

Be Still or Leave

Sometimes writing can simply be none other than an attempt to let the mind think it has found some sense of order from the chaos that appears as its reality, simply due to thoughts. This is an attempt to lull thoughts into believing they are important with some meaning to them when there is none, other than to stop them and leave me in stillness.

No Naming

When we discover something, why do we feel compelled to give it a name? Why not have some things which are nameless, which have no words to describe them? When we discover some one why do we feel compelled to give them a name? Why not have some one who is nameless whom we have no words to describe./Do other creatures give names which fit things like we do or do their instincts of safety, food, comfort and shelter guide them? Does the layer of words as our intelligence cover up our instincts so we can pretend not to be like other creatures? The naked truth is we are no different. We are the same.

Groups

I don't flourish in groups. I don't work in groups. I am solitary and prefer one to one company in all settings. Listening to one person is complicated as there are so many voices present who can't speak who influence what the person says, it is difficult to identify what the person wants. Listening to a group is different because they all speak not listening to each other but want to be heard as one voice and can only have one voice or fragment.

Nothing to Do

Apart from maintaining basic body functions, keeping thoughts repelled by the desire to be conscious of stillness is the direct route to inner happiness.

You Can't Make It Up

You couldn't make it up because it is life. When you make it up, the lie loses the energy of truth just as you always know when an actor is acting. The same loss of energy is felt when our ignorance of believing we are the ego is uncovered.

54. ORDINARY

Ordinary Aspects

Many tame lines can be read, then unsuspiciously out of nowhere, like a hidden tiger breaking cover, pouncing on unsuspecting prey, a few lines knock you over and you are changed.

Who wrote it and what it said, what it showed is not important. It is what I would like to have said and that can be the reason for reading.

It makes us see, it makes us think like a visit to a foreign culture. Remembering, returning home we compare what we are with what we thought we were, only now the ordinary becomes special.

In Touch

What's in the News? It is more of the same old stuff that is new, just because it is newer.

There is nothing new in death but what is new is a baby. We don't get excited unless it is one of our own but news shows us how much we are alone.

Life is more interesting than news. Ordinary everyday people and things mean more than the news and touch us much more.

Ordinary Things

Ordinary things, habits and routines help more than the written word because routines punctuate pain and suffering with some ordinary normality, so at least some normality is felt.

There is little that can reduce pain and suffering because going through them cannot be avoided to move to the next stage.

The inner refuge of stillness and silence should always be accessed, so it is easier to access at the most difficult time.

Ordinary

Ordinariness is something envied, because when the basic simple things are done and appreciated, they make us happy.

Calmness as your Friend

When your focus goes and is lost, great effort is needed to seem ordinary and unperturbed. Calmness is the only path. Hysteria, depression or anger are alternatives.

Depth of Meaning

To have meaning is to have purpose, although it can be anything. When it involves others it seems to have more meaning but it is the same, as it is just about us.

Presentation

Describing important things, events of my daily life is more difficult with each decade.

Things which I used to describe and report are now not as exciting as the ordinary.

The ordinary has been transformed into the authentic, now full of meaning for me.

There is no single reason why nature, beauty and what is done and said seem more vibrant and the sounds are louder on my ear drum.

I have become more sensitive to all ordinary presentations to the senses.

My Secret

Our bodies can be funny when other people find out about them, so I will reveal to you a secret about mine which only my wife and daughter know. It is my face. If you look at it, it all looks normal until you look at one aspect.

Choppers

Sometimes when I need fresh inspiration, I just go to the bathroom and clean my choppers. What's that got to do with being inspired? Like most places beginning with the letter B such as beach, bed, bath, it is probably the best place to be inspired.

Here Now - No Past No Future

Your whole life so far was all about bringing you here, now right now so you could see yourself.

Every happening, every journey, every failure and success, everything you hoped for was only ever to bring you here now.

That you got here, that you are here now means you can never ever leave. Once you have seen this moment, you don't bother with the past or future.

Easy Street

There is no such thing as an easy life and easy street doesn't mean life is easy.

Easy can mean no work because there is money, but every day has to have meaning, a single purpose with yourself.

We will always search for meaning because it is everything. Searching for easy street is not being interested in yourself.

55. BEING YOU

Be You

You don't need approval, accreditation licensing or permission to be you but there is opposition everywhere. In the garden, in the shops on the streets, in the fields, at the end of the day and even in your dreams.

The Real You

Finding out who you are can be a shock. It can be a sudden unexpected surprise. Of course what you know is correct about me in that I fulfil the roles I'm trained in and I do my duty.

I'm not the person you will see when you call my name, though I answer to that name. I am not even the person you thought you met. You can't see me in my duties. I am still, only reflected in what I write here. Just as you are.

Being Us

We need to turn inwards, into the world which quietly is itself. It doesn't try to be something outside itself. We only need to be us, not something which stops us being us.

Your Path

With clear sight of the present path and where it seems to be going, there is nothing else to be, do or wait for.

A Small Crack

Why am I so serious and sometimes sad? Why have I always been so serious? Where does this come from? Was it my orphaned, traumatised Dad? Was it passed on to me from the person I never met, the stillborn brother just before me? Was it my mother's grief about both of these or mine about them and her? Is the sadness really sadness or is it just a seriousness others see in me or I see others don't have or both. I accept it, never wallowing in it. It is stuck as part of me. The rest seems fine just this small crack.

Beauty and Happiness

Beauty is something recognised outside. Happiness is always inside. Beauty is delivered from the senses. Happiness is revealed inside. Beauty is a synthesis of fine thinking. Happiness is simply being in the heart.

Protective Skin

I am renewing like a snake growing a new skin but this one is thicker. I can't be crazy any longer because it's too crazy to be vulnerable. Thick skinned, protecting the sensitive heart within, is more difficult to hurt.

For me

It is not possible to express the relief of not having to write
for anyone else, only just writing for me. I didn't realise until
now I needed to write just for me. This is to say how happy
I am in words, which don't reflect the release in my heart at
seeing these words for me.

Restoration

I am the man with no neck. The angle between the chin
and neck is now like a frog. It has gone. All the things that
happened to me in the last year were heavy and piled on
me, as did my weight. They were weighing me down. I am
lighter than that, I am lighter.

The tension in my neck made it shorter. Now they have gone
back to what they were, with what they are, I can be me
again and stretch my neck, stretch myself again. The physical
change was a result of coping.

Hello in There

Hello in there, hey you, yes you, from me over here. What
has influenced you to be what you are?

My influences have been my family history, our history of
poverty, psychological trauma, fighting back then trying to
help people like me and worse than me to find happiness
within. This is what made me what I am. What about you?

Being Your Own Self

To hear what can't be said. To see what can't be seen. To know what can't be taught, is being all we share.

No interference

Whatever created this world will look after it. Whatever maintains this world has its own ways of doing it. I keep my life simple, just getting on with what I have to. My job is maintaining me and I have my own way of doing it too. The world and me look after ourselves and it is not our business to interfere with each other.

The Cave

There is a place where we are drawn to usually during a crisis, unusually in normal times, rarely all the time. But in endless chaotic turmoil no other place exists, the cave of refuge is the only place we can know. Our first and final resting place, the place which knows us best because it is our most inner self.

Inner Cave

The more we make outer progress, the less we make inner progress. The more we know, the less self-knowledge. The more time we step back from the world, the more we step inside. The less time in the light of the world, the greater the light in the inner cave.

Increased Effort

How strange it is to suddenly become aware it may be that our hero is no longer seen as so perfect. It may be that we are not so perfect or that there is a need to make more effort to do less.

True to Itself

Of all the places how could I end up here on the ground, the most unexpected of all but the only possible place.

Would you trust a memory device which concluded from the stored information or would you trust the nature of the device?

It is only our nature, not thoughts, which we need to simply focus on. We should trust nature for guidance when things appear complex because nature is true to itself, as we should be also.

Being Sad

You say I am sad but what you are seeing is my reaction to you not being happy.

Forget It

Time doesn't exist, so try ditching it as a burden; a distraction from being you, as whenever is always now.

Cheer up

Don't be so sad you say but perhaps you should be silent until you understand your perception of me. Perhaps you have not seen my happiness. Maybe you have become happier.

Maybe you really believe when you tell someone to cheer up you will make them happy but you are only trying to cheer yourself.

Happiness is boundless, always present, nurturing like the sun. It has its own time to be seen like things which have no words only silence.

Prompts

Unprompted by material things, the intangible calls with no words to be obedient to complete surrender, true to the self.

Obedience

I don't have reasons for what I'm doing. I don't have reasons why I go to India and I don't have reasons why I've been to India so many times.

I don't have reasons why I wrote those articles, those books, those notes. I don't have reasons why I do what I do.

I don't have reasons why I'm passionate, if I'm right or wrong. All I know is I'm doing what I'm supposed to do. It is my duty. It is obedience to how I am what I am.

Control

I have not given up as I need to do my duties not let my duties do me.

A habit controlling me is what I can most easily drift into if I don't take enough control. But not if I walk away and don't stay.

Enlightenment Myth

There is no-one like an enlightened person. It would be impossible for there to be anyone who is enlightened.

An enlightened person would not say it because their enlightenment would make it unnecessary and so impossible.

Their enlightenment would abolish the need for ownership of anything including thought.

Would you know enlightenment if you saw it? How could you not because it is only you in your reflection.

Up to Me-Down to Me

Nothing can be blamed for my unhappiness. Nothing external is the cause. It is all down to me. It is all up to me. Up or down whatever it is, down or up wherever it goes, my happiness or unhappiness is only due to me. Whatever happens, I respond or not remaining what I am.

Truth

There can be no truth with anyone until you are true with yourself. There can only be truth when you know yourself.

Truth is singular and everything because it is universal and has to be contained in the beginning and the end, so is eternal.

My Side

Don't strain my brain with your pain. I've got just enough puff to keep up with my own stuff.

I've got just enough time to keep up with what's mine. There's not much spare to give because we all have to live.

I have to start right here and I don't want to seem mean, but before I think of you I need to keep my own self lean and clean.

Uncovering

When I stayed, everything seemed covered and hidden so a passion for personal truth and understanding arose. A passion for truth in community gatherings to continue what we are is what we need.

I'll Tidy My Things

I'll tidy my things, I say when I don't know if I should sing or be silent. I'll tidy my things, I say we say when I'm not sure what's going on. I'll tidy my things; I say when I want to be alone, when I'm fed up with the phone.

56. FEELINGS

The Weather Inside

The weather today is good outside. Inside I'm full of change. This is what I need. Protection from how I was formed.

What I am is not anyone else's to have to cope with but sometimes my coping has to close its eyes and let the weather just be wild inside. Today is like that. I will bury myself in silent intense activity of stillness.

Anger

Anger is not always a weapon used against someone. It can be self harm, a weapon against yourself. Anger is feelings which are drunk because of not halting them with the mind.

Embarrassing the mind with its wildness, anger jeopardises all other thoughts and colours the picture we give others about us when the true picture is unfinished.

Expression Not Hidden or Wallowing

The emotions are more present than ever as time goes on. The only way to keep them under control is to give them a quiet voice but, never not heard, never not felt, so they are always understood.

Why We Look Back

Almost at the end, why is it we look back? Is it to make sure we are happy or to regret or maybe both?

Differences

My thoughts may be different and are different but we are the same. How could anything otherwise be?

We share the same time here and respect is how we all work together under the same sky. So we all need to keep trying.

Reeling the Neck in

To reel the neck in is to think and see what the other person is seeing and thinking of our impact on them.

Change or Timing

I can see how wrong I am being irritated but not at the time it happens. How do I bring that time from being reflective to being present at the time? The answer is, quicker each time.

57. HABITS

War Stories

We think the story of our war with our addicted parents
is unique but they only different in aspects of details, the
nature is the same. The late night footsteps of their return
followed by the rattle of keys. Then the unintended neglect
and emotional abuse due to selfishness forms the invisible
scars no one can see apart from other similar survivors.

Survivors of Alcoholic Parents

He was sometimes there, enthusiastic and cheerful. strong
and artistic. Sometimes he would break into song.

When this was gone he was drunk, eager for a fight any time
of day or night. Fear reined instead of security, chaos instead
of calm.

He found no cure for his condition then no good outcome
was possible. Now it can be shared with others and we are
able to stand like hardier trees. It is so common it is now
normal.

Adult Child of an Alcoholic

The sound of his or her steps coming up the path. Of her trying to get the key in the door, then the sound of her trying to close it quietly, ends with the sound of her relief at closing the door.

The nausea from the familiar smell of the booze on her breath and listening for the noise of her clumsiness, waiting for the fear to rise at her shouting whilst trying to avoid the terror of her violence.

The restlessness until she sleeps, then anger at her sorrow, followed by sorrow for her misunderstood state, but still hoping for a better future.

Unknown, the peaceful secure childhood with balanced views and a happy heart. Instead the need to neutralise the pain of restless chaos searching for the silent inner spirit.

The only cure for us is to see the spirit in others who have survived the experience, who have the strength to detach and let us hope.

Helpful Companions

What helped me most was listening and talking with others who had been or who were going through similar things in their lives, to find out how I could cope too.

I would meet and visit again if those events revisited me but I know those companions also visit me as we all do in our thoughts, dreams and reflections.

345

It's Not the Buffet Car

When you step across a railway line, it's not the buffet car that kills you, it's the engine. When you relapse into an old habit, it's not the second drink of drug that does the damage or all the ones after that, it's always the first contact that gets you

When you see that small sign perhaps a light of hope, it's not what comes after it that gets you; it's that small light of hope which can guide you forever back home.

Give Me More

Addictions are being obsessed with something taking us away from our usual happy self. The A-Z to choose from can be being thin or fat poor or wealthy, over or under achieving but the pull is a persistent thought taking up all our time so there is no time for our own already happy inner self.

Just like when a cuckoo lays an egg in another mother's nest, the host is compelled to feed its chicks just like her own, so we feel compelled to keep on doing something even if we know it harms us.

Industry pressurises and compels us to feed off its products to satisfy the message that we need them, when it is they who need us. They say to be happy and successful we need wealth, position and honours but that apparent truth is a lie. Happiness is always inside.

Antidepressants and Alcohol

Look at the child standing in a dusty public space humming one of their own tunes. Not a care.

Look at the graffiti on a wall and beside the child is a homeless parent living beyond the edge of the city inside a tent.

Don't waste any time listening to psychobabble from psychiatrists and politicians trying to tell you it is all in the mind. Look at their paymaster the corporations.

They bulldoze children's playgrounds to build production plants making alcohol and drugs to alter the homeless parent's brain chemistry, instead of letting them smile as they see their children playing on the grass.

But the grass is gone and tear drops bounce on the concrete forming rivers instead of reflecting the sparkling eyes of smiles between parents and children.

Free to Be

When I ask what is the most positive thing, I always say a group of individual people who offer their help for free just for me. When I look at what I wanted to be, it was a person who could help someone like me for free.

Nothing has changed with all the years. Those people who helped me to see, the greatest gift we have is giving our gift for free, are still here.

58. RESILIENCE

True Resilience

Resilience is not about rapid recovery but about being the same, unchanged. Resilience is not being what others expect us to think, but is being what we are. Resilience is about being our self so we are not changed by anything. Resilience is coming back to our self no matter what, as it is the only place we are.

Fake Resilience

Most of the things resilience training tries to teach you, try to change how you think. But they cannot change what you are, your resilience.

Resilient

Resilience is more than any training to survive torture. No amount of training to survive torture can produce as much resilience as being our Self. Our Self survives everything.

Key to Endurance

Knowing that happiness is hidden but always here, is the key to endurance.

Endurance

There is only so much pain we can take if someone is trying to harm us but there is no limit to the pain we can endure if we are doing it for someone else.

Endurance to See the Resilient Self

There has to be unacceptable pain for wanting to see the truth about ourselves. It has to threaten what we think we are; our conscious lives. We have to go against all our conditioning, everything we were taught and be empty. Rejecting conditioning is removing ignorance, so don't be surprised if everyone else is convinced you are crazy; that is their conditioning. They haven't got the same neediness, so let them carry on, keeping on our own path.

Withdrawal

To stop the pain and suffering inflicted by others, only one form of resilience works; detachment from the things of the world. To annihilate the suffering inflicted by ceaseless blows, withdrawal from the things of the world offers protection.

There is a solitude which brings happiness unaffected by the intentions and actions of others; it is withdrawal enjoying the Self.

Resilience

We are fragile and insecure and can appear to us and others to almost fragment or breakdown. Maybe it is because the foundation on which we base what we think we are, the ego, is simply incorrect.

We are told to be true to ourselves but instead we have been lured and programmed to believe in this thing called the ego which is just a bundle of thoughts.

We are encouraged by the outside world to believe in the ego as real by fear of memories in the past and dreams of happiness in a future. Perhaps we are driven by thoughts of escaping past fear and thoughts of being seduced by future happiness. The past and future are thoughts dependant on the existence of the ego.

The inner self is completely resilient, deeper, stronger, silent and only found in stillness, when we are in the world but detached from the things of the world. It is not dependent on thought, unable to be described by thought's best tools; words.

Wounds for Growth

It may look like someone is broken by wounds, but the wounds can be encouraging new growth into what seems like a transformed resilient person, but who has all along just been waiting.

Detaching With Love

There is so much devotion, too painful a cord, thread or chain to cut and break forever. Death would come first. The bond that was made could not be strengthened.

Sentimentality will always remain until we are just ancestors but we will not be gone. What does remain is intangible, shared nakedness of spirit, indestructible.

Detached

There is a hopelessness, a strain in the voice saying it can't get through this but there it is, the groan of pain from not wanting to get used to it, knowing being used to it is inevitable. There is a dread of what has to be gone through; no hope yet in the form of balance, only carrying on. But the detached know all the things are in place for a perfect ending.

Overwhelmed by Relentlessness

Spiritual but given the wrong type of example. Sensitive but immersed in other's chaos. Resilient and almost overwhelmed by our relentlessness, we always find our way home to our self.

Enduring

I would endure a whole week of strain for one happy day
and if that is what it takes to do it, I would do it again
and again. Happy days are rare as there is so much to do.
Knowing the happiness is hidden but always there is the
only key to endurance.

59. TORTURE

Access All Areas Denied

Every bully and every torturer wants one thing; to get to your centre. They want to destroy what keeps you strong, yourself. When they cannot access you by your body they turn to your mind. But by this time you have learnt the inner harbour which has protected you and sheltered you from them, is yours and only for you to access

Sneaky Beaky

SERE, Survival Escape Resistance Evasion are what you have to endure to be military air crew, Special Forces, MI5 or MI6. Without giving consent you have to be tortured by your colleagues who are trained experts, so you can learn how to endure it and how to do it too.

You escape from them on Bodmin Moor with nothing, then they come to capture you. In the back of a truck you arrive still blindfolded at RAF St Mawgan Newquay. Stripped naked, genital humiliation by a blond female alongside being hosed with water, no food and no sleep for days you are made to stand hooded, with lights, and in darkness. You are slapped a bit but not beaten, as they say.

Once an individual actually did escape from this. He was labelled defective, failed, something wrong with him. Then discharged and forced to return to civilian life.

Medical Moral Gymnastics

No pain relief given. Instead pain is administered in doses very close to death, the torture postponed by a short rest so the doctor can go and collect a medal for her contribution to Defence Medical Services.

Psychiatric Moral Gymnastics

She survived Auschwitz, her family didn't. She was tortured, beaten and raped but that wasn't the worst. The English psychiatrists in 1983 at St Bernard's Psychiatric Hospital in Ealing voted to give her a lobotomy for her depression.

Neckless

The Ugandan soldiers came and sat him down outside his house. Aged twelve he was told to pull the trigger of the machine gun which killed his parents, grandparents, uncles, aunts, brothers and sisters. All fifteen.

The neckless of a rubber tyre filled with petrol was lit but someone managed to pull him out as soon as they were gone. Hideously overgrown scar tissue covered his nose, mouth and all of his face. With his inner and outer wounds he can still talk about trying to forgive them.

Evin

They sat there usually for a year. Every day was the same. Sometimes food and sometimes not. Twice every day someone would be taken to see how much water electricity or other things their genitals could take or even take other's genitals.

Every two days the screaming was so bad it stopped and the person didn't return, so they protested. Then one of them would come in and casually take your hand, break your arm or remove an eye.

If ever there was bread it was chewed many times over for days and the pieces were made by everyone to form kings, queens, knights and pawns, to play chess after they took the blindfolds off at night.

I knew six people who survived. One gave me a brown solid chess piece which felt like stone. One committed suicide, another died ten years later from his wounds The other three are here in England. Evin goes on and on.

Tenderness

As long as you are a victim in a relationship, you cannot detach.

When you can detach you can love and only then find compassion.

Compassion is the tenderness which no torturer can remove.

Religious Moral Gymnastics

Don't start war in the name of God. Don't blame it on God because he or she has got enough blame.

Be honest with yourself and blame it on you.

60. ABUSE

Use and Abuse

Who has not abused power? Those who know the effects of
power either use it or abuse it and some try to do both which
is abuse.

Against the Unnatural

How do we let an abusive relationship continue and let
abuse happen to us? What does it take to stop it no matter
what it is or who is doing it to us? Abuse does not stop
unless one thing happens, we stop it. Only we can stop
someone abusing us but because we have usually been
programmed to accept it, stopping it might seem unnatural.

Ritual Childhood Abuse

The effects of an isolated country tear through all standards
as there are not enough people to check what goes on.

But in the heart of the London the same standards are
identically trashed by the people who check what goes on.

Words to Control You

Words tell you what is happening. Words tell you what you think is happening but the words can be the opposite of what the speaker is doing.

Words can tell you what you are hearing is what you want to hear and you need to stop believing words.

Greetings, kisses, flowers and gifts can reinforce that you are being treated well when these things just buffer the reality. You are being used, lied to, mistreated and abused.

Words can be used to control worse than spears or bullets. Amplify what is really being done and you will see their control.

More

"How much more sir?" Asked the boy.

"Not much," came the answer.

"How long?"

"Just a bit more."

"No more, no more, no more no more," said the silent voice.

Taboo

It sounds like one of the first words man spoke to describe fear. Fear of the dark boiling pots full of skulls which you imagine yours being be added to.

It is a word I am passionate about because it is forbidden conversation in the corridors of power, where it is simply hushed. Disapproval silences truth and screams.

Its nakedness and the people who perpetuate the need for the existence of the word are clothed in infinite layers of protection.

Like sex and religion, it is always the powerful and the weak, the sacred and the sinful who use that word. Taboo is always bound and hidden by fear of truth

In the Name of God

She said, "I was told by the religious elders my mum was not allowed to speak to me because I had accused one of them of sexual abuse. So if I don't talk it is not a problem for them, but it makes it even worse for me.

My mum was told no further communication with me was possible because I was no longer one of them as I accused them of abusing me."

These people think they have protection from their God. In the name of their god they used to burn or drown anyone they didn't like by just naming them a witch.

Education for Girls and Boys

It is nearly always someone you know who knows your
parents too. A stepfather or mother in law, an uncle, aunt
or friend will do. But if not, a teacher or a priest will appear
as will a doctor, policeman or politician. It is always those
who you believe are looking after you, caring for you, like
workers in homes and schools.

It happens to you in secret and you are told it is your secret
with them. That no one else is to know, then you are told
not to lie or cry or else. Strange feelings start to grow, then
thoughts, dreams and feeling up and down everywhere.
Withdrawal, being emotional or not emotional, you know
things are still wrong and have to be put right.

Betraying Children

Their stories were similar, usually like this. I was a child
four to twelve. He was a friend of the family, an uncle
a stepfather. What shocked me as much was my mum
denied it. She didn't stand by my side. She stood by his side
supporting him. She wouldn't let me go to the police.

Thirty years later, I kept a journal and gave it to the police. In
court, other adult children appeared. Where it happened to
me, it happened to them and now they have come to tell and
see him sent down.

The judge informed the court, 'The stories are the same, the
fifteen you have heard but there are over one hundred we
know of which is average for a paedophile before they go to
jail. They are too scared, ashamed to tell. He will stay in hell.

360

61. SHAME

Melting Shame

Things you do that are addictive make you feel shame, but also small things you do for you make you feel good and melt shame.

Shame

Shame is feeling bad about what us or others did or didn't do. Letting go of shame is seeing it as not ours and letting go of it.

Remove the Coat of Shame

Shame is hating ourselves now for how we think our past mistakes can still be seen by others. We wear shame negatively like a dirty embarrassing coat which we think others can see. If we remove and throw away the coat of shame, we can let go of guilt about our self and start to enjoy our inner happiness.

Our Shame

What would our elderly parents say to us if they were younger and didn't depend on us? They would gently show us a reflection. The reflection could show our selfishness, our coldness and our greed.

Melting the Coat of Shame

Things we do that are addictive make us feel shame and want to hide but small things we do for us make us feel good and start to melt the coat of shame we wear.

This can change our attitude, so we see our true self as us and not wearing the coat of shame. This can change your life.

Buffer

There are ways we don't look at things which are too painful, too awkward, too embarrassing.

Sometimes it is simply too early to look because we are not ready, the support is not there, or there would be losses we couldn't cope with.

Then there is no choice. The door has opened and denial, our soul's buffer, our mind's shock absorber, has gone.

Shame's Name

Our whole life can be based on fear of anyone discovering our shame. It could be a simple thing. It could be our name, our parents or anything in our family but it could be a little thing we do, did or didn't do but is our secret shame.

Fear of being accidentally revealed, we have to cope with shames name. With everything we feared now named, there is nothing to fear except not disowning it.

The Spell of Shame

It can be where you are from. It can be you are not good
enough. It can be you have failed or you have succeeded. It
can be your friend or your family. It can be your success. It
can be you have changed or you have not changed. It can be
you have done well. It can be you are happy.

But you are not ok about you. You have a spell on you like
you are branded or like having a tattoo which keeps you
covering yourself up.

Stopping you breaking free, the spell on you says, 'Don't
think, don't do, don't say, don't even be.' Break it by
accepting everything about you is ok and every little thing
about you is alright.

62. CHAOS

Over-control

The human condition is an attempt to control chaos, changing it into ordered, disciplined, rational behaviour, even if it is destructive.

Now chaos is something we don't understand and can't work out, so we cannot let it be what it wants to be in its own ways and time. We need to see it but not be in it.

Be Still or Leave

If you stumble on this almost endless stream of words, which are merely filtered out and sorted reflections from the early morning and late night, they are simply an attempt to let the mind think it has found some sense of order from the chaos that appears as its reality, which is simply due to thoughts.

This is an attempt to lull thoughts into believing they are important with some meaning to them. It is an attempt to stop them and leave me in stillness.

Human Rights-No One Else's Right

Human rights really begins with our self not wasting the opportunity we have to know our self first before all else.

Give Chance a Chance

I was brought up a child of chaos organised by others, so I have tried since not to organise or be organised by anyone.

What happens by chance, a different force can lead to more openings than all the closures of chaos.

Ordinariness

When there is nothing to write about, life is often in full swing because everything is normal, as ordinariness is the usual thing.

But when things are not in chaos, change has already taken place. The only thing that makes sense is to record it all in the present tense.

Chaos brings volumes of words trying to understand what has happened but in ordinariness, where it happened, writing is not recalled and heard.

In ordinariness our foundations are most clearly seen, our true self is seen as solid and ready, much more interesting to record, read and see.

Not getting Drawn into Others Chaos

The daughter of an old friend sent me a message asking me if I still heard from either of her parents but I could not answer and stand in their shoes as they were too chaotic.

Letting Go Of Chaos

Chaos is not natural because it is created by ignoring nature. Nature works by the rule of forces, always balancing, action, resting, giving and taking.

Man is the only chaotic animal not working with the forces of nature. Thinking creates fear, denial, anger, sadness, not balancing action and resting, not giving and taking.

Ignoring signs to stop or move, ignoring where to be, ignoring how to be, ignoring our order, man ignores nature and chooses chaos.

Chaos on the Road to Bliss

Coming from the land of chaos, discipline is at first the opposition. Slowly a frame is seen which consists of boundaries. Slowly we see having a mind which is free, a body which can be strong, a heart which feels and which accepts changes. Not having to second guess what comes after the next outcome allows peace to be expected unless there is actually a war.

Loss of Interest in Chaos

I can't take any more chaos. It must show on my face as I am relaxed and just not interested. There's no smile from the corner of my mouth. No approval or disapproval, just no interest at all. It is not my way but everyone can have their time of chaos.

Not everyone's life

Your childhood days were not like his, hers, theirs or mine. His childhood days were too painful to bear so he took to the drink and is still there. She was bullied so took to being in control for power. But this has not made either of them happy. My childhood days were chaos and all my life I've had to find a place inside me to be calm. I'm still working on it here.

Identity

Living and working with others without boundaries and rules is chaos.

When walls come down, everything becomes un-boundaried, people, authority, power and rules.

The only cure is to make rules, create boundaries and build walls so authority, discipline and identity are restored.

Thick Skinned

I am renewing like a snake and growing a new skin but this one's thicker. I can't go crazy any longer because it is too crazy to be vulnerable. Thick skinned, protecting the delicate heart within makes it more difficult to access. Sometimes my skin may need to be even thicker like a crocodile's.

Detachment from Dependency

There are passionate reactions to things which should be thoughts. There are my inner feelings about things and people which should be thoughts.

I have feelings about how I am treated, but when I am with someone I just seem to treat me as if none of this is happening. I say to myself 'That it is all alright when I really don't know.' But it is not alright to ignore my feelings.

Is it because I don't ask or they don't tell or I can't read them or maybe it is my blindness. Things just have to be. That's all they can ever really be but how do they seem to see it all the time and I don't? They don't. It just looks like they do. We are all the same.

Brought up to survive the most chaotic, I am stable enough myself but only if I have something in me which is stable and constant. It can never be you, anyone or anything or anywhere else apart from what is inside me.

Our Own Troubles

The night he died I had troubles of my own. Our own troubles eclipse other's troubles. We may notice others troubles and remember them but they shouldn't take over our own and trump our own.

Sometimes

Sometimes we must rest. Sometimes we must do nothing. Sometimes we must just be. Sometimes we should at least see this with some regularity.

Sometimes Only One Thing Works

Sometimes the only answer to questions is the same. Sometimes the solution to all problems is the same. Sometimes eloquence is lost as sometimes there are no words. Sometimes in the midst of chaos there can be only one thing that is wanted and seems to work, chocolate.

Basics of Chaos

People with chaotic lives may seem different, as they may seem interesting but their ways are usually self-destructive as well as drawing in others for attention.

63. LETTING GO

Who has to Go?

You have to let go of everyone, your parents, your husband, your wife, your children, then finally yourself.

All Along

How often if at all for most, can they detach from the world? Rarely someone can forget about the world and let the world forget them. Most want to stay connected, convinced the world can make them happy, when all along happiness lies waiting inside.

Because They Can Be

Sometimes people are difficult, just because they can be. Sometimes people are killers, just because they can be. Sometimes people are destructive, just because they can be. Sometimes people are dishonest, just because they can be. Sometimes people are unhelpful, just because they can be. Sometimes people are cold, just because they can be. Sometimes people are funny, just because they can be. Sometimes people are what they are, just because they can be. Sometimes this is being kind.

Detached from all

There are intellectuals, academics, teachers, lawyers,
bankers, doctors, priests, musicians, poets, singers, architects,
sculptors, painters, writers, grazers, the takers, the gossipers
the losers, the pretenders, those who play games and there
are those who are detached, who you do not play games,
because they just are.

Stick With the Humble ones

Avoid trying to be surrounded by interesting people who
want their sense of self-importance broadcast for a fee. Better
to avoid interesting people who are important. Stick with
humility and the humble.

Walking the Walk

I walk the dog once a day when I'm working, twice a day
when I'm not. I don't have a dog but you can't just talk the
talk, you have to walk the walk.

Humiliation

We can be humble and have faith in our self or follow our
thinking and have the ego humiliated.

Letting Go

The last thing we have to learn in life is to let go of life.

Letting Go Sets Us Free

Allowing others to be themselves lets us be more ourselves. Letting go let's us go.

Stopping talking and listening more speaks to us, giving us our inner voice.

Giving up control frees us because power does not give us freedom.

Give Up Being the Victim

Focusing on someone else can turn us into victims because they are getting attention which should be ours.

Letting go of thinking about them frees us to be happy, free to use our precious time for us.

Letting Go of Time

Sometimes let go of outcomes, let go of the future, let go of thinking, let go of the past, let go of memories, let go of resentment and let go of regrets. Then let go of letting go.

Separation

At some time, some stage when it is right, when we see it, when we want to, we have to let go of other people, their attachment to us, their desires for us and their demands.

We have to pull back, detach and change all the connections so there is no reliance. They can be placed somewhere in our heads and hearts where we are happy for them to be so we can be.

From Denial to Crisis

There are different ways we use not to look at things because they are too awkward, too inconvenient, too embarrassing, too painful.

We don't look at things because it is simply too early to look. We are not ready and can't access the support which is there. We think there would be losses we couldn't cope with. We can't look at things because we have not had enough pain. We have not been brought to our knees to ask for some kind of help. We have not reached our rock bottom, the gutter.

Then suddenly there is no choice because the door has opened and denial, our minds shock absorber, our soul's buffer has gone forever.

For the first time, we see we have no power over what has happened but it has stopped having power over us.

No Future Plan

There must be a plan which I fit into but I can never know it, I can only grow into it.

Letting go of knowing un-stifles me and lets me keep growing as long as I let go.

Surrendering to the future, whatever it brings, at last lets me relax.

Letting go of Imbalance

Look at the bigger picture of your life. Look at the presence of balance and where it is upset. Is there balance in inner and outer life, in personal life and work life, in physical and mental life?

Is there balance in what you consume, in what you eat and in your needs? Is there balance in looking after you, in listening to you and in letting go?

Letting Go of All Negatives

Let go of everything negative. Why keep it to take away the positive because it will only moan and groan. When it does, cheer it on as it goes.

Letting Go of the Unnecessary

We eventually have to let go of life so why is it so difficult to let go of things we don't need?

We don't need approval, permission, forgiveness, success, memories, a past or a future, or to be a victim.

We don't need other people's business, promises, time, chaos, lies, deception, failure, or betrayal.

We don't need anger, denial, guilt, shame, fear, perfection, fear of abandonment.

We need our love, happiness, simplicity, compassion and humility, detachment, boundaries, to look after ourselves with patience and love.

64. RELATIONSHIPS

Un-Trapped

How can you so easily be trapped working unless you are stuck down a mine?

You may be stuck in a job but it's your choice to stay in that job.

How can you be trapped with someone unless you are conjoined or handcuffed?

If you can walk away, you choose to stay or leave.

Being Listened To

When someone doesn't listen, stop talking. If they ever want to listen they will find you.

Repeating yourself, raising your voice to attract their ears won't help if they can't hear or won't listen.

Relationship Dynamics

Thirty years ago I was frustrated that I was aware of my ignorance of relationship dynamics. Now knowing them better I am frustrated because you cannot learn them any quicker.

376

Radical Change

Intimacy had changed, was changed, but I didn't know it.

I didn't know intimacy because what I thought I knew was only the wish of my own projection of what I had always wanted. But it wasn't what I thought it was.

Thrown into chaos, not knowing if there was anything to salvage, the tears flowed and flowed because now I knew that I didn't know her.

Gathering myself, I let go and didn't cling on. Detachment with love is the only way, going our ways, together, forever.

Sharing

There is nothing as difficult as relationships as they cannot be predicted and they cannot be controlled.

They cannot be what you want them to be because there is always the other who has their say.

They can change or not, give you the greatest sadness and joy but they are not yours but shared.

Breathing

You no longer have to communicate to say that you are still smiling, still standing, because breathing says it all.

Projections

Perhaps there are no relationships, they may just be projections, our best guess of what we think is there, often what we want to be there.

Relationships can be projections of thinking someone cares when we don't even know what we care for.

Relationships can be two people sending out projections which they believe.

How could we be someone else's invisible projections? How do you see who is really there especially if you can't see yourself.

65. DECENCY

Decent

How could you the prison guard be so kind, yet my fellow prisoner beat me into unconsciousness?

How can you, who keep me here because of my beliefs, be so considerate and kind yet my colleagues trample over me for the next meal?

Our jobs, clubs and class do not define us or sculpt our choice to make us decent. The clothes we wear or do not have are not badges of honour.

Being True to You

If you are conscious of yourself you cannot be false.
If you think, write, speak and act for yourself you cannot be false.

Solidarity

It is the smallest things we do for our self, the secret treat of a tea in a café in solitude, when we listen for a long time to a lonely stranger.

Connecting our self with others in solitude, in solidarity is our best human quality.

Ways of Life

We only have our jobs, position and influence our way of life because we are allowed them by those with principals.

It is quick and easy to be overpowered and lose our work, position, influence and our way of life by those with no principals.

Our self cannot be taken away by those with no principals, even though they torture us with their ways of life.

Decency

Behind windows with iron bars and bolted doors of the modern domestic material prisons, which many aspire to accept as home, decency is frequently excluded.

66. SUICIDE

Egoside and Suicide

If you want to be free of your ego, you have to think of it as nothing and let go of it and you have to completely surrender to what is left. Only then you are free of it to be your true self.

When we cannot see what is behind the ego, the self, we can be mistaken that the ego is all that we are. Without some kind of guide showing us this, especially if we are in pain, the ego may be destroyed, mistaking it for all that we are.

Egoside

To end all misery permanently and to always live in happiness involves a different kind of death than thoughts of suicide. Destroying the illusion created by the mind that we are the ego, a bundle of thoughts, is egoside. Of course the mind is resistant to egoside, the killing off of its proudest creation, so the self has to be used to silence thought by observation or surrender. All that is required is stillness. Nothing is lost apart from the illusion that something was there and there is a massive relief to have finally caught the sneaky imposter.

Suicide and Character Assassination

They are both easy, quick, irreversible and mess on a lot of people for ever.

Death by Thinking

You didn't die of cancer or get killed in an accident. Your lungs were good and your limbs were strong.

You didn't die of a heart attack, infections didn't overtake you, your eyes and ears were good and your speech was strong.

But what killed you was intangible. Few understand being overwhelmed and fewer still the freedom your thinking presents with its lethality, easier than reality.

Suicide

Sometimes suicide is difficult not to do because suicide is the least painful way to end things. It wanders in and out of our life uninvited but not unexpected; considering the circumstances.

Not something you want around and something you sometimes cannot control. Part of us that is wanting to take part of us over but only part of us.

Maybe the part of us that has poor projected sight of the future tries to deal with it this way whilst the self, which sees all cannot let this be, is ignored.

Permanent Solutions

Despite everything most people say, life is better than death. Even with the things that people do, life doesn't look as bad as death.

But some, with just minor things out of place, decide to finish it. Can this be dignity shooting yourself and everyone permanently in the face? Those left will give the answer.

Non Suicidal death

The priest listened to the mother about her son who jumped from a multi-storey carpark.

'I know he's in Hell. I've lost him.'
'How do you know your son is in hell?'
'Because that's what happens if you commit suicide as there is no other place, so you go to Hell for eternity.'

'But what if, after he jumped whilst he was actually falling, he changed his mind, as many do? What if he decided he no longer wanted to commit suicide, then he would not have died with suicidal intention, so he would be in Heaven.'

The mother changed her mind and the resting place of her son by a simple 'what if.' Perhaps we should not just assume someone thought a particular way. It might be wise to discuss it with others before we make a conclusion.

Suicide and Self

Suicide is mistaking the restless ego for the ever happy Self.

Suicide American Style

Suicide is not always what it seems as male American war veterans who die by a single shot from a gun are registered as accidental death whilst cleaning their weapon, never as suicide.

Suicide is not what it seems as male American war veterans who die in a single vehicle car crash on their own are registered as accidental death, never as suicide.

In America suicide is not what it seems because if you've had enough and want your family to collect the insurance after your death, point and hold a toy plastic gun at someone and the cops ensure, 'suicide by cop.'

67. STRESS

Blood Flow to Our Brain

Under pressure we do simple things because our higher brain functions get less oxygen under stress and lower brain functions get more oxygen and work best.

Breathing deep and slow, from the belly not the chest, widens the arteries to the brain and opens up the higher functions again.

At the peak of stress it is not what you do, it is how you breathe, deep and slow that lets you be still, think and know.

Endless Positive Thoughts

It is an endless effort to stay in the light, to stay in stillness detaching from dark thoughts, by having endless positive thoughts.

My disappointment in others is only mine with myself, which I also feel sad about for us all.

We don't all appear the same but we all have the same potential for the darkest thoughts and behaviour.

Spiritual Stress

I was given the opportunity to show my findings and compete in the world of psychological stress but something in me called me and I followed it. It took me to more simplicity which has increased in value more than the investments I could still own instead. Stress originally took me inside so it is a friend not an enemy, always trying to help show us the way inside.

Production

Are you a product, of an era, of a decade of a town? Are you a product of a family, of a school, of a sport or some other tool? Are you a product of money, of the business of law, of a trade of education or medicine? Are you a product of a situation of circumstances or of yourself?

Self Portrait

Uncomfortable reading, inconvenient, truth, with teeth and passion.

Our Only Duty

Our duty is to see what we are here for and to do what we are here for. Our duty is not to be concerned with anything else of have any other duties. Our duty is to have no other duties except our duty to our self. When we become conscious, we see our duty is to everyone and everything.

Pressure

We only take so much then we change, stopping still, doing nothing. Maybe silent, perhaps talking or shouting, then walking away.

We know damage is happening and try to slow or stop it but we can detach and watch it as we walk away.

'I sense Hostility' the social worker said

There may be reasons why you sense someone else's hostility. It may be perfectly placed, timed and appropriate but none of your business to point out.

Confronting someone else's feelings without intending to understand and defuse them can be like jumping into a boxing ring with a prize fighter. You do not usually get thrown in.

Easier to Tell The truth

Men and women lie about money, food, sex, relationships. They lie about themselves, their origins and about their training.

Men and women lie about what they have done, what they do, what they can do, what they want to do.

Men and women lie to make things easier, giving reasons for lies, then they lie about their lies, thinking they won't surprise you with lies.

Over Precious Rights

Our happiness and shortcomings are like the patterns of a woven carpet intertwined by contrasting threads, only visible because of the other threads.

How do we exist as this mix of opposites present and ready at any moment to react without thought and knowledge of the full consequences?

Our intellectual laws say one thing but we let the guilty go free to continue offending the innocent, who are not allowed to speak, who are always the losers.

Freedom to be anything human is not affected by fear of punishments, as the worst crimes by politicians go unpunished. But this can only happen if we keep quiet and say nothing.

Frightened of losing his rights by over controlling himself and others, man chooses instead to let abuse of the innocent carry on, so that he can still say he has his precious rights.

Failures and Faults

Our failures and our faults have the most important function, more valuable than our success and strengths.

Our failures and faults keep us in check circling success and strengths and show us how to be humble.

Solitariness

Each in our own room, solitariness is our family unity
through music, art, writing, meditation and being our own
self.

Sometimes it seems strange to be the same but be together
separately, but then we are happier when we meet.

Our paths are different, yet seem to have the same aim,
happiness seeing everything through until the day is done.

Health

Health can be used well or badly. It can be spent frugally,
generously or squandered away. There is no way of
changing how it has been used. There is no second chance
and no way of predicting it. There is no way to control the
health you have. You can strengthen or weaken its supports
but not itself.

The old regret this, the elders teach this, the young ignore
this, the sick see this.

Full Light

I have drained the batteries using the light to shine on life
as bright as I see it. Not dim but in the full light of black and
white or colour. All seen, the batteries can't be recharged
only discharged.

Choosing Nothing to Do

How often do we decide to do nothing when we have nothing to do and are not tired?

How often do we decide not to think and be still?

Do we ever experience being still? Do we ever stop and just be still?

Light from Inside

What a difference light makes, not the kind from the sun or power but inner light.

What we think we sense and know, perhaps we imagine much more than we would like to.

What we can sense and know is only visible if an inner light is turned on.

The inner light can only be turned on by turning around, looking inwards not outwards.

The things of the world become secondary, then they too become brighter.

68. CHARITY

Why we give

Do we give because we feel an obligation to religion, an obligation to the community, to our parent's values? Do we give because we are too scared to say no, out of shame of what we are, what we have done or not done? Do we give out of superiority, wanting people to like us, wanting people to depend on us or are we giving so others feel like us. If we give because we feel better, then it is good as we are not concerned with anything else.

Doing Others Work

Helping so much that someone doesn't help them self can be worse than doing nothing.

Sometimes extreme difficulty is needed so that extreme effort can be recruited to move an obstacle.

Anonymous Benefactors

Not long ago the wealthy used to be benefactors to artists, writers and the poor to ensure they could survive. Today to avoid tax, they only give charitable donations to corporations which have pension funds, investments and CEOs.

Self Reliant

If you come across someone who is being treated unfairly. If their life is awful. If their life is too difficult. If their life is so hard. If they have pressure from everywhere, you may feel you want to help them but be careful before you help.

They may be playing the victim. They may want you to feel sorry for them to receive things from you, but don't want to help themselves. So see what responsibility they have taken first.

Me First This Time

If you have trained to care for others and your work is looking after their needs, your training and work can hamper you in your own family and relationships.

You are trained to find out someone's needs and ensure they are met but unlike most people, you don't tend to think of your own automatically.

We are on autopilot to think of others first. Even some religions condition us to think that we must be selfless and we don't even come into the equation.

So it is a shock to find you have to think of you first, not other people. Accepting it can be like new clothes but if they don't fit, change them and just try something else.

Helping Others

When you do something to help someone, it makes you feel better. If it made you feel worse you would stop doing it, so do help others but know it is for you.

Service

Let's ditch the word charity and instead imagine going back to where it started, service, yes a servant to something needy, not to be advertised.

Only anonymous volunteers allowed to do the work, no paid workers taking money from a pension fund built on widows' donations, who go without food and heat.

No chairman or chairwoman, deputy director, pension fund director or director of human resources. Come and help if you can show up anonymously in your own time.

Silent Ghost of Service

She arrives unannounced at any time in your life when you can only look back or while you still have time.

She wants to know about anonymous service only. How much of your time here did you devote silently helping animals, people or plants, their world, the world of the sky and the sea? The only things counted when she lets you look inside you are silent service for anything but you.

69. CHANGE

Change is something you do naturally, out of choice or because there is no choice . . .

Change

Giving up expectations cannot be stopped because
we always expect something, especially life, but most
expectations are wishful thinking.

Hoping someone will change, trying to change someone, are
more difficult than self change.

Failure to Change Others

I'm pretty rubbish at resentment, at being aggrieved and
bitter because it keeps on coming back with things I just see
as black.

I want to be able to accept the things I cannot change, which
won't change them but will change how I see them and will
let me change to accept them.

The things I want to change for others are attitudes in me to
them. I can see what I can't change and what is possible to
change, my attitude.

Don't Change

Why would I want to try and change anything, as it is all as
it is meant to be? I can't become because I already am all I
can be which is myself.

The Only Possible Change

We teach that you can change anything especially how
people think. Some believe this and die trying it because you
can't change how people think.

You can only ever change yourself. If what you do with
yourself influences someone and they change how they
think, you will have proved this right.

Change Resistance

Where did you go to? What did you do with your life? Are
you still living? I have thought of the paths you may have
taken and I've wondered if I've been right.

We don't change. We don't like change. We avoid change
Those who make changes often don't like change. You were
one of those and I expect you are unchanged. Like all of us
formed hardy to withstand change.

Walk Free

How many times do we come close to death in our lives to
show us what we are?

How many times do we learn how to relate so that we see
love in others hearts not hate?

How many times do we travel this road until we finally see
only by giving up all roads we can walk free?

Seeing What We Are

Imagine there's no image only what is now.

If we couldn't think of alternatives how would anything have changed?

Change happens because of imagining things can be better improving how they are.

How often do we imagine changing how we are so we can be different to how we are now?

Perhaps what can be changed the most is seeing what we are.

Still Hoping for Change

Since I was a child it is conditioned to be the state of my head to have a sense of dread for an hour after I get up.

It can happen that in time in the mornings I won't still be waiting to see if it shows.

Let It Stop

Whatever they say, whatever they do, don't react with your mind, respond from your heart.

They may never change so step off the merry-go-round. Let it all stop.

At the end of Today

At the end of today, at the beginning of tomorrow, will I
still think the same, will I have shed things, will I still be the
same?

Will I have shed what I've decided should go or is it too
embedded tonight and tomorrow it will still show.

As long as another change doesn't displace this time, the one
I have chosen for now.
If I stay with now all will be fine.

Changing Form

I know I am unconventional, do not respect boundaries and
break them down to see if there is something else.

Perhaps there were influences which I still need freedom
from or freedom from an individual who has too much
power.

Art and even the English game of cricket can take a new
form so what about me?

Retire

What fear do we have if we stop? What questions would
persist? Aimless thoughtless, we are not taught how to just
be now.

Changing

People don't change until changes happen, then they change.

Hats

When you are introduced to someone, when you are wearing a hat, they can never see you without it.

When you are introduced to someone, when they are wearing a hat, you can never see them without it.

Mother, father, brother, sister, aunt or uncle doctor, teacher, banker, soldier, lawyer and farmer's hats are fixed.

But a friend, an enemy and a stranger's hats can change.

Can a hat be seen as only one of many hats the person under it has to wear.

Everything must go

Everything must go, all possessions, all collections, memories, nothing left to be shown, nothing left to know.

We have to let go of everything from the start to the end. First it's the womb. Last it's of all letting go, all without choice, let go.

Everything must go, me first as the ego, then the last thing of all, consciousness must eventually go.

Working on Ourselves

We can contribute more by having influence on ourselves rather than on others. We can give more if we give more to ourselves rather than to others. We can help more if we spend more time on our own rather than with others. We can change things more if we change ourselves rather than others.

Me First

It is easy to look out at others and criticise them. But how difficult it is to look inwards and see what is good, positive and right about what we are before we criticise anything or anyone. Stop trying to persuade another before persuading yourself. Stop trying to correct another before yourself. Stop trying to help another before yourself. Stop trying to love another before yourself. Stop trying to live only by thinking not by authenticity.

Being able to see the faults of the world but not our own is always easier and preferred but is being superficial and irresponsible as everything has to begin and end inside here.

Who Needs to Change

To understand someone, pretend to be them for an hour to feel their weight or lightness. Are there things holding them down or maybe things that should be? Do these make them repeat what they do to others and to you? Is it up to others and them to change or is it just you?

There is No Cure for Life

There is no cure for life. How could there be? What would it be? More life, a different life? Changed consciousness?

Unchanged

I would rather no one knows me because I want things to carry on as they are, unchanged. I'm not looking for reactions or surprised faces.

Adjustments are Not Change

You see that there is not a single thing you can change because you have already chosen it. Any further adjustments are not change, just more of what is meant to be.

Changed

All the chats we used to have so casually but passionate about all the things wrong and right in the world, were so beautifully simple and extraordinary, but are gone.

Enough is Always Enough

One thing we know is that we have been asking the same question about ourselves for several thousand years and we are still asking it. Is it time to just stop thoughts and be happy?

Chronic Suffering

What have I got when everything is going wrong? There is
nowhere to turn except to what I know, what is inside me. I
am hoping it will end well as I actually have no control. I am
near to being on my knees praying for it to end well, then in
myself I am on my knees.

I think it is fate and I think it will be a positive change into
something better. But what if this is the last of the good times
and there is now permanent suffering like this? Perhaps
this is the only way I am able to surrender, to give up every
single thing and just be my inner self.

Creatures of Habit

We get caught because we are creatures of habit. We stay
in and live chaotic lives because we are creatures of habit.
We stay in abusive relationships because we are creatures
of habit. We live and hate because we are creatures of habit.
We stay addicted to things because we are creatures of habit.
History repeats itself because we are creatures of habit.
Habits are easier than doing new things

The Most Trusted

The unmaterialistic reformed thief is the most honest. The
recovering reformed addict is the most sober. The reformed
adulterer is the most pure. The repentant reformed murderer
is the gentlest.

Habit and Hope

Most creatures seem to be ones of habit and like us they prefer habitual behaviour.

Many of our behaviours become habits because being familiar with something we know makes us feel secure.

Most creatures seem to be ones of hope. In times of crisis they hope and look for ways out. In calmer times they try and maintain the calmness, living in hope that things will stay good.

Fear of Consequences

Pain seems to be our best motivator encouraging us to do things we would not necessarily consider.

Usually before the threat of pain, better alternatives are considered. It is only when these are not that pain becomes likely.

Happiness and Suffering

When you are in darkness you can't see any light because your vision is unreliable, so you try not to stumble and fall. When light arrives you adjust and forget the fear of stumbling and falling, then darkness arrives again and you try not to stumble and fall. We really do not know when either will go or come.

Things change on their own

When we are not watching or listening, things are then ready to change. We think they have changed when we look at them again from another point of view. Have they changed or is it just us?

No Change Without a Cause

Thinking doesn't change much without a cause. Mental health doesn't change much without a cause. Feelings don't change much without a cause. Behaviour doesn't change much without a cause.

It seems we cannot become anything only be what we already are.

Already Me

Those who have been saw it; what they are. Those to come will see it; what they are. We do not change; we only see what we are, so we can become what we already are.

Only Us

As much as we try to change, we cannot become what we are not. If we don't think, feel or behave like this, this too is only us.

How to Change Other People's Minds

We should say hello on the street, yes because it is polite but most of all because it is friendly and it is kind. Maybe we don't see any opportunities to be kind each day. Passing someone is one of them because even if there is no reply, you have reminded that person you said hello, which might make them change their mind.

First Ray of Sunshine

Life would otherwise not be over but empty, then a ray of sunshine come in. In the form of a child who changes the colour of everything.

Change Addiction

There comes a time when we discover a difficult aspect of the way we are living. We see we are restlessly addicted to change, which can only be resolved by being still.

Change Inside

Geographically thinking we believe that change is found in the best place to go, or that change is changing where you live or going on holiday. But they don't work because you take your head with you. It is not on the holy mountain or in a monastery because you take your head with you there too. There is only one place go to change.

70. FORGIVENESS

Communication

When someone's reason is understood, when pain and vulnerability are understood, we understand what may not have been communicated was too difficult to. What's not known can't be forgiven. What's not acknowledged can't be forgiven. What's not understood can't be forgiven. What's not understood continues to hurt.

Letting Go of Shame

Victimhood is something to let go of because by creating forgiveness, resentment disappears and revenge is not necessary.

Focusing on yourself, not the perpetrator of your pain, lets you heal yourself to be whole again.

Meeting your perpetrator as a happy person leaves no guilt or shame in the wrong hands or heart.

What We Want We Need To Give

Being ordinary, straightforward is what we want, not mystery or insincerity. We want forgiveness, not resentment. The more straightforward and forgiving we are, the more of these we receive.

Forgiveness and Permission

The sun does not ask for forgiveness after it has burnt your skin. It is the sun. The wind does not ask for forgiveness after it has blown away your washing. It is the wind. The rain does not ask for forgiveness after it has wet your face. It is the rain. The snow does not ask for forgiveness after it has stopped you. It is the snow.

You should never think of asking for permission or forgiveness for being your self.

Risk Taking

Leaving forgiveness behind, exploring what is not allowed, encourages further exploration. Perfection is the enemy of progress because it stifles looking further. Perfection halts all growth, whereas progress with imperfection stimulates the growth process.

Limited Forgiveness

When you acknowledge you are hurt and want to stop it, you need to understand why someone did it so you can stop hurting, forgive them and move on. You have to understand them but understanding may be left up to you. It can exhaust us beyond a point, so we have to accept our forgiveness may be limited.

71. BEING HUMAN

Tolerating Imperfection

Our mistakes allow us to tolerate the imperfect in ourselves so we can be human.

Looking In Each Others Eyes Again

Man's habit of making everything easier by making them habits has led to everyone using things instead of themselves. He doesn't walk, talk, play, give eye contact ,communicate or physically take part in life. Maybe only when the inner man is close to starvation and annihilation will he raise this with someone who might hear him.

TURNING INWARDS

72. FAMILY LOVE

You

Watching you grow up cannot be compared to anything. It is the showing of the inner self in its most brilliant light of happiness. The singing like a carefree bird. The skip still in your step. The uncontrollable laughter. The love you show.

Gone Too Quickly

I miss my parents and the times we had but I will miss the times I have had with my wife and daughter. Though we still live together, I miss these times already.

Of Happy Family Times

Time to start clearing out all the things of what has been. Everything needs to go, so we are ready to go, ready for the next phase, which we can't control or know, ready to move over to let you be where we've been. There is nothing sentimental. There will only be things and images left after our memories too have moved on of shining brilliantly happy times.

Singing

Hearing your child sing is like no other voice. Singing from the heart, their heart takes you to your own.

73. FRIENDS

What We Receive

What does it take to bring war to an end, to bring greed to an end to stop harming ourselves? What does it take to start loving ourselves, to start making amends, to start making friends? It costs nothing because it is free, a gift we receive as precious as what we give.

Love and Friends

I know I have to be told. We all do. Being told our destiny of doom doesn't have to be permanent gloom. We still have choices, especially to be happy to enjoy our love and our friends.

No Memories

Most of the close friends I knew are gone; some have been taken over by rotten luck. They have left me to remember them which I do but not how they were. What they do for me still is what I know. They gave me these gifts of their self.

What is Needed

What friends are left to call on in devastation? How can they help apart from being with you? Sometimes just the silent presence of another person is all that is needed.

411

My Best Mate

I don't see him much but when I do it's like when I was a
kid and we have each other's total attention. He makes me
happy. He makes me see our lifespan, how much we as
friends really mean. What were our core values and what
they are today? We had youthful looks and smiled a lot and
when we see each other we still do.

Stick with the Winners

Stick with the winners not the losers. Stick with happy
people, not with partying people. Stick with people who are
interesting to know, who are interested in knowing you, who
you feel good about being with.

Staff

If you have staff, they are not friends. They are the hired
hand, not the shepherd to the lambs. If you have staff who
you think are friends, they are not because you can't pay
friends.

Friendship

To wake up breathing easy with no effort. To wake up
comfortable with no pain. To wake up with shelter with no
exposure. To wake up with nourishment without starvation.
To wake up with warmth there is nothing better.

Help

We fear accepting we need to ask for help, perhaps because we don't want to be a burden. Or maybe because of our upbringing, we want our dignity intact as long as we can have it. But there are times when dignity needs to take second place to help.

When help arrives and is accepted, it is all the help we need, not too late or too early, on time, at the right place, by the right person.

Help never affects our dignity because help shines a light on who we are by those who see it and see us in themselves.

Stuff

What do we value apart from our own self? Only our family and friends come close. All else apart from the intangible in us is first as all else is just stuff.

What Are We?

Our race, religion and the story of where we come from mould what we can become but our family, life, education and friends continue to change this too. Consciousness also has different levels which change because ultimately there is the happiness of consciousness, of being stillness.

With friends from nearly fifty years ago

We were only our potential and now we still see the world the same, only coloured by our different experiences.

Opponents as Best Friends

All my opponents are my best friends. Who else would care so much about me to spend so much time plotting against me?

Sweet Music

The only way to cope with a baby screaming when it wants to scream just because it can is to listen and hear it as sweet music. Then the sweet music must be invited to stay like you want a friend to stay. Making friends with sounds changes sound to positive input to the heart.

In the Company of the Wise

People keep on coming up in my life from everywhere and there has been little control of this at all for the last forty years.

Wanting help of some kind, psychological, medical, spiritual. But less than a handful don't want any of this and we are just with each other.

Beauty

Why does beauty come with so much pain? After years of happiness it leaves you knowing you'll never see it again?

Why does beauty have to be so very cruel, always ending by displaying there is no more renewal?

Why is beauty so skin deep not like hard earned love but very cheap.

But beauty can be the calling card of love, sometimes the only clue of things from above.

So beauty can be cruel, cheap and pain or the only hope that we can love again.

Mistaken Identity

I didn't form an attachment today. They are gone with no trace. No loss or gain. No risk of pain. No concern their path is sealed. I know my place. They're gone with no trace.

Protection Against Your self

Some people need protection against themselves because they are damaging them selves. How do you provide protection to someone who doesn't want to be protected? You cant protect them if they don't want it. Convincing them they need protection may only be possible after the damage is done.

The Jackal

The old Jackal lives on the hill in a cave on his own planting trees to try and help stop the soil being washed away. Lightly tanned he has a temperament with spikey short grey hair.

A keen look in his eye the old Jackal with that all knowing look in his eye. Getting on with his life always stopping to see if you are happy with today.

If he finds you wanting he cheers you up. You listen searching to you see how happy you are inside.

Friends

Friends are not lost as it is not possible to lose them even in death. People who are not friends are lost after it is discovered that they were giving you something which was supposed to be nurturing you when it wasn't.

Friends are always with you. Even when they are not here, they support you and are in touch. If you can't hear or see them, friends encourage you from anywhere all the time.

If you think you don't have a friend, imagine one and nurture that relationship like someone in front of you. With all projections withdrawn, all connections open up and your best friend is found.

What Do You See

I've seen what they do, how they behave, how they think, how they feel. I've seen what they want, how they relate, how they devour, how they carry on. I've seen what they pretend, how they run, how they cheat, how they end. I've seen what they desire, how they try, how they fail, how they mourn. I've seen what they worship, how they are kind, how they dream, how they help. I've seen their love, their protection, the look in their eyes, the look of a friend.

Hidden Encouragement

Opposition is not your enemy, it's your best friend, stretching you further than you can imagine. So keep best friends with the opposition, they are encouraging you as you encourage them.

Camaraderie

Camaraderie changes with age. You no longer communicate to say that you are still smiling, still standing. Breathing says it all.

Companions

I don't need protection from others but from myself. I need to protect myself from changing my attitude too late. I need to protect myself from not turning inwards to see myself, from not seeing everything as the same. We are all companions no matter what.

Giving up Fishing

You can write about romantic love to make people love you but that kind of love is the loneliest path to choose as you are always alone fishing for love, trying to not be on your own.

Giving up fishing, turning inwards to rely on your inner resource, you find you have the company of others who want something more than romantic love. There is no need to look anywhere for company because it is inside and all around you.

Progress

There are so many layers, levels, polarities and inter-relationships. How we get to speak and hold a meaningful conversation so that we do not destroy one another is progress.

Eating Out

There is less solitude yet the chaos weaves itself with the help of the human hand into a pattern not seen alone.

There are reactions full of the night, everyone trying to be heard, no one trying to be humble and everyone is on a diet.

74. AGE

The True World

So few see and understand their inner world, only seeing and judging it like the outer one, by apparent results and effects.

The inner world can only be experienced by repeated experience of it. Only then is it seen to be the only true world.

Seeing

There is so much to see, hear and sense, it seems it could last a life time but time and the material things of the worlds we see only encourage us to believe the worlds we see are real. The worlds we see can be of poverty of wealth of the busy world or people of solitude.

There is one who sees us inside who is our self.

Not thinking

If there is nothing after this life, does it change anything? If nothing changes then this is it.

Running On Empty Tanks

Would my heart be able to follow my head and accept what is currently unacceptable if it happened?

Where would I find the strength when the tanks of energy are already drained from just living?

Where does someone get the energy from which seems so unbelievably never ending?

Fulfilment

Why is it some of us seek happiness? Is it because it was so denied us, or still is? Or is it because we have seen so much unhappy chaos?

Is it people have made us unhappy or has the world made us unhappy and we have just not been able to find it yet?

Do we seek happiness because we know it is there. Is it because we know it will make a difference because we know we will be fulfilled?

Stop Writing

Am I condemned to write my thoughts down? Is this what I have become, a recorder of thoughts? This must stop as it is just an avoidant escape from actually just being still. Maybe it is just a pressure valve to release some thoughts.

Not only Chance

I can't change direction now, only slowly embrace the future possibility of it, when times are easier. That's what I tell myself. But I don't accept that, so I keep trying to be somewhere to change it, hoping luck will see me.

To Think or Be

I have reached a plateaux where thoughts neither entertain or please me and have lost their amusement in what I am.

I try and have less of them but it is only stopping them in meditation and when I am at peace in stillness that I am happy.

I have tried to have a visual mind but it's no good, I think rather than see, so my task now is to see and not think, to be and not know.

The Worst and Best

Is this what will be remembered, finding some writing about mid Sunday afternoons. The only time of the week I dread more than waking an hour early on Monday mornings. But then there is the morning of a day off to get up early, to indulge in the leisure of an arduous walk or waiting for the post or a loaf of bread to finish baking.

Switching attitudes sometimes helps but the only thing which normalises is seeing each day as precious present moments of the truth of our stay.

Moving On

You are surrounded by things which have meaning to you. They bring up memories you know you must let go of. Things can trap you from moving on to where you are better.

Unreliable Tools

We think that thinking can make us happy but happiness is in the heart.

Our thoughts imagine, hope and believe, but what we are, is what we are.

We think something is finished when it is still going on and we think something is not over when it is already finished.

Reality of Truth

Truth is not in books. It is not in words. It is only inside.

Truth cannot be spoken of. It cannot be taught. It can only be experienced inside.

Being Stillness

Thinking is not being still. Being still is conscious stillness of no thoughts.

Unity of Truth

This is that. That is this is truth.

Alive

With passion there is Fire. With fire there is heart. With heart there is life.

Not Only Thinking

The human state is it just being an animal, is it just consciousness? The human state, there are so many things it isn't, it is not only thinking.

What's Left

What else could we leave except for what we have seen and can pass on?

Out of Sync

Why do we seem to freeze at some age inside? For some it is twenty one, for others thirty one. We even believe our body is younger too until we are embarrassed or humiliated by it. Why are we so out of synch with what we are? At what age does the ego let the inner self be covered up? Yet for some, this is resisted, the ego is ignored and the presence of the inner self is all that is felt. It is not an age, it is the moment we see our ignorance.

423

Life Is

Just as it comes is how it is and it cannot be changed.

Feeding the Fire

I live a life which would shock most people who know me, monastically simple most of the time, almost no television or entertainment, no outings except pilgrimages.

Pilgrimages which help keep the inner light burning by whatever fuel others or I can feed it.

Elderly Risk Takers

Why are the old not listened to? Of course the young must have their bets chance at changing things but ignoring experience is not always wise. The risk takers are the change agents.

Sometimes the biggest risk takers seem to be the elders because they often see the finer points younger people with other interests cant see because the elders have less to lose.

75. ELDERS OF THE TRIBE

Your Last Home

Will you end up in a facility for the elderly? If so what sort?
A residential home to keep you clean? A nursing home
to help your organs cope? A psychiatric home because of
officially labelled demented behaviour?

Will you be part of a group labelled just like you, stooped
walking stick users or Zimmer frame shufflers? Will you be
playing games you never would have before with people
you would have previously avoided.

Could you live in a serviced comfortable apartment which is
stylish and has a great view but never sees visitors and you
cannot leave?

Or will you take your chance with the inner room, trusting
everything to fate, to stillness, being kind and enjoy every
moment?

We Are Forever Young

At any age people are the same as they have tried to be.
Opportunities given to people who are about to retire are
not rejected based on reality but accepted on the basis of
thinking they are forever young.

Old People's Home

I don't want to sit in a room with pictures on the wall of people I can't be with in places I can't visit anymore. From infant's school to college and then through work I avoided being in an institution and never want to be in one.

I don't want to sing and dance with others and be told what to do with others in a final institution when I never fitted in with any of the other institutions I was in, apart from my own.

Last Dignity

Old people's homes, I'll try and give a miss. Unburdened family, friends or hired hands first please every time.

Be What Others Think You Shouldn't Be

The young sing about what they want to be, the old sing about what they still want to see. The old can't give as much of what they know because no one else wants to know. The young don't go after the things they could because no one thinks they should. Is the answer to the problems of age, 'Maybe be what others think you shouldn't be.'

Old Friend

What better surprise is there than the face of an old friend with their stories of them and us and their news which cannot be trumped.

Aching bones

I didn't deliberately harm my health; I just used it to do what I was supposed to do whilst I was here, so it is as it should be. The effort of getting here, then the effort of finishing challenges wears out body and mind but not the inner self, so it is as it should be.

To Sit and Stare

Daily essentials which arise, so what is there to really do, only food to prepare, otherwise we can sit listen and stare.

Reclining

Reclining on a bed having to have a routine of walking just to ensure exercise or all would seize up. No pressures from business or securities, the only purpose, happiness whilst we are here.

Most Mornings

To wake and whisper to people I would like to speak with and listen to them before the day starts is what usually happens.

Life and Ending

Rarely things get stopped in full flight as most reach a natural landing.

Relief From the Mind

No more questions of life or death. No more worries
about health, just the slow decline in breath and change in
consciousness.

What News In retirement

A note from a friend, a walk with different weather, a change
in health and steady wealth. Perhaps it is time to stop it, be
of some use, to make someone happy apart from you.

Holiday Island

Forty years later I am back where I was, but older, worn and
torn. One more large cycle to start but this time with my
family.

The Doctor

The old doctor has a smiling face. The young say he has
no understanding of the feelings they are immersed in. He
smiles because he didn't drown in them.

The old doctor smiles because he knows as he sees with eyes,
what your eyes cannot yet see and listens with ears to what
yours cannot yet hear.

Memories Eye

All times gone by are in memories eye like all ships which pass. They hold us in their memories eye. Memories eye is not ours but everywhere.

Unknown Message

I feel an underlying feeling of something. Something is not right, almost like an anxiety but this is physical. Maybe it is a warning saying stop and investigate.

Maybe it's just a clock message saying you are this old now. Sometimes with these, you just never know.

Eternal Youth

Be a child now because you will be grown up for so long.

Be a child now and never stop being a child as adults aren't so much fun.

Children want to be adults; the elderly want to be children and they don't know they haven't changed.

Retirement

Retirement is handing over the fight you have trained and fought for all your life.

Secret Teachings

When you grow old, you adjust and accept letting others be first, striving to be behind anyone you can, knowing winning is losing because someone else has that thirst.

It's not like running a race where you can't come first anymore, it's because there is nothing to prove, except seeing someone prove it to themselves.

Stepping back is not stepping down but is watching with the ones at the back who want to be at the front and slipping them a few essential tips.

Outer Happiness

Loss, suffering and pain, no outer source of happiness, sometimes give us an opportunity to look inside again.

The gains and losses after thirty five years are not likely to change greatly with the passing of more time. They are neither less noticed nor less influential on us.

The coming and going of people, of opportunities and circumstances become routine change, guiding us to happiness, showing us if we are drifting slowly away from them.

Who Knows Why?

I am happy and I enjoy my life. Of course, there are highs and lows and what for who knows. It is not ours to question endlessly; just to be.

Where Do You Want to Be?

Do you want to be a product? Do you want to be a brand?
Do you want to do this? If you want to do this it will mean
sleepless nights, it will mean endless nights. This is how
you do this; this is how you get there. If you don't want to
be there, would you rather stay here? Would you rather be
here? Would you rather be still?

Afraid to say the word Dead

The more we try and avoid the words, 'He died, he's dead,'
and instead use, 'He passed, he's passed,' the more scared,
fearful, distant, and removed we become about accepting
what we should try and become closer to, so it does not
overwhelm us when others die and we start the last process.

76. DEATH

Not Me

I don't want to be left in a coffin forever underground. I don't want to burn in eight minutes. I don't want any of it.

Slipping Away Unknown

I never had a big appetite or thirsted for more. I confess my simplicity has left me materially poor. Probably in my last years it will hurt me the most. Compared with my peers, I will seem like just a ghost but I won't have much to give up or leave behind. Lawyers and estate agents won't even be involved. If my job is done well, there will be nothing about me to forget, as remembering me will be impossible if I am not known.

I am Just

There are two ways of looking. I can see myself as rich for having just enough money and being what I am, or poor for just having money.

Bread and Life

Baking a loaf of bread and seeing how it turns out is like our life. Is it good, satisfying, do we want more and does it make us happy?

Not Early or Late

Perhaps it is my time to die soon. Maybe I'm just waiting to be told. A shock but not a surprise. I will feel and think then try and be normal.

If I go into denial, it buffers all from talking about it but that is not fair because they may want to and I should be able to deal with it easier.

How strange to write about what has not yet been confirmed or announced to me. I hope my timing is not early or late.

Exemplary

When you are dying, apart from being yourself, there is nothing you can do to show others the way. You cannot be more exemplary than this.

One Way

Most people don't know the people who lay down their lives for them. There is no reason why they should but I mention it because the ones who give their life, do it without expectations.

It is something they just have to do to be what they are. They don't see an alternative and for them there is no choice. They see it as their own way, the one way.

Last Rights

Last things are sometimes first like what we are, like what is gone when we are gone. No intellectual thoughts of the unconscious, only conscious of consciousness.

No Missed Appointments

We all attach so much importance to the body, to our age. Disease threatens us, death becomes us, so we try and run. There is nowhere to run or hide as death keeps all appointments.

Too Many of Us

Wouldn't it be terrible if we didn't go, I mean we were replicated when we die so we are always around?

How would the world get rid of everyone if there was no natural wastage? Man would get fed up and find something to get rid of us with.

We couldn't just accumulate as there would be far too many and it would just get worse.

The thing is; it already is worse and it cannot get better. It can only get really bad.

Who Knows?

You can tell everyone how it ended after we are all gone.
Would it surprise us, probably not.

Just as you won't be surprised when someone sums up your
life and the world you lived in, but it's only from their point
of view.

I only half know the people my parents related to and how
they got on when they were young, what silent influence
they had or the gossip that goes with all of us.

Which Way

I can't work out how to be disposed of. Unselfishly is it
better to be degraded into gases and bones by bacteria or
burnt for eight minutes into carbon? What is better for the
planet, more gases or more carbon and what happens to all
the gases produced by cremation?

Then there's the waste of burial ground. Direct committal
sounds very quick, all over with no fuss. But with burial you
can be stolen then ransomed for, to be put back. You can't
put gas back.

External Hard Drive

What interesting things we are, all this learning, acquiring
skills, relating, loving, traveling, eating and entertainment.
Then it's all gone with the death of the body no external hard
drive to plug into to copy us.

Be Seeing You

Soon I won't be able to write anymore because just like you. my time here is limited, so I see it as precious and I don't want to waste any of it.

This is just a reminder to you that you have to go soon too, so spend it well, be happy. Be seeing you.

Discovering the death of a Friend

I found out just this hour that my old friend Richard Mckane died three months ago. He was a poet who helped translate for victims of mankind. I knew him for seven years during shared work. We had just lost touch for twenty six years but his obituary enabled him to touch me once more. Masterly he hid his mental state, unswerving in his one pointedness, not distracted even by his humour, amidst all diversity.

Power of Graveyards

They make you want to walk quicker, to wear out every joint, to use every fibre in your heart to stretch your mind, to travel far, deep inside, to die with wealth overflowing from within.

What News in Death

Nothing new to recommend, just memories from the living soon too to be dead.

Paradise

There comes a realisation there are only precious moments left, so have them now instead of trying to have them then.

Like Instinct

What we hand over when we leave are not the memories of what we did or what we said but what we are. We show others how to be, so they can show others before they leave. Not spoken about, like an instinct, it seems to be our primal duty.

Intellect feeling of the Dead

The emotions we feel around death have no words, for words are of the head. The intellect is no use for feeling about the dead.

Remains

When your partner dies, what about them dies in you and what about them keeps on living in you? What about you keeps on living? Is it your thoughts, your actions, your body, your sense of awareness of consciousness?

Light

When you see time and space are just words, you see how much light you have. Being conscious of happiness is all you have.

Nothing to Change

When you see the length of the wick, you see how much light you have left. Everything is now perfect. Everything is as it is meant to be.

Inevitability

When it's your turn, it is different because it is you. You lose your detached logical thinking and get immersed in the challenge.

The inevitability dominates everything. Some things mean less, some people more. You seem on a different track, even though the path and pace are the same.

Nightmare

First a nightmare about me restrained to a vertical plinth, overwhelmed by self-righteous people dressed in flowing white robes, holding night lights under my feet for longer than I can stay asleep.

Followed by my sisters going to the same place for Christmas and only able to avoid their company by having to cut short my precious time with my parents.

Then not having quite passed my medical finals lingering in front of me, stopping me enjoying my life, never quite good enough. Finally one of unavoidable death, the scythe cutting all blades of grass and the mercy of not having to take medicines to try and alter its course, my path.

Slowly

Lower me down slowly inch by inch. I am not in a rush. I want you to have time to see, to think while I slowly go sink down.

I don't wasn't my last movement on earth rushed because someone feels uncomfortable. I want the slowness and the time to be lowered slowly down.

One Way Ticket

You realise you got a one way ticket and there is no way back to where anyone younger wants to listen to you. But perhaps you can write about your foot prints and describe what is at either end.

The wisdom of old age is something we seek when we are young but cant see it until we are old. We cannot accept the inevitable until we become it.

What Remains of Us?

All that is left is our name and date of birth with the date of our return from earth.

Perception of the end of life

The body of physical organs including the brain is the temporary vehicle for what we regard separately as our self. It appears everything else of us must die, but not the Self.

Life is Understanding

So much of life is understanding. All of life is understanding. Understanding is seeing until seeing no more can be understood and there is only being.

Understatements

Euphemisms are buffers ,understatements to the English masters. The long sleep is the one for death.

The Long Sleep

Soon it will be time for me to sleep the long sleep as all of us have to.

I thought this forty years ago as you think this now. You will say the same in forty years.

Isfahan

The man with the scythe meeting the servant in the market place who runs away, only to be told later that day by the man with the scythe, 'I wanted to tell you about this meeting here earlier.'

It is only now I see it is about me. I knew then it was about us all, but not about me.

Guests Resting Place

I cant be regarded as Irish. I cant be regarded as Ukrainian.
I cant be regarded as English. I am pleased because I have
lived in many places. Why should they or I choose to own
what is only a resting place for a temporary guest.

Wake Up before You Die

Maybe the only point of this scare, this very real threat on
my life is to wake me up even more. How awake can you be?

Sleep

If you sleep well, value it because like everything it will pass.

Heart Attack

Having a heart attack is being attacked by you for not
looking after you. It's no one else. You are not looking after
yourself, your heart.

Heart

You cant get later what you could only get in youth. Later
you get different things but not the heart of youth

77. ANCESTORS

Respecting All Our Families

My Irish ancestors ascended to power then were slaughtered
by the invaders of their land. My Ukrainian ancestors
survived until they were slaughtered by their friends whose
minds had changed.

Irish, Ukrainian, slaughterers and all are how I got here, so I
can only respect them all.

I can't know what happened and who in the future will
know how you and I have moulded the world for them.

Ripples

What has been done to your country has been to your tribe
to your family, to you, to your children.

What has been done to my country has been done to my
tribe, my family, to me, to my children.

What you do to another country you do for you but also to
tribes, to families, to each person but also to their children.

Wrong Focus

We are so concerned with our similarities and differences,
we forget we are companions on a unique experience in
consciousness.

Our Heroes Gone

When all your heroes are dead, you realise they weren't so good or great. Some of the things you do are better, so are some things you said.

When you see how complete you are, how you have been all along, you feel more complete now they have left and are gone.

Questions and Answers

How does it work? Not all of it, just life? Ok then, all of it? It works as you make it work, that's how it works, it's the only way it works.

How do I conduct myself, what do I think, what do I do? What conducts everything conducts you also, so what you think, won't change what you do.

When We Are Here

What do you know about someone from a few generations back? What surrounded them, the events of that time that were the external world? How could you know them? Do you know if they knew themselves? If they were aware of how happy they were when they were here?

Intangible Steppingstone

The illusory connections of information give us our identity. Look at this photograph. I can name the people in that photograph. I can tell you about each of them. The year and probably the month but they are all dead. Each one of their memories and experience vanished with them. Only this photograph is left and any meaning it had will vanish when I am gone.

Memories naturally fade then vanish to enable us to live and be in the present. But there are some, they are intangible reference points like steppingstones from our ancestors and in our age, we must lay down our own intangible steppingstones to pass on to become intangible ancestors.

Respect

It seems strange when you read the obituary showing that someone you knew had done things they had not talked about. Perhaps it is out of respect that we leave the past where it was and let the present be what it can be.

Passing it On

Before summer is over, preparation for the next one must begin. Like having children, their children are thought of before they are born. We strengthen ourselves to prepare, not us but the unborn.

No Words for the Dead

My reference points are all gone. My heroes have all passed on, cremated or buried, but their voices linger. Something they used to do or just say suddenly brings their face, their eyes in front of mine again.

Knowing That

Your world view or mine are choices of your mind or mine which are moulded and sculpted by ancestors, education, and culture just as our brain is moulded and sculpted by our actions and our thoughts in our time. Does anyone or anything direct this or that? Perhaps it is not just chance that I know I am that or the divine dance.

What We Leave

Like a river flows, our thoughts and millions of people have to flow. We flow through birth, growing through pleasure and pain, knowing disease and death will arrive but we also know we survive in those who are behind. They always keep our spirit alive.

Frozen

The thirst for expansion of our ego, power and money is unquenchable in search of desires. The hidden price of ignoring our inner world leaves us at the mercy of a cold life, a cold end.

No Change at All

This is the final part of the journey. It is the beginning of the end and the end of the beginning. There will have been no changes, then it will be realised there are no changes. After, when you look back you will see this with more certainty than you do now.

Permanent Consciousness

The choice of marriage can produce so much but it can end with a remaining partner sometimes left for years with memories. Aging alone when this was the deal, but it still feels a surprise that it has happened.

But by some other means there is the togetherness of life. In all the beauty and growth which becomes degeneration, a new awakening, higher than any perceived beauty, radiates out to the universe from within.

Trust in the Self

At fifty three with her husband just dead I had no words as my intellect couldn't respond. I felt the pain radiate from her heart. She had been struck leaving a difficult wound no-one else can heal. This is our nature. Just existing is what she says she is doing. She doesn't want to carry on living if this is what it is like. She knows the pain is working at something, perhaps positive. There is trust in herself.

Fourth Time

Yes, we are alone. Yes, everything is subjective. My friend is dead and only I have memories as his are gone.

Now this at least records it for a while but your recording, your sharing, after the fourth time it will probably vanish.

Happiness Not Dreamt

Four generations have been born since my father was born and like passing clouds, wars still come and go because the same instincts then still seem to be needed to survive those competing against you.

There is still hope and we try to be happy. We imagine better times like our parents did. Like them, we teach the presence of happiness is the most precious thing to have and to hold. It cannot be dreamt of in the future.

Love of Life

Like a Baby and a chieftain, innocent and knowing truth, no other intention other than to live life according to truth is what we can be.

Beams of Communication

In that moment, where rays of light beam down through spaces in clouds, is where communication with the living and our ancestors is.

Our World of Flesh, Sticks and Stones

Live glistening tissue with warm blood pumping through it as part of the organs which form us, support us in our transient stay. We build out of words, sticks and stones slightly longer lasting things but we no longer seem to understand us.

Forgotten

I hope they don't forget their ancestors, history books, paper, canvas, handwriting or drawing.

I hope they don't forget religions, childhood, wars, to search and find their inner self.

Stillness

If you are still, you realise almost everything is moving. The plants and animals are growing and dying at the same time. The plates of the earth are forever shifting. Our planet moves around the changing sun which also moves.

We slowly become our family's ancestors. Our thoughts move in directions which we only see if we are still. If you are still. you will see only one thing is always still. Since you knew it, consciousness has not moved.

Life Bread and Death

Bread is like our life and death, created by nature, harvested from our ancestors work and our efforts to continue and pass it on.

78. THINKING

Hope

We may not need to remove hope but we cannot lie that the truth is usually simple, hope complicated.

Thoughtlessly

We are addicted to thinking as much as we are to chemicals because we prefer to think about things rather than experience them. We prefer to think about what we can do and what we can be, rather than experience us and our true self.

Not the Body, Not the Mind

We can drive a car until it is worn and the road is worn but their state doesn't affect us because we know we are not the car or the road.

Similarly though we direct our thinking and our bodies we are not our body or our thinking, we are the one who is conscious of them.

Being Thoughtless

Having no thoughts is being constant, being in the same state we arrived in and that which we will leave in also.

Mind the Gap

It's not that we can't think enough to work this out. It is because it cannot be worked out by thinking. It cannot be understood by thinking because thinking itself is the problem.

Thinking will not leave us alone. It will not stop and let us be still. Thinking will not cease as long as our heart beats. It can be distracted, made to go another way.

With a partner of our senses, such as going with our breathing or a sound like a mantra the rhythm of our inner sense of breathing can slow down thinking, so only the gap between exists.

Some Times

There are times when things don't work, our thinking, our bodies, the desire for stillness, when thinking won't stop, when it won't be tethered to let us be what we are.

When we are not talking, not doing anything, thinking won't stop to let us be what we are.

Compassion

Having no thoughts is our best state, our state of natural happiness, heightened consciousness, with compassion.

Forgiveness

Thoughts can interrupt love but thankfully they can
interrupt hate and temper our feelings.

They can open things up or close things down, make us
remember when we have forgotten and can make us forget
what needs to be forgotten and they can let us forgive.

Thoughts

Our worst enemy is not anyone else but our own thoughts.
They interrupt silence. They interrupt stillness. We interrupt
our natural state of the happiness of just being still.

What We Can't See

Most of our time is spent looking for what we already have,
thinking we will find the happiness we want outside our self.
Sometimes after decades or trying to find it, we realise it was
inside us all along.

A Single Choice

If happiness is my nature why would I choose to be anything
else than be that?

Greatest Gift

Finally, what I had been longing for, waiting for arrived. It just became obvious. Its arrival was confirmation that what I suspected all along was true that I am already happy.

Equal but different

How can anyone knowingly follow anyone who doesn't insist on equal pay for women? Unequal pay for women is irrational, unfair, cruel and denial of their rights and inhuman thinking.

How can anyone knowingly follow anyone who doesn't insist on the same protection for children as animals? Less protection for children than animals is irrational, unfair, cruel and denial of their rights and inhuman thinking.

How can anyone knowingly follow anyone who doesn't insist on no poverty, no homeless, no sick or cold which is irrational, unfair, cruel and denial of their rights inhuman thinking? How can you and me not do these things, not protect, not be fair, not help, not hold, and not house which is irrational, unfair, cruel and denial of their rights and inhuman thinking?

Fully Empty Mind

Full of rubbish, ready to be emptied, to be full of thought, to be full of nothing. To be full of emptiness, the aim is to be fully empty.

Broken Moulds

Against all their conditioning, against all they were told, against all that they were taught and all they were sold, the chance of it happening are remote. Someone breaking the mould for an unknown reason, not tempted by silver or gold. What will become of them in the stronghold? They won't be thinking too much. They'll be working on how our future unfolds.

Stemming the Tide of Thinking

There is a dangerous rising tide which threatens us faster than the oceans, our thinking is the tide, rationalism is the force.

Rationalism reduces everything to being logical.

There is no time for helping or laughter, no time for art, poetry, dancing, mourning, hope or unifying mankind.

But there is hope.

There is an answer.

Belief in yourself, consciousness, happiness or even God, stem the time of rationalism so rationalism can step aside.

More or Less

There is only one thing that drives us mad. It is not traffic, our neighbours, the news or the weather. It's thinking. It's not what is done to us or what's in the food water or air.

It is what we do to ourselves by thinking. It is what we let ourselves think about, how much we think about it all the time.

Hypnotised by thinking we continue to think, thinking that thinking more will make us feel better. But not thinking is the only way to experience happiness of being.

Monsters and Angels

Thinking should be our servant, not our master but we are encouraged to see only thinking, not our spirit and heart.

We ignore and forget the past so we can be part of the brave future. We forget how to be just where we are now, distancing us further from our roots in the past.

We end up with no culture, because it is our past. We desperately want the history books back which we destroyed, but we used them as fuel for the furnace of new technology.

We delude ourselves we are progressing because the monster inside us always rises up from its sleep and counterbalances our angel.

Belief in Thinking

Thinking has dismissed belief as illogical and not real.
Belief in our sense of our self as anything but the brain is
regarded as not fully sane.

Belief that things have got better, belief that we are happier,
that we are more prosperous. Belief that we are in control are
promoted, so regarded as true.

Belief that consciousness is more than the brain, that there
is a spirit in us, that some people are good, that we will be
looked after are against sane logical thinking.

The limits of thinking are not mentioned, that our dreams
can't be measured, our memories can't be assessed, that the
future can be anything.

We can't work out why we are here or why we think so
very much or why we live more in the future than now,
except perhaps now our belief is not in us or any god but in
thinking.

Wave

Humour is a Mexican Wave to the mind bending it into
a more relaxed shape. Humour is a Mexican Wave to the
mouth curving the lips into informal expressions. Humour
is a Mexican Wave to the breathing making it heave with
emotion. Humour is a Mexican Wave to the heart opening it
up to all kinds of possibilities.

Virtual Happiness

Catastrophes happen in the world all the time but sometimes they are just in the mind, then our thinking is catastrophizing.

Anxious to protect securities, sometimes our minds take cruel liberties, blind to the naked greed of what we think we need.

Over attached to other's affections, we don't take our own directions and then what we should never do, we easily approve.

Being naked with greed, approving wrong deeds, letting thinking stink, too much happiness is virtual and real happiness nearly extinct.

Decompression

Do I want to sit for hours travelling, watching unfamiliar mental scenery pass; wandering what they are doing out there or wandering what they are doing back home?

Would I rather be somewhere not on the tourist road, which they tell me, broadens my vision or would I rather be in familiar company?

Do I need psychological decompression, time travelling away, only to see and appreciate I feel better at home?

Purposefulness Thinking

You are taking up this space which I have created for me and you have moved in on my words trying to interpret them when they were not written to be interpreted.

They were not written for anything, just written to be written. These words have no purpose but you can't stop trying to find one. If you stop reading, the purpose will go.

But you can't stop looking for something meaningful because you are concerned with purposefulness ,when this is purposeless. I hope you succeed in purposelessness.

To Be Honest

To be honest the only honesty seems almost like being dishonest, so why not start by asking for forgiveness not permission about honesty?

Thinking Soap

Soap is not natural, so does it harm us and if so why do we continue to use it? The presence of soap assumes that our bodies can't clean themselves, a mistaken leap to mass production. Like promises, money and therapy, thinking can create more problems than there were to start with, just as soap can create more dirt than we think it cleans.

Speaking of Eating

Pizza, pasta, curry, soup and bread are all elevated by man
to anchor him to a place before during and after eating,
irrespective of all else like the company or the silence.

They are what are in focus and when they are not in focus
there is too much thinking and outer chatter and the focus of
food is lost. We try too much not to just do one thing.

My father's elder in his orphanage always told him, 'When
you are eating you are not speaking and when you are
speaking you are not eating.'

Wallowing in Dreams

Back to work because of its utility, ignoring reality and
sticking with futility. Wallowing in dreams more appealing
than thinking, so when are we going to just allow dreaming?

Psychoanalyst's Brands of Thinking

Of the two most highly regarded thinkers on human
thought, one promoted cocaine then his thinking as a brand
of thought.

The other promoted the synthesis of others thoughts as his
own new brand of religion.

The Height of Nurture

Plans are the mind constructing its own future, thinking they will protect and nurture us, when without thinking, nurture is at its height.

Stopping Thinking

We try and control our thinking but we are not in control. Our thinking controls us, so how do we stop it making us fear, worry, remember, regret, resent and want to be in control.

First, we are aware there is one inside who is conscious of it, so seeing we are not actually our thinking opens the door to freedom to separate us from our thinking.

Always turning inwards to the one who is conscious, just being, in silence and stillness, with thankfulness, thinking has nothing to do but stop or be stopped.

You Can't Get What You Already Have

Happiness is our nature and that's why we all look for it, but some say they have the secret key to it for a price.

Happiness is our inner stillness which no one else can give us. They can't give us what we already have, our inner solitude, silence, stillness our nature of happiness.

I Am

Before light is seen for the first time, there is one inside us who is aware of the first light of dawn.

Before our ears can hear, there is one inside us who listens to the heartbeat of the world.

Before our skin is touched by air for the first time, there is one inside us who senses the world.

Before our flesh is given food by the world, there is one inside us who feeds us.

Before we take our first breath, there is one inside us who wants us to have life.

Before we cry, there is one inside us who wants us to communicate.

Before we speak, there is one inside us who in silent stillness knows 'I am.'

Now

I wouldn't want any time back as I have all the now I could have ever wanted.

I don't want to look back to distract from being completely here now.

79. THOUGHT

Reasons

Why do we do the wrong thing for the right reason and the right thing for the wrong reason? Studying not studying, marrying not marrying, getting divorced not getting divorced. Eating and drinking, not eating and not drinking, having children and not having children, moving country and not moving country.

Perhaps we want a reason to do everything but as life seems to happen irrespective of reason, maybe we should stop looking at reasoning and reasons.

Clouds of Thought

You have to come up with your truth not anyone else's. You have to see what is true for you even if someone else's truth sounds better.

Your truth is the only one that exists for you. Other truths are no truth for you, they are others thoughts.

Our own truth is always present like the light and warmth of the sun, present but hidden from us by clouds, clouds of thought.

Only Two Types of People exist

The Greeks first thought of personality typography but were plagiarised by astrologers who were plagiarised by psychologists. Then came psychiatrists, then the war.

Greek Choleric were astrological Fire signs for the Intuitive type

Melancholic were astrological Earth signs for the Sensing type

Sanguine were astrological Air signs for the Thinking type

Phlegmatic were astrological Water signs for the Feeling type

Psychiatrists now think they lead with personality disorders for which there is no cure and no proof. There are the eccentric- paranoid, schizoid, the dramatic -antisocial narcissistic, borderline, the fearful-obsessive compulsive, avoidant, dependant and the unstable and many more . . .

However, most likely only Viktor Frankl was right. An inmate of Auschwitz who decided that to survive man has to have meaning and that there are only two types of people, decent people and unprincipled people.

Personality Typography

So there are two types of people decent people and those with no principles. There is no telling the difference when you meet them until they run into you.

Hidden Personality Typography

There are those who present as ill who are hiding crooked thinking and want to be a wolf among the sheep, ready to take everything they can.

And there are those who cannot give much because they are so needy and can't work to live or give anything back.

But there are also those who are unwell and make mistakes because of their illness which brings trouble to their door with almost everyone.

Anyone would think it was obvious which type a person belongs to but not even the quickest most experienced person gets them right.

Another Way of Looking at It

Sometimes it's better to avoid the intellectual and see things in emotional and physical ways. Things can be seen in other ways by refusing to see them as others expect you to or as you think you should. Look in a mirror or at their feet. Look at the breathlessness and see what comes in its silence.

How We Finish

Our last year or two say more about us than all the rest before. We also carry the heaviest burden of all our life. We are under more scrutiny from others and ourselves than ever before, right until the end.

Ignore Logic

Seeing someone's problems and solutions are not always best looked at with the mind. Seeing them visually, seeing them in patterns of growth and decay in circles of becoming.

Hearing them instead of seeing them, let them walk on you then you on them. Is there a difference in your step, in your intention?

Mental Blocks

Mental confusion is being blocked by the effects of too much coming in.
Mental constipation is being blocked by the effects of not letting go.
Mental coldness is being blocked by the effects of being frozen with fear.
Mental health problems could be a result of any or all three.

Judgement

How we are judged like justice itself is not fair. How we are judged like justice may not be truth. We are judged for what we appear to have done not what was hidden. We are not judged for what we are but for what we leave.

Competition

Near the very top is where most fall. The top is where no one falls.

Weight

How thin and how fat we become are for different reasons.
Fat is rarely due to illness or drugs, just the habit. Thin is
frequently due to illness, drugs or poverty.

If you don't eat you will lose weight so our main problem is
not malnutrition but habits and wealth.

Doing the Wrong Thing

How do you know if you are doing the wrong thing?
You always know it but don't act on it until it makes you too
unhappy.

Doing the Right Thing

When do you know if you are doing the right thing? You
always know until you find yourself unhappy because you
are not doing it.

Mental Stamina

We can walk until we are dead, that's the power of our head.

Off Mode

The body likes being lazy sometimes. The mind is less
willing to be lazy sometimes. That's when fuses blow and
candles should glow.

Evaluation

Why do you evaluate a day when it's over? When it's gone, it's gone forever, so why evaluate it after and not at the time.

Differently the Same

In trying to look the same, we always look different. In trying to look different, we always look the same.

Rules

Rules are guide lines for those who need guidance but for others they are a nuisance.
Rules are sometimes there to stop some behaving as fools.
Rules are sometimes there to stop other types from becoming elitist.
Rules are there to guide, to boundary and to protect.

Snaking Along

We move through life like snakes snaking through this, wriggling away from that, hissing at some, lazing in the sun, biting at others and swallowing our prey whole.

Epitaphs

Been this way, had a say, now away. Transformed into stillness forever.

467

No News is Better News

The mind is fascinated by the dreadful things we do. That is why the news is full of negativity about man. The mind is not fascinated by compassion or kindness because it is so conditioned by the news. He or she in the media who makes the news sometimes makes it from what is not real. They can disguise selling their power, their protection and goods they want you to buy. If you choose not to watch news, you will see it everywhere on the street and in others trying to find you. Not looking further than yourself cancels the negativity and exposes happiness inside.

Life

I can just stay here and grow old, that's all I can do. However there are many things I can be.

Weather

The weather can change us just like a tired parent coming home or the angry dog in our way.

The weather is everything from our enemy to our friend and is always around even at the end.

More powerful than any weather is your attitude to weather, not letting it get inside you.

It is outside us, desperate to get in like we are hunted by it. That's the only separation between us and weather.

Our News

As the media becomes more individualised, we will
be sharing news with each other which will be our
interpretation and not what a journalist has reported as their
interpretation.

Was delivery of news by a pigeon better before? Have we
become so distracted by news of others that we have lost
focus on the integrity of our own life?

Who is Interested

Who is interested in you, not because of your job, not
because of what you have, but interested in you for just you?

You should be interested in you, but only in what you must
do. No one needs to be interested in you, only you.

Hoping for Sleep

No more thought tonight please. My overused mind needs
some switched off time.

Darkness with closed eyes in a room on a summer lit night,
trying to shut the door tight on thinking tonight.

Let's see what the night brings. Maybe no thoughts, only
dreams about people.

With or Without Thoughts

Do thoughts really have a function? Have they helped us to survive or hastened our destruction? We can't conclude yet.

Would we be better off with or without them? Would we be happier with or without them? This is where it is clearer.

Thinking makes us unhappy. Not thinking gives us the peace of stillness, more time for consciousness of happiness.

Thought Greed

Sitting still or walking, thoughts come and we explore a subject from all sorts of directions, then the whole subject is forgotten.

Like all things we consider like this, they are all forgotten, so what function do they serve? Is the mind's appetite for thinking thought greed? To feed the ego?

Unification

Why can I understand thoughts and having no thoughts, especially words? But visually I am like a blind person unable to conjure up images.

Someone else can only imagine visually but not words. Others can only imagine sounds but not words. How do we communicate these when we meet?

Thoughts and Being

Thinking less plus being still is happiness is the most important equation.

80. RELIGION

Hidden Women

In Islam the Hijab is worn which keeps women hidden but
in other's religions the women can be as difficult to find.
The women in other religions are not hidden but forbidden,
degraded by the men's immediate masculinity in their
voices.

What is exquisitely hidden is preserved by a few who have
learnt a secret dance to dodge the masculine at every chance.

The Pearl Within

During life you can pick up all sorts of things. Religion used
to be common now it is more common to pick up diseases,
drink and drugs.

An alternative is diving like a deep sea diver but inwards to
find and pick up the inner pearl.

Searching for Happiness

Happiness is everyone's main desire and our search for it has
turned away from religion and more towards psychology
but psychology is limited to the study of thinking and
behaviour. It is not competent to look at the inner self. The
only place to search for lasting happiness is to turn inside.

The Best

The best songs are about what we can't see. The best songs are about nothing to do with things. The best songs are about what's inside us. The best songs are about what we see as our self in others. The best songs are about what we see in our self as God.

Religion

Wandering around the market stalls, products are for sale but the traditional stalls sell so much that they are no longer manned. Selling their products like self-help books by mail order, no human touch is required.

The other stalls sell more unusual products maned by individual loud sellers who want to expand so their stalls too will no longer have to be manned.

There is a place where there are no stalls, nothing there is for sale. It only has one authentic thing, which is in the inner room.

Holy Men

The holy part of us can't be holy all the time. We must get clean, exercise and eat. But it's only through being holy that the spiritual in us can exist.

For Sale

Religion is for those who see the word as God, spirituality is for those who see what comes before the word as God.

Religion is for those who can put it in a book, spirituality is for those who know it can't be written.

Religion is for those who like security, spirituality is for those whose security is surrender of everything.

Religion is for those who want others to be like them, spirituality is for those who have no wants.

Religion is for those who want to have power in the world, spirituality if for those whose world is inside.

Religion is for those who want their religion to be displayed, spirituality is for those who don't want to be seen.

Inner Life

There used to be pilgrimages to the inner life to connect with what we believed. A journey with fellow pilgrims. A journey inwards to the truth we each perceived. We had retreats into the inner life and into ourselves. We left the business of life and with fellow inward travellers we dived into the inner self.

Here and There

Religion keeps you thinking there is a better place.
Spirituality shows you that you are already there, which is
here right now.

No Religion

The Buddha's, the crucifixes, the Natarajan's have gone, the
incense the candles, the beads and the gong, the Quran the
Sutras, the Bible's gone too with no Tanakh or Vedas, all
that's left is you.

81. SPIRITUALITY

Apparent Duality

Although the point of life is being fully conscious, just like being holy, you can't be holy all the time.

Full consciousness once seen cannot be lost but other things have to happen which appear to eclipse it. Like the sun eclipsed by the moon, the sun is there partly in the shade. Full consciousness is only appreciated because of its apparent opposite.

The Last Things

The only writing or singing whose meaning lasts as long as man, are those of the spirit. The last verse will be of the stars. The last song will be a hymn. The last sound will be silence.

Satsang

People on nothing but their own self, not on any high.
Not on knowledge or ignorance but on the removal of both.

The Spirit Inside

The Spirit inside is not the mind. Its strength more than the mind could ever find.

Complimenting Everything

Once your path has begun, you can't go anywhere except from suffering to happiness.

Once your path has begun, because everywhere without it is misery, you cannot leave it.

Once your path has begun, you have surrendered and there is no longer anyone to save you from being devoured.

Once your path has begun, it compliments everything and the path is everything.

Pathless

She had her time in the world. It was short because she found a secret path which rescued her from the world. At first she couldn't let go of the world because she thought responsibilities would suffer. Then, when she could see her responsibilities were not in her control, she let go of the world. Now the path looks after and is her. Could this be you?

First Step

Unbeknown to anyone who chooses a spiritual path, everything changes forever, and you are gone.

What is it that Remains?

At the end of each day, reflection reveals thoughts which pass but consciousness remains.

Rooms

There are different rooms which suit people at different levels of attainment. Those with little aspirations of the world have simple small happy rooms. Those who want style and grandeur usually get complicated large unhappy rooms.

Simplification

I no longer care. I no longer stare. I no longer dare. I can see there is more to see than I see. I want the time remaining to be mine so I can appreciate my time. This is my only wealth.

Wrong Spirits

How could you like the drunk who is always in good cheer but not in good spirits? How could you like the drunk who gives you money but criticises those who control you. How could you like the drunk who is not angry except with all the people who lock him up? How could you like the drunk who is always relaxing, not concerned with the practicalities of pain?

Return

Stop Travelling. Give up the search to find anything. Stop travelling everywhere to find happiness which is not out there, because you always have to come back to yourself to find lasting happiness.

Cups

The cup you drink from can be anything but sometimes we forget that it nourishes what we think, then what we say and then what we do.

There are cups we can drink from which nurture our attitude, our stance in life, how we are in everything.

Then there are cups we drink from which change every one of our days because what we drink is from the cup of grace.

Padres

When the last padre has gone from the armed forces they will be lame with lack of strength. It is not religion which they offer but a perspective when others don't work.

The surrender needed in going to see one results from doctors, psychiatrists and counsellors unable to help and is the first step away from the outer world of blind authority into the inner world of command.

Fire Extinguisher

When thoughts sustaining the ego stop, there is no fire extinguisher for the light of stillness, no fire extinguisher for the light of surrender.

Planes

What is left apart from the ash, molecules of carbon in the air? Or is something else on another plane somewhere?

Unaware

Consciousness of today is all we have but the many thoughts are memories or dreams obscuring consciousness of today.

Searching in Secret Words

In trying to be civilised, man has ordered all the things outside but he has moved so far away from inside, his soul has nearly died.

How do you get back inside a place you've rarely been. A friend says it's not unknown but secret words can be seen.

There are many words, texts of instructions and advice but most have to be with holy men to see inside and look.

480

Spirituality

The most liberating principle of consciousness which makes you happy is freedom from religion. It can be anything you see it as so long as, it's what you see it as.

It can be 'Know the self' or 'Be still' or 'The kingdom of God is within' or 'To thine own self be true.'

When you choose, you have to look within to choose yourself and be still.

Anti-attractive

Man is attracted to complexity not simplicity, to thinking rather than being still. to the future not the present, to distractions rather than non-attachment, to mystery not truth. In essence, simply be still now, non-attached, true to the self.

To Keep a Gift

When you see something which is a gift, to charge others is to see it as a business.

What you have seen in yourself can only last if it is passed on for no fee.

What you have to give can only be passed on if it is given free or it ceases to be.

Sight

Gurus come in all shapes and sizes. Some will suit you and some will suit you until you see your short-sightedness.

Their purpose is for you to make them become redundant when their task is done.

They have a function which needs accomplishing in you, so you can use your full sight to see the guru is you.

Extension Everywhere

When you are fully conscious, the Guru can go. When you are fully conscious, God can go but then you see they are only the self in you, a family of an extended you everywhere.

Guru

It is good to hear someone on a spiritual path just as long as someone else is not just having a laugh.

False Gurus

When you see that which shows the spirit in us all, passing it on for a fee is business and without exception, it ceases to be.

Spiritual Guidance

Asking for anything in exchange for spiritual guidance is fake.

Spiritual guidance can only be given freely or it is a business and is fake.

Spiritual guidance can never be promoted. There is only an attraction to it or it is fake.

Spiritual guidance does not work using the mind but deeper inside or it is fake.

Spiritual guidance is not a single thing. It can be everything or it is fake.

Spiritual guidance encourages supreme effort, complete surrender and stillness or it is fake.

Gurus

The Guru has no more knowledge than you, only less ignorance. The guru can't see you better than you, but he is a mirror of what is inside you. The Guru can't remove your ignorance, only tell you how to remove it. The Guru can't show you yourself, you have to look inside. The Guru may do everything by doing nothing. The Guru may communicate everything by saying nothing. The guru is the help you want to be yourself. The guru is only the truth in you.

What Lies Beneath

Between sunrises and sunsets, battles, plants and animals seem to come and go but below the earth remains still. Ships delivering their cargos capsize and passengers see storms which seem in charge of the air but below the sea remains still. Comedy, horror, crime and romantic tragedies entertain us on film but below the movie screen remains still. Waking, dreaming, memories, people places and things appear real but below the self remains still.

Beyond the Stars

If you are going to go for a walk, leave everyone else behind, including the dog. Walk free, open to anything, to experiences sudden revelations, happy or sad, good or bad. Don't take the dog, walk without another. Think of what you are here for. In daylight try and see the stars beyond the clouds, yourself before everything else. Perhaps that alone exists.

Humble

Humility is not thinking, speaking or writing but accepting it is from somewhere else, given to you and putting this first.

Humility is knowing there is nothing you can say, nowhere else to go, nothing to do, nothing to be.

Humility is being the lowest not in competition but in service to the greater. Humility is acceptance of what you are and being still with that.

Humility and Insignificance

Insignificance and humility are relations, the difference only seen by a keen eye.

Insignificance is felt as lack of an ego. Humility is felt as a happiness of the heart.

But when seen by someone with a closed eye and heart, humility can be seen as lack of success and insignificance as simply comparison.

Concerned Sight

We don't know anything, god included, the nature of the universe, life or even our self. We are mostly deluded and cannot see ourselves even in the brightest light. We do not see what we do or have done as we have such poor sight. There are no excuses for our lack of concern about what we are here for and what we have learned.

Stepping Stones

Stepping stones are there to get across, there to be remembered, left there for others to cross. Rafts for crossing rivers shouldn't be carried on our backs. Not letting go of painful memories lets our mind start showing cracks. Stepping stones can't be taken with you like mementoes to collect; they have to be left for others to connect.

485

Why Can't Some People Meditate?

Why can't some people meditate is because they don't know that they haven't asked how to. Why can't some people meditate is because they don't know the person to ask. Why can't some people meditate is because they don't know they don't know. Why can't some people meditate is because they don't know they are not meant to. Why can't some people meditate is because they don't know they can't. Why can't some people meditate is because they don't know there isn't a way to. Why can't some people meditate is because they don't know there is no one to meditate.

82. ATTAINMENT

Attainment

When you are yourself there is nothing to attain.

All

Our understanding has an end beyond which it can not go because there is nothing to understand, only putting it into practice.

Stop looking

Stop looking for what you have as you can't find what you have. Stop looking for what you haven't lost as you cant find what you haven't lost.

Sound of the Self

Silence is the sound of the self, something that happens inside you when you have let thoughts go.

83. BEING THANKFUL

Thankful Either Way

Who will teach you the most this week and are you humble enough to be open to learn. Will it be the kindest person or the meanest and will you be thankful either way.

Being Within

Seeing what the inner world of our own self is like changes out attitude to the outer world. We become thankful that our inner happiness can change our attitude to everything.

Respecting

I don't hope for a good week or try to work out how to make it good. Whatever circumstances I find myself in, no matter what happens, I will be polite to everyone; my manners will be as good as I can make them. I will be kind and be thankful that I'm not the person I am having to help.

Time to say Thanks

To everyone who has ever given me a book, thank you. To everyone who has taught me freely, thank you. To everyone who gave me a chance, thank you. To all those who did the reverse, thank you more for making me stronger.

Experimenting

Thanking the cause of our distress seems like an error of thinking because gratitude may not be what we think it is but the opposite.

Yes, maybe it seems like an error of thinking to thank the cause of our distress, but thinking can be wrong.

If so, then we can rely and trust on a part of us that comes before thinking.

Ok, so actually just have a go and try it once and see if it works. See if your attitude seems changed if you thank those causing you a problem.

Thank You

Saying thank you for this even if it seems painful changes it into a gift like nothing else can. Saying thank you makes things right, by turning darkness into light by showing us what was hidden in us and others. Saying thank you shows us lessons only learnt one way, understanding other ways. Saying thank you lets us grow in ways we didn't know, letting us move on when we are stuck. Saying thank you releases us when we feel trapped, showing us how to move on to the next stage. Saying thank you turns mistakes into opportunities, losses into gains, problems into solutions. Saying thank you shows if we can fix what is broken and shows how to make the past good in the future.

Keeping Our Self Clean

Keeping ourselves in reasonable condition means keeping ourselves free from as much negative as we can clean out.

Keeping our selves clean is sometimes all we can do when someone is doing something we don't like.

We can't do anything about where we don't live, except be thankful as we can only keep our own place clean.

Respect for Strangers

Treat friends with love but strangers with extreme respect and thankfulness as you don't know how you will meet them next. A stranger you meet can be a tramp, a king, a relative, your healer or your nemesis.

Eternal Thanks

If this is the last thing I write, I am thankful for being able to write and to write this. I am thankful to nature, to life, to truth, to all I could never see.

Preserving the Thread to Pass On

We are lucky to have so little, so there is little to worry about losing. We are most lucky to have the intangible to pass on, which needs the energy of every breath to preserve.

Love Those

Thank all of those who gossip about you, especially those who try and pick a fight with you. Be particularly kind to those who criticise you behind your back.

Most of all have the deepest thanks for those who try and annihilate you with rumours and lies. These are the friends of justice and truth in the end.

Illogical Perfect Solution

When you are under pressure. When you are in a difficult situation. When you are cannot find a solution, say thank you and be thankful for it.

Being thankful for difficulty helps you accept the problem is showing you something.

When you are aware the problem is trying to show you something, you can stop trying to control it and only then can it disclose its message.

Saying Our Thanks

Expressions of thanks to a God with or without hope or wish are to yourself.

A New Day

Nothing is as good as seeing the early morning sun, not simply because you are alive but because you are saying hello not goodbye to a day.

The Best We Can Be

When we look back on life and think that didn't go like everyone else's, maybe it was because it was perfect.

Still Grateful

We are not grumpy but we are old men and women who don't criticise or complain. We are just thankful in our life we don't have to moan ever again.

We are thankful whilst we stand and watch life's lessons learnt by the child we once were, that we can still remember, stand and can see.

Being Thankful for Us

I remember when I have not been thankful more than when I have been, because something is missing from me. I am incomplete. There is a compulsion to go back and say thank you, so that I am complete because being thankful is for our own self first.

Familiarity

Perhaps we have hobbies like writing because our day jobs are repetitive. There are a limited number of ways you can express the same knowledge and skills you learn at college.

On automatic pilot for years, monotony has to be broken up like the day or it can creep in like weeds into the most beautiful garden.

Old areas of gardens cleaned and replanted with seeds may bear fruit or even flowers. These beautiful same fruit or flowers just like us will not be seen again.

Eternal

Trying to be immortal cannot be, as there is no one to be immortal because what we are is eternal not immortal.

Us First

Thankfulness is not for someone else; it is for us. We show that we are thankful, that something has made us feel good but showing thankfulness is secondary to us experiencing it.

Showing our thankfulness might make someone else feel good but the primary person who should feel good is us. It is easier to be thankful for receiving than for giving but both are done for us first.

Being Thankful for Opposition

Why do we ask questions which we will never be able to answer? Is raising the question raising consciousness or do we live hoping for all answers? It is probably best we don't have the answers to some questions, like suffering and death, as our strengths could be weakened.

Like many things in nature, we are stronger for being opposed and would be weaker like a tree if there were no strong winds threatening us. Perhaps like a tree is thankful for the wind, we should be thankful for what opposes us in others and in ourselves.

Being Thankful for Nothing

Sometimes we have to try hard to be thankful. The harder it is, the more thankful we usually are for seeing what it took from us. Thankfulness can be for what someone gives us and sometimes for what they don't give us, didn't give us, or couldn't or wouldn't give us.

Our Best Teachers show abuse

So many people respect other people it is wonderful to see but just like in the rest of the animal kingdom, there are those who don't respect but abuse.

Challenging to the last moment, they can show us our weakest points, so we can strengthen them for the next time. So we should thank them; they are our best teachers.

84. PATHS

Eventuality

We don't see this until we have searched everywhere, then suddenly we see where else could we be except at home, already on our own path.

Mistrusting Security

Even though my parents struggled and I was shown the importance of the material in life, materially I didn't go down that path. I didn't trust the insecurity security gave me, so I have and I am with my self. There are no words for the only thing I have which is stillness.

The Means are Actually the End

With increasing knowledge of the world and stars by the best microscopes and telescopes we know less of our self as there is one place we don't look. Consciousness which above all else we claim to have, we cast aside like a tool.

We think the destination is more important than the journey, knowledge not consciousness the aim. Just as we don't see the path and journey are the actual destination, consciousness is what we are, not what we can become. The means are the end result, which ends all searching.

When Distractions are Gone

Your thoughts can lead you up or down paths to interesting places but you will always come back to just consciousness, as it is what you are.

Final Path

Our whole life is finding our way by separation, finding our way separating from others. The womb, parents, then family and friends until we reach the final path, still on our own.

Our Path

If we keep looking, we see all paths lead to the same final path which is the path of happiness found in stillness. Whether in solitude or with others, we find it on our own.

Non-Inevitability

When it is your turn, it is different because it is you and you lose your detachment and get immersed in the challenge. The non-inevitability dominates everything, some things mean less, some people more. You seem on a different track, even though the path and pace are exactly the same.

85. SUFFERING

Suffering The Road to Happiness

How do you realise happiness is inside? You only know if
the world has shown you naked suffering which it cannot
ever make up. Then the only place of happiness is found
inside.

Inside Happiness

People who think they are perfectly happy don't need to
follow the path inside to find happiness. Only those who
have suffered want to be happy inside because they have
seen what the outer world happiness is like.

Authentic

Suffering for our self goes on with no alternative because the
alternative is not to be authentic.

Being Stillness

To surrender is not to anything other than what we see as the
heart, truth, stillness.

To surrender is not to words or images of the intellect but to
being still.

Kindness

When kindness is not present it is time for extensive looking. Why has all the pain hit so hard that it takes away kindness to the self and others?

The Strength of Letting Go

We try to determine our fate by trying to control everything we think we can but the more we try and control the less control we see we have. The less we try and control, the less fear we have of losing control and only then do we feel secure in trusting the fate of everything.

We Don't Know

When we think we have chosen the wrong thing to do in our lives, sometimes it is because unbeknown to us, we have chosen it as we need to learn from it. It may be showing us what we need to move away from or it may be shining a light on where to go. It may just be introducing us to people or places where we will be happy. We do not know.

86. TURNING INSIDE

Only This

There are journeys and places I remember but there is one journey which cannot be compared, one place which is the best. That first turn inwards when the light inside went on is the journey I've been on ever since, always turning inside no matter what. No other place exists anymore, nothing more exists. There is only this.

What Appears Different

There are different ways to turn inside but suffering is the beginning, meditation and solitude are the middle, stillness is the same at the beginning, middle and end.

Agendas

Often when we read to find out about a story we are looking for our story. We don't know we are not reading but looking for a mirror.

Turning Back In

We return to our centre no matter where we go, to stillness which we have lost, to happiness which we have lost. The business of the world lets us go as we let go of it, to return to where we have been all the time.

Final Common Pathway

There is no single formula which works for turning inside but whichever way we get there, this is always the end of the path.

Eventually we see we have been shown the way so far by someone who has also been this far. But this is as far as they can take us as we have to do the rest on our own, keeping on turning within to contact our inner self.

87. KNOWLEDGE

What we know

Probably all we know is that we don't know what we don't know.

Disconnected Elite

Words of knowledge not shared keep power in their hands and their hearts disconnected.

Heart on Sleeve

How can I be personal about me when I have already revealed it all. There is nothing left to show that is not you as well.

Knowledge

Knowledge can be stored as numbers, drawing, paintings, on paper, cardboard, wood, canvas, written by the smoke trail of a plane or even electronically and sent anywhere. Consciousness cannot be stored.

Only Being helps Being

Knowledge of being conscious does not help being
conscious. Only being conscious helps being conscious.

The Best Present

Of all the presents we can give, showing someone the way
inside is the greatest. It is not material things, legacies of
possessions but opening the door to the inner treasure.

Strange How

Only through solitude you learn how to be with others.
Only Through silence you learn how to communicate. Only
through stillness you learn how to move. Only through being
you learn to know. Only through knowing you learn to be.

88. SIMPLICITY HUMILITY

Homeless

The high priest may have more ignorance than the homeless. The Queen may have less happiness than the homeless. The landowner may give less than the homeless. The judge may have less honesty than the homeless.

The homeless are their own self. It is all they are and all they have to give. They cant give what they don't have and don't pretend what they are.

Death of Arrogance

Being more in control of our work, our health and life opens a door to let us be as happy as we can be. More autonomy lets us see how much we are interdependent on each other. We know we are not as important in matters of the world, which can carry on without us. We see we do not have as much influence as we believed and that our humility determines our humanity.

89. CONSCIOUSNESS

Seeing What we Are Without Ignorance

Thought is the gift we have to show us our ignorance.
Consciousness is what we are with our ignorance removed.

Awkward Strange Foreigner

Just like a bodybuilders muscles are only good for the world
of body building, our brain is best suited to the world of the
intellect. We spend so much time thinking about being the
self, so little time being the self that the self seems awkward.

Consciousness is being still but we have restricted just
being still so much that stillness seems an awkward strange
foreigner.

Consciousness and Thinking

The input of our senses is received, assessed and processed
by the mind. We then conclude and believe this is what we
are, a collection of particular thoughts.

Whereas consciousness is existence and happiness which the
mind cant explain in words, consciousness sees the limits of
the mind as consciousness is what we are.

Hallucinating what we Are

Only at the beginning and end of a day do we remember we too began and will end. Thinking hides what we only hallucinate. We see, hear, touch feel our world of the senses, then imagine we are the organ which senses these, failing to see what is conscious of the sensor and all that it sensed.

Conscious of That

Man's most difficult challenge is to accept the point of life is life, not what he thinks comes after it. Being conscious of that, all knowledge becomes secondary.

Consciousness is Stillness

Everything in the universe moves except for stillness. The only thing we need to be aware of is our stillness because consciousness is stillness.

First Things First

It was perhaps an error to assume the importance of the unconscious before looking at consciousness first. Like trying to get to another planet to find a new one to colonise when we have not understood this one. We do not understand and accept what we have not yet understood, so we could be more conscious.

Last Word on Consciousness

Consciousness is not about being responsive to our surroundings which can be measured by others because you can choose not to respond or not. If you choose not to, it can be mistaken for not being conscious.

If consciousness can't be measured or defined by words, perhaps acceptance is the best way of dealing with our self.

Consciousness is life

You can think about consciousness a lot as it misleads us. Consciousness is the gift of what we are.

It is not about thinking or thoughts. Thoughts are not life. Consciousness is life.

Consciousness and Thoughts

You are not your body. You are not your thoughts. You are taught, conditioned and programmed to believe you are a bundle of thoughts called the ego.

You are not just a bundle of thoughts. You have consciousness which is not a thought. Consciousness can make you think but you are not your thoughts; you are consciousness.

All There Is

Days are powerful. They repeatedly show us consciousness which some like me are concerned with. So much so, it seems consciousness is all there is.

We Are The Same But Differently so

We are all the same consciousness but with different levels of consciousness of who we are.

What We Are Not

It is important to know what we are but much more important to know what we are not. We are not a collection of thoughts we call the ego. It is just a collection of thoughts. We are not the ego with its past memories and future dreams. All we are is consciousness.

We Are Not Our Thoughts

Thought comes from consciousness and cannot exist without consciousness but consciousness exists without thought.

You Are Not Your Thoughts

Thoughts are a creation of consciousness, so consciousness cannot be understood by thoughts as thoughts are the servants of consciousness.

Unforeseen Long Term Companions

We all travelled together all working, skiving and relaxing trying to make the most of what we chose from what was in front of us. We all travel together not knowing we are companions, not just for a while but for all the time, eternity.

Walking the Talk

Books can't show you how to do what you know, because knowing is not being. So many can talk the talk but almost none can walk the walk.

Consciousness

So I am gone where am I? Into the organic atmosphere of the universe or on some other plane of existence of consciousness. Why would that be? What's the need for more than one journey? Why have a graded hierarchical system of being conscious?

The State of Being

Consciousness is our self. Being conscious of our existence is consciousness. The self we are is consciousness. We are consciousness and nothing else

Being is alive. Consciousness is awareness of being. Not being conscious is being unaware.

Consciousness and Knowledge

Consciousness can understand all knowledge. Knowledge cannot understand consciousness. Consciousness is a state of being. Knowledge is information.

Knowing and Being

Books can show you information which increases knowledge. They can show you information about the self, which increases knowledge of the self. But your information and knowledge of the self are not being the self.

The Ceiling to Thinking

Thinking doesn't have the capability of seeing beyond itself. It cannot be what consciousness is, which is consciousness. Machines can be shown how to think but they cannot be shown how to be conscious because consciousness is not a process.

All The Time

We cant be conscious all the time. We cant be holy all the time. We cant concentrate all the time unless we are transformed. If we are transformed back to full consciousness before our conditioning by removing it, we can be conscious all the time.

Total Significance

There is no other thing more important than the inner self. It has to be the most important of all things. It needs to be constantly the basis of our consciousness, the basis of our being and happiness.

Mystery of Truth

Reality seems to come and go in our changing consciousness but it doesn't because it is always here. Reality and truth are our great mystery. We think about them the most but the more we think about them the less we are in touch with them.

Precious Time

When I want to sleep, sometimes I cant and just think, so I've learned to do what I'm told. I sit up and see what is here. Sometimes I have to sit up and write. Sometimes I have to meditate or just be still, then I reflect and see if I am right. They are all the same.

All We Can Be

Each appointed time arrives. Seen or unseen the appointment moves to be present, then is gone.

There is no control, only being conscious of the present. Its arrival, presence and passing is all we can be to do anything.

Our Inner Nature, Our Master

In this the place where the presence of your master is felt? Do you ask how this comes about here? Why here to you now?

Don't avoid asking if the presence of the master comes from your desire to find your own inner master, to find him in your self.

If you can bring him up in your self as your self this is the greatest gift you can ever have, as the presence of the inner master is our very nature.

Light Within

I am fully aware I have spent my life focusing from the inside on the inside. My investments have been inside of unseen value.

I can only see by holding a thread made of light which gets brighter the longer I stay. It is passed on because you have to hold it in your self.

In the Dark

Growth takes place mostly unseen and like a seed growing, it takes place unknown in the dark. Growth cannot be forced. It cannot be made to happen faster. It cannot be slowed down. Growth is not fate. It is not nature but something resulting from both.

Futility

I do not understand how and why we wake, sleep, work or live. No one has given an answer to any of these which is acceptable. Perhaps the answer is not to ask the question after one attempt to answer it. Any answer becomes less important, then it is seen as futile.

To Be, Stop

The only sensible thing is to stop everything, offer the ego to be crushed and be what is left.

Equality

The sensitivity with which we defend a baby should apply to all.
The tenderness with which we handle a baby should apply to all.
The care which we plan for a baby should apply to all.
To apply this to all has to be applied to our self first.

Our State of Being

Consciousness can understand all knowledge but knowledge cannot understand consciousness. Consciousness is a state of being, whereas knowledge is information. Consciousness is our self. Being conscious of our existence is consciousness.

Repeatedly Awakening Now

Sometimes twenty or thirty years can be re-experienced in a few hours which is no dream but another awakening now, showing more.

Psychological Decompression

Working days are overfilled with work so much that there is no time to rest and recharge. There is only time to psychologically decompress in the car but this is not rest, only a necessary thing to deal with work.

The days off feel like full days which are so full they are almost bursting. Sleep comes without any effort, then the days are repeated in fullness.

Learning to Be

How do I lose sight of me inside? How do I let everything take me over? How come I let myself drown in the world, forgetting who I am?

I am human and make errors repeatedly and stopping repeating them is not automatic just because of knowledge of them. It is being the same.

Too Much Information

Access to vast amounts of information does not help us become better people. It does not help us become what we are. Encyclopaedic knowledge does not fulfil us to become our full potential.

If we try and stick with what works, what is in front of us, what is inside us, it is more valuable than all the vast information because we are the only thing which helps us be our self.

Piper of Our Heart

Our nose is our best friend in meditation. It is an organ of sound, the piper of our hearts breath.

Special Places Inside

We think special places are somewhere else but we always find them inside, seeing they are always our self.

Meditation

Stopping thoughts so there is stillness is being conscious of that stillness, which is happiness.

Happiness Inside

Happiness is what we all want. Happiness is what we are, our nature but we seem to have lost it.

But if we haven't lost it, it's just we can't see it because it has become hidden inside us.

Seeing it is inside, there is only one way of getting it, going inside by turning inside.

Stillness Can't be Pursued

Stillness cannot be pursued. It happens when thoughts have stopped, so giving up the thought of wanting stillness must be given up.

Silence the Sound of the Self

Silence is not something you aim for, it is something that happens inside you when you have let thoughts go. It is the sound of the self.

Solitude Inside

Solitude is not a choice made without seeing suffering. When suffering is experienced, the only thing to do is to not embrace it but to detach and surrender to what is inside.

Detachment Inside

Detachment is not a thought and idea which you can be because you want to. It is where you go inside when you have had enough pain.

Perfect Mantra

The nose is the best mantra because it makes a noise when you breath which tethers your thinking to stillness.

Wordless Mantra

I never really gave my nose much attention or even a second thought until I found out another use for it. When I keep on getting distracted by thoughts the high pitched buzzing of my tinnitus, I focus on one sound. It's the sound of the movement of air through my nose. It is the wordless mantra. It tethers my thoughts back to stillness.

When thoughts are tethered like a goat to a post, they cannot wander, no damage is done and there is solitude to enjoy the stillness.

Stillness Rules All

Looking out and everything is still with nothing moving is rare. No wind, no branches moving, no birds singing. It is respect for the darkest hour before dawn, when stillness unknown to most rules all.

Back to Full Consciousness

If consciousness is all there is, we are in a lot of trouble. Because we are not conscious of this, the ego of thoughts has taken over.

How do we get consciousness back? Only by having too much pain from suffering. Yes, only through suffering do we desire the pain free state, leaving us conscious again of the happiness of no want.

We are Like a blank piece of paper

We have a lot of sensory input from our body organs to our brain, which the brain can make us conscious of or not. The brain as an organ sends its own input of signals as thoughts to itself which the brain can make us conscious of or not.

We can be conscious of the bodily senses and thoughts. Without them we have consciousness alone like a blank piece of paper. But the body senses and thoughts greedily overpower the blank paper and take away the perfect peace of the blank paper.

The blank paper has no sensory input and no thoughts. It is none other than our true nature of perfect happiness which we have as our consciousness.

We Are the Same But Different

We are all the same consciousness but with different levels of consciousness of what we are.

Presence of Consciousness

The sacred place gives me a message. Over the years it is the same. I didn't hear the mountain at first. Not for a long time. Its language is not silence. It is stillness. Its stillness is not telling me, not showing me. It is just its presence.

Only Consciousness

Sequential logical thinking creates the concept of time. By memory and imagination thinking concretises the past and future as concepts, so the past and future are inventions of thinking.

But past and future can only stand in the present so only the present exists. But even the present is created by thinking, so only consciousness exists without thinking.

We create and hold on to the universe as a concept with time as the creator and destroyer and if we do not see ourselves as spirit we are then subject to the future and the fear that time creates.

Then our whole life tries to fight against time, whose inevitable consequences we try to avoid. Instead of continuing the battle against time we can drop the useless weapon of thought. We are then bodiless, hallucinating the world no more, existing only as consciousness.

An Inconvenient Acceptance

Consciousness in all its forms of waking, sleeping or dreaming cannot be understood by the mind but by what we truly are.

What we truly are is not accepted as known, so the unknown is also part of what we truly are.

We can go on an endless search with the mind or we can accept that we cannot know what we are. Accepting this we have to just be what we are. Accepting what we are and being what we are is everything that man can be. A dynamic combination of opposites, known and unknown. A contradiction forever in a living moving struggle.

Opening Consciousness

Opening a door of consciousness is not necessarily by knowledge; it can be by desire. Desire for happiness, a refuge away from what this world is like. No courses to do, no money to pay no religion too. All that is needed is to look inside you.

Unmaterial

How can we be of the material when nothing adds or subtracts from us. We cannot go beyond consciousness.

We are Consciousness

We are consciousness from which thoughts arise but we are
not thoughts.

Thoughts arise from consciousness.
Thoughts are not conscious of consciousness but
consciousness is conscious of thoughts.

Thought comes from consciousness
Thought cannot exist without consciousness but
consciousness exists without thought.

Thoughts are a creation of consciousness, so consciousness
cannot be understood by thoughts as thoughts are the
servants of consciousness.

90. THE WORLD

The World

What you perceive as the world is your perception and is not
the world. There are seven billion versions of it which are
not the world. The stillness when you do not perceive, no
thoughts, is consciousness.

Returning Within

Others amass more land, more buildings, more investments
and I wonder if their dreams are free. Maybe they are more
free because of these things. My dreams seem to reflect who I
get involved with and are not about material things. Sharing
my journeys, paths, silent places, the eeriness of when chaos
seems to have gone, seem to be my world. They always bring
me home.

Imagine

Imagine toady is your last day of life. What do you need?
All you need is what you need for today. You can only be as
happy as you can be today.

91. GOD

Behindness

What a foolish thought to see God with a beard up in the sky, when all along everyone knows it's a lie.

What a terribly foolish thought to think God is not a woman. The only ones who believes this must be men.

What a terribly foolish thought to think you have another life. Those who want one haven't had enough pain in life.

What a terribly foolish thought to think you are your mind. You will remain forever behind.

With God on Our Side

The bad attack the good, the strong the weak, the rich the poor, the happy the sad, all in God's name.

No surprise because man cannot improve himself, or help himself and history cannot stop repeating itself in God's name.

The inconvenient truth, seen adjusting and compensating for it is better than attempting the impossible of trying to change our nature in God's name.

Same but different paths

When we see what inside us has been projected outside us as our image of god, we either surrender to what we project outside of us as god or to what is inside. Then we see they are the same.

92. GURU AND GOD

No Guru No God

The function of a guru is to not need them. The Guru helps you remove the darkness which is you think you don't need them. Only then can see without them that you don't need them. It was only them in you that helped you see. The function of a God is to not need him. God helps you remove the darkness which is you think you don't need God. Only then can see without them that you don't need them. It was only them in you that helped you see.

People Do

Prayers don't save people, people do. God doesn't save people, people do . God doesn't kill people, people do. God doesn't abuse people, people do. God doesn't choose people, people do. God doesn't punish people, people do. God doesn't poison the rivers and oceans, people do. God doesn't give you diseases, people do.

Do You Need a Therapist a Priest or a Guru?

The guru is the perfect mirror of yourself. The priest society's accepted messenger of God. The therapist the registered, regulated, insured solver of problems. The guru is the mirror. The priest is the message. The therapist is the solution. A mirror is not needed to see the message to solve a problem which doesn't exist.

93. I AM THAT

I am That

What I see is not what I am but that which sees I am

I am that I am

That thou art

Be still and know that I am God

The kingdom of God is within

Maybe suddenly you will see this.

94. REFUGE

First and Last Refuge

We are our own saviour. We can only protect ourselves
and not rely on outside forces. The inner self is the ultimate
refuge from all the suffering and torture the world can seem
to give us. The presence or the refuge never fails even if we
cry out that it has, as it is all we have that is always here.

Harbour Within

The one safe place which is our own, safe from everything
and everyone, safe from the past and what is going on now
is always here waiting. Life's temptations and difficulties let
us move further out to sea away from our harbour until our
harbour can't be seen and we don't seem to know how to get
back. We only have to turn inside.

95. LIVING IN THE PRESENT

The Present

All our yesterdays and tomorrows are taken care of if we live
in the present. To stay in the present we need to find out how
to let the past rest and just be the past.

Being After Understanding

Life is understanding that seeing all of life is understanding.
Understanding is seeing until seeing no more can be
understood. There is no more understanding, only being.

Over the Next Few Hours

The weather over the next few hours is as far as I go into the
future. Tomorrow and next week will be taken care of for us
all inside and out.

The Life of Your Time

Do you live in the present moment, conscious of the life of
your time, conscious of existing today? This is the exact time
or your life. The moment now is the only present time you
will ever experience.

Today's The Day

Why shouldn't today be the happiest you have ever been? Because happiness comes from inside. Yes, you create it. It is only up to you if you want to be your happiest ever.

Another Chance

You might want to look at this because you may not want one of your last thoughts to be, 'I wish I hadn't been so negative but more positive.'

With no knowledge of when that will be or if you will have that moment to reflect, it may be wise to start being positive now.

From Illusion to Today

Coming at me today is the unknown, the surprises which could leave me in a mess if I ignore the present.

Today is the only day I will ever have as the rest are an illusion to keep me from the present.

The Same Change

Being in every moment, beaming inside with fullness of happiness, even though it is raining, even though it is different, happiness inside is raining the same.

Critical Times

Critical times are always now. A critical time calls for completely focused critical action. Everything else is ditched to survive. All of life can seem critical, not a moment to waste on what is not necessary to survive fully conscious.

No Time

Seeing what was and what I went through all those years ago, I have gone through it again today because time is a great illusion, an invention of the mind.

Being Here

The present is being attentive now but only you can be present now. No one can give it to you as you have to be fully here not distracted.

Goodbye

The facial bones stand out now from the flesh. Nearly a full life shows, not a flicker of desire left as they say their last goodbye.

Inevitable

We hold some time in the future. Maybe it is an event, an age or even our death but we have something we think of there which we know is inevitable.

As Above So Below

There are layers to the sky, layers to the stars, layers of our consciousness; as above so below. Under the night sky this we always know.

Time

The apparent sense of being conscious of time passing is not the sense of passing time but consciousness of being.

Boomerang

You can offer all the things, all the experiences to explain everything. At the end you have to come back to yourself.

Bathing in the Light

The world has not changed as the plants and animals come and go struggling with each other to bath in the light.

Future Worrying

The future is not ours to worry about. It is a waste of energy worrying about the future. If we focus on what we are doing now, the future will always be sorted out. It is not ours.

96. HAPPINESS

Why We Are Here

What trace is left behind of why we are here? Offspring,
buildings, a painting, poems, books, records of others
people's memories of us. Were we happy and did we pass it
on, sharing it with someone to understand and to be happy.

No Want

When will I have what makes me happy? Asking the
question prevents looking at how happy you can be now.
The happiness of anything new only lasts until another
desire arises. Not accepting the futility of this encourages
endless pursuit.

Do you know of a person with no want? Have you ever
heard of a person with no want? Do you know what it is to
have no want? Seeing what they are, Kings and queens, the
powerful rich and famous are no match for the person with
the happiness of no want.

If you died today would you have had everything you want
for today? When will you look and see that today you have
everything you want; that there is nothing else you need?
When will tears of joy roll down your face. When will you
start laughing with how happy you are with the bliss of no
want.

Call Off the Search

Happiness is not complicated once it is experienced, the search can be called off as happiness can't be lost or found. It can be mistaken; it can be covered up; it can be ignored; it can be put second but happiness is always here wherever we go, everywhere. Where else could it be?

Stop Looking

If so many people look for happiness but almost none find it in their lifetime, we must be looking in the wrong places, so where is it to be found? In success, wealth or fame, friends, family, a lover, in security or in power? No. This leaves only one place to look and it's not what we are taught or teach our children . . . to turn and look inwards.

Surprise

The surprise answer to our greatest question . . . how can we find the real true meaning of our life and be happy, is that after much searching, we eventually see that we have had it all along. We are already the truth that we look for. We are reality just like everything and we have all the happiness we need. It is all inside.

Disappearance

In suffering, there is no escape only disappearance. The only desire is happiness which is only achieved by no thoughts. Disappearance is what we all want most.

Perfect Days

How could a day feel complete without thankfulness and without surrender to stillness? How could a day have meaning without being no one and without any purpose other than to be still? How could a day be full of happiness without any wants and without anything at all apart from stillness? How could any day in the future be possible without the happiness of today, without the stillness of today, without being aware of now?

The Only Time

When can we realise we have messed up what our ancestors gave us? When can we realise our ancestors were right? When can we improve what we do, what we are, not what we were, what we can be now? When we can detach; when we can be still we can be happy now.

Not Far from the Shore

There's an island not far from shore where people live who have enough. They have only what they want, which is all that they need. It's a place for the quiet, whose riches are intangible. There is just enough with nothing left over. Nothing is wasted and nothing is gained. There is no money or religion. There are no leaders. There is consciousness hidden from the outside world. The island is not as far from the shore as you think . . . it's just inside.

Days Off

A day off is not a rest day when everyone else is working because a serious sense of life appears. The traumas and deaths behind and not knowing what is ahead, fire the sense of purpose of today and tomorrow, allowing enjoyment of the day, just being happy today.

Expectations

We are taught to have expectation to hope things will be better than they are but we are not taught how to accept what we have now. We are not taught how to be happy without expectations of other people. What we already have is permanent happiness. Being thankful for what we have, instead of wanting more, is not the first step in being present, it is the only step in being happy now.

Far Away

Striving for happiness in the outside world of desires is usually a faraway move from the inner home of happiness. Straying too far away, it may be difficult to see how to get back to be close to the inner home of happiness.

Inner Commander

Happiness is not in other people in material things or in futures hands. It's not in some other place or in a faraway land. Happiness is an inside job. It can be shared that you are happy but it has to stay in your command.

Happiness . . . the Most Difficult Desire

Withdrawn from attachments, who is left to be unattached?
The occupier of the body internally devoured. There was no
destruction only a simple removal of the illusion, there was
some one here in the first place.

The desire to want this is the most difficult thing to want and
only happens because the ego, made up from thinking, could
endure no more suffering and embarrassment.

No Apology ever needed

Is it true you don't want anything? Is it true you are happy
with you? Don't you wear to match what others think? Don't
you do your hair for how others care? Do you never say
sorry for being yourself? Do you work how well you feel?
Do you go to places of silence when no one knows you have
gone? Do you spend days on you own, happy with yourself?

One Sided Diet

How can you a trillionaire have everything and be so
unhappy? This is what you wanted so you've brought this
on yourself. The properties, the people, the power; any
relationship you could desire but inside you are an unhappy
pauper. You've ignored the inner man. The one-sided diet of
your soul has led to the most serious disturbances of balance.
The only cure is everything must go.

Choose

How can so many people be content with little money and so many people with so much money be so worried about what to do with it. How can so many people be happy with so little and how can so many people have so much and be so unhappy. The connection is that what you go after you may get but you can't go in two opposite directions at the same time. There is nothing wrong with whichever way you go as long as you don't complain that you want the opposite too.

Inside-out World

These ears, eyes, nose, tongue, hands, feet, stomach and skin did as much as they could to make my world happy until that happiness was repeated so many times there was no pleasure and the world became undesirable. Inside another world was found which nurtures all I ever really wanted. All desires transformed into happiness.

Breathless Impulses

We used to only have one job now it's as many as we can do. We used to leave our work outside but now we take that home too. Where are we trying to get to? What are we trying to do? What are we achieving? Where will we end up?

With a breathless impulse to achieve, obtain, and possess, the outer world is all we have in our sights but we can settle for less. For one minute close your eyes and try to still your mind and see who is behind the curtain.

Exile Street

Most dream of a pension, of life on Easy Street. Some dream of blue skies a beach of white sand in some foreign land. We dream of another place in a different time, in different circumstances at the end of the long old climb. But dreaming makes us exiles from our happiness now, a foreigner never at home, always dreaming far away from now.

Intangibility

We can follow the sacred books until we die but walking away from thinking is harder. Against what we've been taught; against what we know; against what they tell us and condition us to think. The answer inside is clear. Freedom from thinking is living in the heart, at the complete mercy of the intangible heart. Intangible being in intangible silence is intangible happiness in intangible stillness in the heart.

Tears of Happiness

Sometimes when a memory of times gone by appears, it makes my heart heave and bring tears of those times gone by to my eyes. My cheeks are wet with tears my hands can't dry but it's a heart of bliss that cries. It's usually me with someone in a place and I was happy or sad, sometimes with my mum, wife, daughter or sometimes my dad. Memories bring up emotions which break through time and are just like being touched by their love. Without these tears I have no heart to heave and I am as happy as I can be if this is all I too will leave.

Happiness Cures Resentment

Resentment can only be cured by forgiveness inside but you can only forgive what you understand. If you feel resentment ask yourself for forgiveness to understand that someone is unwell, to hope that they recover. You can ask yourself for forgiveness to understand someone, so that you can be compassionate to them, wishing they can seek the happiness they see inside you.

Happiness

A day of no events; nothing has happened; no one called around; I didn't have to do anything. But I stayed at home pottering, small tasks accomplished. No time was saved or wasted. Conscious mostly of existence and happiness.

Ocean of Being

All memories vanish when the oxygen stops just as the ego does without thought, so why hang on to fading memories. Instead, learn to swim and just be in the ocean of happiness where the ego cannot exist. There are no storms, unsinkable, unperishable, unspeakable is the ocean of being.

Celestial

To be celestial you have to give up the terrestrial. To be eternal you have to become a child. To be a child you have to come from the heart not the head. To come from the heart the ego must be dead.

Subjectivity

Where has all the love gone, the ninety year old asked me. Still here I said, looking in her eye. In thousands of years we have not changed and the illusion of progress has not altered us. The non-changing inner world only awaits the presence of the externalised outer person.

97. REMOVAL OF IGNORANCE

Meaning

The point of life is that maybe there isn't one. Thinking keeps us deluded that there is a point to life. But if there is no point in following thinking, then we might as well be happy.

Solitary Stillness

Pursuing celebrity status, praise and recognition of intellectual eloquence are an expression of external superficial happiness. Solitariness, avoiding promotion, humbly, quietly existing in stillness are a reflection of inner happiness.

No Weather

The only interesting aspect of people's lives is how they found out about themselves, how they discovered consciousness, the only permanent aspect of their life. The inner directed wind carrying them inwards which has only one aim, only a single purpose, happiness. Having turned away forever from where happiness cannot be found, because it is a clever illusion sustained by those who gain from it in money power or ego, there is nowhere else to go except inside. Stormy outer weather continues, whilst inside there is always, calmness in the refuge. Weather does not exist there only stillness.

Between Thoughts

It is right here in the space between. That is where it is;
not hiding but right here. It has to be observed by slowing
thoughts until there is a halt. When thoughts halt, their
journey has stopped for a moment. This moment is the space
between thoughts; thoughtless consciousness. This is where
the search ends. It is where happiness exists, peace, the truth
we are all after. It is stillness.

The Way of The Self

The way to the self is not in books or in thoughtful
understanding but reached only by loving surrender to
what is deep inside us. Suffering is the key to the door to the
way inside on the path of happiness. By being vigilant of
the wandering mind, once controlled and steadied we can
surrender.

The Beauty of Age

The beauty involved in ageing is eclipsed by the negative
press of its health. Forgetting is only remembering in
reverse, emptying the mind rather than filling it. The falls
are the unsteadiness of the child and her falls, in reverse
is unsteadiness. At first gently propped by sticks and then
by walking frames until finally even the nappies return as
continence pads. There is great understanding and wisdom,
reflections and memories almost touchable and the bliss of
finding happiness in the self. The process of life is a no less
than the flower unfolding its petals in the early morning
light then closing them again at night.

Hungry Road to Happiness

I was so lucky to come from hardship. I was hungry and I needed to nourish myself because only through suffering can you see.

Happiness in Existing Consciously

Almost everyone believes they are someone because we believe we have an ego with millions of thoughts, memories and experiences which connect up together with threads to others.

This immensely complex world we see is a playground for the body and mind.

There are very few who see this is not real but these few see bundles of thoughts as an imagined ego that is not in any way real. It is a clever illusion, a trick of thinking consisting of just thoughts.

Ignoring

How can I be helped if I don't accept I need help? How can you show me if I can't see? How can I understand if I am not ready to understand? Perhaps something very different to what you think is needed. How much are we aware of what is happening to us or of what will happen to us.? Maybe by ignoring what we think and just accepting what happens, all is understood.

Welcome Back Home

So you decided to follow the intellectual and not your
ignorance a while ago and you find yourself here. Welcome
home: this is where you were always meant to be.

The Simple and Small Count

Allowing a tiny small mistake can cost us dearly. It is the
denial of small mistakes which matter because the big ones
are usually seen.

From the moment of being conscious that the seer the seen
and seeing are the same our nature is understood.

Sleep is only rest from the mind, dreaming sleep's reality;
being awake, both are left behind. But in full consciousness
rest from the mind only takes place when thoughts are left
behind too, then sleep dreaming and awake are no different.

Kingdom of Exile

We live outside the walls of the only great city we know is
safe, where we know we are happy.

Through forgetfulness we think we don't know and
eventually we believe we don't know. We live in a kingdom
of illusion because of forgetting our true self.

Our whole life is spent seeking what we have, which is what
we have forgotten.

Stillness the Remover of Ignorance

No one other than you can find out about yourself and I don't mean the things you say but the things that you cannot say.

All the things you cannot say are a sense of consciousness inside you. It is not thought but the presence of awareness. Whatever name you give is not right as it doesn't need one because it is itself and is not qualified by words.

Wordless is the best way to experience yourself which means being silent. When in your own inner silence, stillness is found, you will see ignorance has gone.

What we Are After a Wash

Soaked with life trying not to become the various environments which have rained on us, we survive. All along seeming worn, torn and repaired, struggling not to be overcome. We are not transformed, only shown and brought back to what we always are.

Transcendence of Assumed Duality

In the silence of meditation, stillness shows us as abstract without form which we imagine, then draw and paint as the divine. Then inner stillness shows us more, that there is no difference between the self, the image and the divine.

544

Not What it Seems

Ignorance cannot be removed instantly. You have to be aware of it and want it removed. Then work has to be done to change what you think you see in front of you to remove thoughts of what you think is there.

Removing ignorance is not straight forward but like walking around something so it is seen from different angles. You see new perspectives. Ignorance is like looking at an object the size of a car in front of you and not knowing what it is. Walking around it repeatedly, you see it has different facets but that eventually it can only be one thing.

It can't simply be named so that it can be communicated and understood by words alone. This can only be done by walking around it, looking and seeing what is there.

No Key No Door No Path

There is no key to happiness because there is no door and there is no path to happiness because it's already inside.

There is no such thing as suddenly gaining enlightenment. You can't obtain what you already have; you just have to see you have it.

Happiness is your actual nature and all that needs to be done is to see this and be it. What can be easier than being still to see this, being yourself, you see you already have happiness.

PhD in Mind Fullness

Following the sacred books of truths, man begins the cycle of filling the mind, engaging it, trying to achieve mind fullness. In the end the mind and its theories have to be given up to go to its source which is always there. To engage further with the culprit of thinking which starts all troubles is not a way out of trouble. The trouble, like a PhD just gets Piled Higher and Deeper. You can't think your way to stillness and serenity; you can only stop here now . . . be still.

Epiphany

The only thing to see in life is the removal of ignorance. The aim of life is not acquiring knowledge only the removal of ignorance. The aim of contemplation; the aim of prayer; the aim of meditation is the removal of ignorance. Realisation cannot be acquired; enlightenment cannot be acquired because there is nothing to suddenly see except removal of ignorance.

Removing Darkness

Enlightenment is not something new which happens like saying someone has switched the sun on when it has always been there. Light is always there from the sun but clouds may be in the way of seeing it. Similarly when our ignorance is seen, the self is seen. Light is always there from the sun but someone may be busy looking at something else; then only effort is needed to turn inside to see it. Just letting the sun shine in you is realisation.

The Unknown

When all the words have been practiced and all the practice
lived, the redundant scripts of teaching are given away.
When all the work is done, it carries on without words in
consciousness. Our teachers like ancestors have to be kept
inside with high regard. Perhaps our only duty; the only
thing we are here to do is to pass on what we do not know.

'I am' Invites You

You are invited to turn all your attention to the sense of 'I
am.' Keep up with your obligations but don't invite anything
new into your life. Resist the unnecessary. Keep your focus
on being the sense of 'I am.' Just be still. We think we are
this or that but these are imaginary thoughts. We are just 'I
am,' the sense we all have. We think we are our bodies, our
memories but these thoughts are only part of what we are.
Because of this we take ourselves to be what we are not. We
get attached to all sorts of associations, thoughts, ideas, the
future.

Constantly resist the unnecessary. Focusing on the sense of 'I
am' lets thoughts just flow and pass by. You start to see what
the sense of 'I am' is. Just remain still and you will see how
your thinking has kept you dreaming.

That Place

There is somewhere man knows he can go to but wont. The
call of this 'somewhere to go to' gets bigger simply because
he wont.

How Stupid Could I Have Been

To think and believe there will be a sudden acquiring of happiness ensures disappointment. Seeing it was covered up and there all the time is the happiest you can be. Not removing ignorance is living as if you will be happier in the future not seeing that you are happy now.

Just Around the corner

What you are looking for, what you are trying to find is just around the corner in the illusory corner of the mind. Just around the corner is invented by the mind to make absolutely sure you keep on searching to find it.

Just around the corner is a trick saying I haven't got it yet but it's something I can still get. There is nothing to find which you don't already own; nothing new to see which you haven't already known.

Intentionally Ditching Ignorance

If you want to see yourself, look at this first before you take a single step. There has to be unacceptable discomfort for wanting to see the truth about ourselves. It has to threaten what we think we are; our conscious lives. We have to go against all our conditioning, everything we were taught and be empty. Rejecting conditioning is removing ignorance, so don't be surprised if everyone else is convinced you are crazy. That is their conditioning. They haven't got the same neediness so let them continue veering off, keeping on your own path.

Immersion

The only point to life is removal of ignorance unveiling our inner happiness. Seeing our true self. We see truth which has no words, so we can only remain immersed in its stillness.

Seer Seen and Seeing

Complete surrender to whatever you surrender to eventually turns you inwards so you see and experience what is being surrendered to is the Self. The Seer, the seen and seeing are still seen but never again as before as they are one thing which is consciousness.

Non-duality

Although the point of life is being fully conscious, you can't be holy or fully conscious all the time. Full consciousness once seen cannot be lost but other things have to happen which appear to eclipse it. Like the sun eclipsed by the moon, the sun is there, partly in the shade, so full consciousness is only appreciated because of its apparent opposite.

Removal of Ignorance

There is no sudden enlightenment as you can't get what you already have. You can only see it which is the removal of our ignorance. Seeing happiness is our actual nature is the removal of ignorance and all that needs to be seen. It is an unspeakably enormous relief to actually see this.

Captured from Being on The Run

What calls to you, what pulls you from within; something always calls us. When you are not doing anything in particular, it calls to you and you think you might want it, so you go. But is it the true self, the true spirit? Has it got in the way and hidden what you really want, keeping you on the run. It may be in a container, a shop, the fridge or a person. The more you have of it, the more you think about what it is keeping you from.

Knowing Ignorance

I now know I didn't know, so it's much easier to know my ignorance. I knew I didn't know how to overcome my ignorance. My ignorance took most of my life to learn and was removed by knowing it. I know because all I know is my ignorance.

No Other Way

It is correct that we find out who we are through suffering and we find happiness through suffering. It is the way of removal of ignorance of happiness and is the only way to happiness.

Man of No Means

I am a person of no means going nowhere. That is why I am here on the road to nowhere with my ignorance changed into happiness.

The Bridge

What forms the bridge between the ignorance of not
knowing then suddenly understanding and knowing? What
starts it? Is it becoming aware that desires don't make you
happy; perhaps combined with seeing the pointlessness of
endless pain? What quality do we need to see these?

Against Nature

There is no strategy which works; nature has a better one.
There is no amount of effort which works; nature is an
unknown force. There is no amount of will which works;
nature is just herself. There is not a single thing which works;
nature is so many things. Water finds its own level. Wind
stops when it is out of energy. Fire can burn everything. The
earth has its own plan for mankind too. Thought is only an
aspect of consciousness. Consciousness is the gift we have to
show us our ignorance and truth.

Intelligent removal of Ignorance

Having a great memory may help you speak many
languages, solve complex equations, live in comfort,
persuade others, seem clever but . . . understanding your
self, not complaining or blaming others, being forever
thankful, this removal of ignorance is true intelligence.

Certainty

If after prolonged extremely painful torture, death is an inescapable certainty, rather than leaving the decision to the torturer . . . how can choosing when to end life seem like showing mercy? Well, in the midst of extreme pain when the outcome is not certain the same course of action is the only option.

Asking

It is almost impossible to find the answers without asking someone who has looked before. They will have probably looked longer, further and deeper, but sometimes they haven't so we must always look.

Ask the Hill

The answer to your question is not in books. It's inside you and the sacred hill.

Ask the sacred hill the question. The answer is the hill. The hill is the answer . . . because it is still.

Wrong Turn

Most don't want to know and accept they made a wrong turn. When they hear and accept the wrong turn, they are fast to correct it but nearly always too late. These are the ones who know because they have grown.

The Darkest Hour

Suffering increases the size of the cup which you use to drink from the river of grace which can only be seen by those who have suffered. What is drank quenches a thirst which only those who have suffered know exists and is the greatest assistant. It is the final reward. After struggling and crying for help, it arrives at the most difficult time, the darkest hour, the highest honour.

Application

Basic training and education leave us thinking we can do things we can't but there are things we don't know we can do until they need doing. Relationships, marriage, parenting, caring for someone, assisting the dying.

Last Resort

Don't let them take up space in your head rent free. Don't blame anyone, thank them. If you really can't get them out of your mind, change how you see them, thanking them for being your teachers, even pray for them.

Reality is me too

Everything is as it appears to you. It is exactly as it seems to you. It is all there and is a part of you. All you actually have is you. Reality is that there is just you. Just you is all you can be, all you can know. We are the same.

Where Has it Gone?

When will we start being kind to our own, not locking them
up in expensive homes. When will we start inviting them to
stay with us like they did to us when we were young. Where
has the kindness they gave us gone? Where is the generosity?
Where is the love they showed us so we can pass it on?

98. SURRENDER

Surrender When All is Gone

Surrender is always ongoing, like stopping thoughts to be still. Surrender is not a promise because it is when there is nothing left.

The Path

The path going left is the path of the intellect. The path going right is the path of surrender.

I turned left, thought so much and couldn't work it out, so I gave up and surrendered to the path going right.

Having surrendered, I now completely understand the path going to the left which eventually joins with the path going right. Whichever one you choose takes you to the same place.

Surrender

In surrender there are no questions, no questioning, no bargains as everything is surrendered.

Surrender of Everything

Cool water to drink on a hot day. A cool breeze to waft away any worries about securities makes life smoother. No worries about securities makes life easy for everyone, with no talking of money or its consequences.

People, family and friends, if you have any, do you believe they are not looked after or are their fate and ours already sealed?

Is this possible, that you can leave it all to your God, foolish, crazy, free and happy to just be? Can you let go of everything and just let go of trying to control all outcomes?

Surrendering and Knowing

The path of self knowledge leads to the source of thinking where the self is seen and the ego as an impostor. But the path of self surrender leads to submitting the ego for destruction, so the self is all that is left. Through self knowledge and self surrender thoughts in the form of the ego submit for execution.

Surrender and Solitude

Who lives in solitude? Who surrenders? Final surrender can never occur because there is no one left to surrender and there is no such thing as surrender because it came from an imaginary mind.

Secret Key to the Secret Place

We accumulate so many outer things without letting go but we let inner things mount up and grow. There are no rules as guides; no one to take them all away to be re-cycled like furniture for re-use. As inner rubbish accumulates, it gains weight. Remember no one can help you, it's only you who can throw it away. What do you do with it, where do you go and how do you process it to let go? Remember that sometimes the last place to look, the secret key to the secret place, is on our knees.

Default to Complete Surrender

Complete surrender of consciousness removes all burdens, then there is no one to be burdened. The mind may not accept this easily but with enough pain it will surrender. Complete surrender of consciousness removes all burdens so they are not mine anymore; they belong to what I have surrendered to. Complete surrender of consciousness removes all burdens. If I completely surrender, life is not burdened by thoughts and a free life begins.

Genuflection

It's never too late to get rid of fear. It's never too late to be happy. It's never too late to be what you want to be. There is a way if you really want it. It's never too late to help someone grumpy, messy, lost in a haze. Maybe you will show them something new too. It's never too late to lose all that stuff you've been collecting for years. Walk away from it or get down on your knees.

Surrender Time

Surrender the past, the future, the sacred, the universe, every person thing and place. Surrender; just be. When are you going to get it? Your past and future stop you being in the present. They are only a collection of memories and dreams, only a collection of thoughts . . . but they are not you. The past and future isolate you from now but they are not you. They are an illusion . . . not you. Why do you carry this awesomely heavy weight of the past and future around with you everywhere in front of everyone. You will be ok without it. 'You' is the person I see.

When I see you, I don't see the future or the past. Now is the only time I see you. When I'm not with you like now, I can remember or dream about you but I can't see you. Surrender your sense of control to live in some other time. Surrender your sense of power, your attachment to the future. Surrender in the face of being powerless. Surrender what you think you can be to being what you are now. Then surrender that to surrender.

Surrender

Surrender consciousness. Surrender the present. Surrender surrender itself. Then that too. Surrender existence then consciousness of that.

No Return

There is never a return because there is no desire to go backwards.

The Ground

Not all of us are taught to pray but we all know how to call
out to the God we believe in when we are about to die. Grace
after meals, daily facing east, incense, chanting, singing and
recital, remind us we should pray. But the prayer in our
hearts is not the same as prayers in books, our minds or on
our lips. Prayer can be anything as long as it's only ever face
down flat on the ground surrender.

It's True

It is true if you follow the path of surrender it works. It is
also true if you follow the path of consciousness it works.
They both work the same as you disappear, everything
becomes truth.

Devoured

I don't have a choice over what I am any more. I am lost to
solitude, having been devoured.

Few

Fourteen billion eyes see the world each night and day.
Fourteen billion feet walk this way and fourteen billion
hands work each day. Some eyes see, a few hands pray,
almost no knees take the easy way and kneel . . . so how
many know truth?

Gone

There used to be someone I used to know as me but I was taken away and not by fairies . . . far worse. I surrendered to a mountain. At first it was escape from pain and the desire to be happy all the time. Then I realised nothing anymore was mine. Only with surrender I could see for the first time there was protection and safety from fear. There was no worry and the stillness is in myself now . . . in here.

The Origin of Our God

Mankind has a special inner consciousness which he finds an outer image for with a form and name on earth. This he projects up in to the sky to satisfy his thinking and his eyes. This name and form for his inner sense of consciousness he calls God. He finds it easier to see the projected image on earth or up in the sky until eventually he finds it difficult to return to the original consciousness within.

Then meditation, surrender, or prayer can focus away from the mind's outer projections and return him just to the heart of consciousness. The original consciousness of the inner sense he calls God. On his deathbed and after the name and form are gone, all that remains for others is the original sense of consciousness of the inner sense we call God.

The Choice

Wealth and power can make you believe you are important. Detaching with humility and surrender eclipses all importance.

The Old Yogi

The old yogi was right when he said, "It was all accomplished a long time ago. There is not one even thing wrong. We do not know. All is truth."

99. MEDITATION

The Path of Meditation

What we discover about meditating is that we do it our
way, then we find that this is what has always been said for
thousands of years.

Worked Out By The Heart

The stillness we find is our natural state and there is a
natural path to find it which is not a path worked out by
calculations but only worked out by the heart.

Solitary Unity

Meditation is for one person. It is not a group thing with
projections from the mind of togetherness. The unity comes
with removal of ignorance which it is the unity of truth in
stillness.

The Inner Banquet

When on these silent words your hungry eyes search for
meaning, close them, turn inwards and let the inner eye
uncover the banquet of truth revealed in the self which
always waits for you in your stillness.

Though Not Seen Always Present

The gap between thoughts is the only thing that exists, not the thoughts that appear to make the gap. The thoughts which appear to make the gap are like writing on blank paper, only an appearance. What looks like the gap between thoughts is like a piece of paper before it is written on. Blank, the paper is not conditioned by anything. It is what it is in reality. Drawing on it does not change the paper as the drawing can be removed and another one drawn so the paper remains as it always was, just like consciousness. Though not seen consciousness is always present.

Simple Meditation

Meditation is as natural as breathing. Desire for the happiness meditation shows us is as natural as breathing. How to get to it is as easy and as simple as breathing

Look inside yourself and find some way to slow your thoughts and wait for the stillness to appear.

Breath as the Best Mantra

If thoughts bombard you in meditation dim them, dissolve them, and distance them away by your own breath. Your own breath's sound entering and leaving you is second only to stillness. It is a in built mantra to bring you back to stillness.

Path to Stillness

There is no way to meditate as meditation is to just be still. Nothing mysterious happens because there is nothing mysterious to experience except seeing that you can be still and in stillness you are happy. There is no formula to be still as there are no thoughts to have, only to be vigilant to stop any of them interfering with you being still. It is only uncovering how to slow thoughts until they seem to have a gap between them. When only the gap is sensed by consciousness, this is meditation. Resurfacing from meditation after being still, there is an awareness that thinking may not be what makes us happy.

Moving from counting beads to saying a mantra seems easy but changing from mantra to silence can be slow. For stillness to be allowed to just be, the sound of the mantra has to go. With no sound or thoughts, the connection is direct and simple to stillness. When you arrive at your destination, you no longer need the vehicle for any transport. Without a repeating sound there is less mental clutter so more vigilance to the space between thoughts. Only in silence is inner stillness unveiled to be all that is the self.

We meditate trying to find happiness, trying to reduce fear, pain, suffering and uncertainty by stopping thinking and being more conscious. But instead we can pray or surrender to being still in our sacred inner space. If you follow the path of surrender it works. If you follow the path of consciousness it works. They both work the same because as you disappear everything becomes truth.

From all the paths you could choose you have chosen the one you are on now. It is exactly the right one because it will show you how to be where you are now. It is the path we can't see until we step into the inside room. The room is the cave of your heart, pristine, forever unchanged, waiting always, being here for you.

Breath is not life. It is what is behind it which makes and maintains life. It is not the lips, the mouth which speak but the reflection of what is within. Similarly, the mind is a mirror reflecting a light inside but the mind is not the actual source of the light. The mind is only a piece of kit doing a job. The source of the light produces the mind.

How can you live in a city and Meditate? How can you live in a city and not Meditate?

Tethering

Untethered breath let's thinking flow so thinking is free to wander as it pleases. Tethering the breath helps to tether thinking so thinking is controlled. Disciplined thinking allows the space between thoughts to be seen and behind those spaces. Those spaces between are portals to stillness like the stars are portals to the universe

At some stage man will realise that breathing affects his thinking much more that scientists are aware. Alteration of breathing can make you dizzy, numb, unconscious or have a fit. It can make you run on emotions and survival instinct only. Slower controlled special breathing, can open up blood supplies to areas of the brain, expanding consciousness of the self and universe into blissful existence.

Total Concentration

Like driving, I try to stick with essentials, not drift off into related things which are not important to the path, which needs total concentration.

If Meditation Seems Impossible

If you cant meditate, if you don't seem to be able to meditate, there is a solution which will do.

Meditation is only about your inner self, without thoughts and you are the only expert on you, so all you have to do is look inside.

You are looking for your own stillness inside you and you see this stillness when thoughts die down and it is quieter inside. Just be that stillness. This is all meditation is.

100. PILGRIMAGE

Ask

Don't ask me, ask the mountain as the mountain has the answer. It is unmoving massive stillness. It is what you are looking for. It is the actual answer; all you have to do is see it. It is so obvious it shouldn't be missed because it is stillness on a massive scale but it also reflects the stillness, the intangible in us.

Inner Site

When thinking about a sacred place you have to conjure up what you imagine about it is sacred. You have to imagine what is there. You interpret what everyone else has said. You read about it. You look at pictures, then you get there and it seems ordinary. You take mementos, pictures, stones, water or earth. But when you look inside yourself and see what image you conjure up of the sacred site, what is it and how do you project that on the world? How does it connect with the sacred place? Can you withdraw the projection and just stick with what you feel inside that is stillness? Is this the secret of the sacred site?

Pilgrimage

Go anywhere on your own, don't take a phone.

Pilgrimages

Medicine, Psychology, psychotherapy cannot work for problems of the spirit, the soul. Only things of the spirit, the soul can help and heal to build and see the spirit, the soul. Smells which remind us to go within and images which guide us to inner consciousness can turn us gently around to see the spirit, the soul. Pilgrimages seemingly going somewhere else, unbeknown only ever take us gently to one place . . . within.

Types of Pilgrimage

Why do we need to visit sacred sites as our ancestors did on pilgrimages? Is it a break from ordinary life a chance to connect with our inner self or what we regard as spiritual or God? What needs preparation; how long do you stay; what do you wear; how do you get there and back and how do you expect to be changed on return?

Nothing new can be got but what is inside you can be uncovered, returning rejuvenated because ignorance has gone and the self is known once again. But you can also do this on your own, in your room, in your home or anywhere. Go to the place inside you where you would if you were on the pilgrimage and you will see it is the same.

The Place is in You

If there is a sense about going to a sacred site you don't have to go as nothing may happen. Stay at home where it is. Be still and everything may happen.

Our Inner Nature

Looking for the presence of the master comes from your desire to find your own inner master, to find him or her in your self. If you can bring him up in your self as your self this is the greatest gift you can ever have, the presence of the inner master is your very nature.

Right to Wrong

No one has the right to do wrong anywhere for any reason. Doing wrong is a choice not a mistake.

Second Choice

If someone chooses to do wrong it is a clear choice. Making a mistake is not paying enough attention. Repeating either is the same . . . a second choice.

Being True

If you are conscious for your self, you cannot be false. If you think for your self you cannot be false. If you write for your self you cannot be false. If you speak for your self you cannot be false. If you act for your self you cannot be false.

Decent is permanent

Our chosen jobs, clubs and class may help describe us but they don't make us decent. We only have our jobs, position influence, our way of life because we have allowed them by those with principals. It is quick and easy to be overpowered and lose our work, position, influence and our way of life by those with no principals. Even though they may even torture us there is one thing those with no principals can't destroy, our Self.

Kindness

Kindness is treating someone how you would want to be treated if you were in their position. Animals show kindness, so it is not unique to humans but many choose not to be kind. Receiving kindness can make the biggest difference in someone's life. Kindness can restore our belief in mankind, that there are decent people and this can give us a purpose in life . . . that we can pass it on.

It's the smallest things we do which tell someone about us. The smallest things we do say what we are. It can be a card, the x for a kiss or a smiley face at the end looking you straight in the eye. An early morning surprise. A cup of tea can be enough, or just waving an extra goodbye can make it that special day. It's the smallest things that we do which are the most important.

Un-monetise Kindness

When the last act of helping has been monetised, man has
to change and turn around or he is not man. Every move
can be mechanised and monetised. Every breath you take
can be sanitised and monetised. Preventing monetising of
everything could begin to enrich a homogenous, cultureless
future with at least kindness. Perhaps the turning point of
man could begin with being kind and thankfulness being the
most sought after reward . . . not money.

101. PLACES IN SPACE

The Thread

Where does it arise? Initiated only by the one before, then passed along to the next, an invisible thread, intangible but still felt?

What is good for one is the same for each of us. What is good is also for the greater good, for much more than just one.

World of Trauma

I come from a world of trauma. I was brought up in it. I have seen heard and felt trauma, remember it, learnt about trauma, taught it, helped it be understood and still try to forget it.

I go for happiness not entertainment, I can't engage in mediocre small talk for long, but simple tasks and hard work let me be full of happiness.

That stillness not quite in the background which we dive into, immersed totally is the world of the spirit, the only way through what we have seen. Nothing else helps, heals, holds or gives strength forever.

Praying for Help

Requests for help are requests to yourself to see things differently.

Different Roads

Each being spiritual in their way, aware their way and all ways have the same aim; why then are we the same but different?

Biologically, psychologically, emotionally the same but spiritually we take different paths.

Perhaps it is not us but the planet's different characteristics which forge our sense of what is spiritual.

Is it the sacred mountains, the holy rivers, how the sun rises and sets over the holy lands?

Is it some combination of things we don't yet know which make it seem like the choice is in our hands?

What Works Is True

Stick with what works searching inside. For you what works is true.

102. TRUTH

What is Truth

Christ said 'Everyone who belongs to the truth listens to my voice' Pontious Pilate said 'What is truth?' There was no answer and Pilate left.

Maybe the answer is direct and simple. If silence enables stillness to show truth, then truth cannot be communicated by words because truth has no words. There is no recorded answer from Christ and perhaps this is why Pilate left.

Timeless

The wise know truth but it is not that they don't speak, its they can't speak because truth has no words. The wise know truth has no words which cannot be captured by thinking but it can be circled to see where it is. The wise know truth in themselves is everything with no form in a timeless state. The wise know truth here through timeless stillness like being conscious in distant outer space. No division there of consciousness by the sun into hours, days, past or future. The wise do not experience time, only the bliss of stillness connected to everything always.

Freed by Suffering

Our purpose and fate, the unconscious, physics and archaeological sites are only opinions and guesswork. They sound good, luring the mind trapping us in someone else's interpretation or what possibly was or could be. But suffering brings a terrible reality only relieved by gods or faith and hope in something. After the suffering, there is a happy person whose mind's main duty is to repeat the name of what works. When calmness then stillness are invited, something that was there all along is seen . . . the removal of ignorance revealing that happiness is only within.

Enlightenment

The crushing weight of the problems of the world, thoughts of hesitancy, fear and outcomes become meaningless in stillness. The crushing weight of missed personal opportunities add up with isolation and the lack of previous joyful activities, all become meaningless in stillness. The suffering of lost friends, missed ancestors, the pain of disease, loss of tears of happiness become meaningless in stillness. The meaning of the direction, the purpose become meaningless in stillness. Enquiry into our self with complete surrender, practice, kindness and being still let stillness be seen as truth.

Rest Rooms

The absence of toilets in shops raises the suspicion that it is all business but they are not paying attention to what is everyone's business.

Truth is Yours

Truth is your truth, my truth and their truth because truth is in everything and everywhere and it can only be one thing. Truth can come in different forms of beliefs like water, as ice, steam, rain, lakes or streams but back in the ocean, it is water.

Reincarnation

Reincarnation is not just a Buddhist or a Hindu thing, Christianity believes in something like it too. It doesn't actually exist except intellectually as an idea. It's really an invention to imagine prevention of our destruction. But how can someone be destroyed who was not here and like reincarnation was only invented.

Inconvenient Truths

Inconvenient truths can be about anything dark which is uncomfortable to talk about. Your family, your history, your health or wealth or lack of all of these or just about what's inside you. It's not in another country in another place, in someone else's head, it's in my head, your head. It's not anywhere in anyone apart from in us. That's all we need to know to change and get rid of them.

Plagiarism

All art is plagiarism; all sculpture music and architecture
all writing. In art, copying is progressing an idea but
few speak honestly about science where plagiarism is
copying someone, whilst research is copying many. It is a
compliment to be plagiarised and helps everyone earn a
living and maybe influence is why we are here.

Image

Who needs images of what is right in front of you. If you
can't see what's in front of you what are you going to see in
its image?

Non Verbal Silent Bliss

Writing only for me is about my truth. It is not for anyone
else. It is worth all the books ever written in seeing my
ignorance. Uncovering my own ignorance using words is a
reflection and echo from the deep cave within, where I exist
in nonverbal silent bliss.

Being True To You

Don't try to imagine because it cannot be imagined. Stop
looking for an image of what you really are. Don't try to
imagine because you can't be imagined.

Your Self

As knowing what it is to be a parent can only be known by being a parent, so truth can only be known by being true to your self.

Damage

Mental scars are not something you point your finger at unless they are yours. Damage is a cost some pay for experience which allows them to grow. Battle hardened and scarred, the damaged are stronger than the sheltered. Only the damaged recognise the path which the overprotected only occasionally notice. Someone who has mental scars, who understands the language of suffering, is a better companion than the shielded. Finding the path and staying on it needs the right companions who are battle hardened equals .

103. DETACHMENT

Being Detached

Being detached solves a lot of problems. There's no trying to be serious, no involvement in other people's problems, taking the days as days not as anything else, taking things as they are and not as imaginings, taking just what you need, giving what you can, keeping what you want. There are no expectations, no having to find reasons behind everything. Life just comes and goes; happiness is the aim of all.

Detaching

Try and greet the rising number of limited years with welcome surprise, especially the uninvited surprise guests of pain and suffering, for both are necessary friends at their best. Look away from things that didn't happen and away from people you didn't please. Look around and see the chaos, the mess you could have had to leave. You notice as each month passes, being this or that are now almost equal in the tunnel to the light and seeing no one is right or wrong, you don't hold on so tight.

Warning Heaven's Door

Heaven's door is closer than you think; no need to bring it closer, to oil the hinges or to blow the wind in its face. Forever on your mind, knowing what you will eventually find, heaven's closer than you think.

Old Child

A new face is moulded from the younger one but the mind is changed in its involvement. It wants to listen more deeply, hearing only the good. Smiling is a gift to give to everyone. Passions are spent, so no there is no longer any anger of struggling. Effort is trimmed to needs only, so reducing all load and detaching from the tangible. The child inside still there. Elderly but assumed to have changed . . . all along unchanged truth.

Feeling Sorry for Yourself

When the most respected person dies, does where you placed them in yourself change? Do you listen more now for their words? Do you think more about them now they are gone? You assume they are not with you. But you also know we know so little that they could be beside you now silently supporting you as they did before. Perhaps they are asking you to be open to possibilities, to put aside your responsibilities, to share right now with someone the happiness of just being alive.

Siblings

Some don't have them and are sad, others do and are driven nearly mad. Jealous they may be to the extent of ruining your life or helping they can lessen all pain in life. For better or worse they'll always be here. Detachment is the best way to cope; that they'll change is living in hope.

Returning to the Birthplace

Back in the village the opportunist left. Back to the faulty,
to the decay, realising now she is here to stay. The hamster
wheel abandoned where has she been, back now at home to
forget all she's seen. Back to a rented room all her stuff gone,
realising now it was serious not fun. Back to the beach the
sky and sea, the dreams that she chased after have all gone
by, but now the memories strangely form tears in her eyes.
Bliss of the baby returns as her self, before being taken away
she saw happiness can never decay.

Moving Along

Short are the years we live on top but below we will always
be in man's longest lasting dwelling place, suddenly hidden
away from the family. But unlike tombs built as dining
places for eagles, our bones are no longer slowly moved
along the barrow to let the living slowly forget us and
change us from family into ancestors.. Gone from touch
forever, no gentle nudging, no fading goodbyes, a sudden
spent piece of kit.

Let Them Be

Shall I wake them or let them wake naturally. There is
nothing to particularly get up for . . . except for today, so
why try and control the world. I see I have learnt
to just let others be. The world will reveal it self in all its
moods, colours, smells, temptations and actions all directed
to maintaining happiness.

The Rhizome

When someone I know dies, it's as if we are part of the same singular subterranean giant rhizome sprouting up new growths as others wither but are forever the same thing. There appears of course to be a terrible loss but also a gain, which is only our true organic nature. In keeping with the spirit of creation and destruction in the stillness holding the Universe together, we carry on subterraneanly.

Detachment Together

Let someone else live how they want to live and you can still be together.

My Last Note to You

Of all the things I could leave behind it could be a letter conveying love but not to a person but to you about love of everything. How could this be and how could you see what I see? All that I see is that all there is, is to see, not how we think, only how we see?

There is nothing to be gained only things to remove, mainly our ignorance. After all thinking is jettisoned; after surrender is accepted and complete . . . only then is ignorance finally removed.

List of last Regrets

I wish I had . . . been more true to my own self, not
expectations, expressed feelings, been more in touch with
friends, let myself be happier, worked less. I wish I had
said what I wanted to say, said what I had to say, tried to
be friendly every day, tried to smile every day, tried to pray
every day I could pray. I wish I had tried to do my best, tried
to rest, tried to leave nothing undone, left stuff for others to
do, given up trying to have no regrets.

Being Put Down

Most just take the medicine to avoid the distress of arguing
about it and to stop others getting too angry for just doing
what they want. Many ignore what is coming with the
sedation of taking a pill, too addicted to sedation or to
something else just to be still. Silence is exceptional. Many
say the same thing, 'I won't be the first or the last.' Only
seeing this life, just as it is nearly past.

Intervention

The key thing to my happiness today is to let everything be,
to not control it . . . to be detached unless someone is going
to get hurt, then I will intervene as that also is meant to be.
So I will have a day of letting go of everything. I will be
detached, but act as I am meant to, as it is meant to be. I may
not be concerned with the things of the world but some are
concerned with me.

How Most of Us Actually Die

All my youth I thought what I wanted was to be at the top of the tree I chose to climb. Old now, just being able to tilt my head to look up at the top of a tree is happiness. Just as few know that a life without suffering is a curse, few know a gradual painless loss of breath is death. Never expected but the most usual, the last taboo not spoken about. Most of us drift slowly into and lose consciousness then simply lose our breath slowly in a day. There is no fighting for breath, no desperation, choking or any pain. So there is no need to worry about what is usually very peaceful.

Loving Detachment

I don't care if no one listens to me; it is for them I care.

Directions

Dignity with oneself, decency with individuals, detachment from all.

Mentor

Only I can monitor my behaviour and I have to watch it, stopping much of my thought as it could overwhelm me. Emotionally, I try to keep straight forward as I have enough scar tissue. Spiritually, I try and simplify everything. I believe in me being with others in stillness, talking walking, to keep alive but ignorance goes against these. It takes away my time for these.

Elders of the Tribe

Everyone sees older people as being more content but it's not always like that. Elders of the tribe usually carry the most because they carry what has accumulated over their whole life. Accidents which have maimed, illnesses and diseases which have left pain, deformity. Decades of loss of family and friends, deaths and more always expected, right up until they get to their own.

Of course elders of the tribe envy youth but not for youth itself but because it is lighter free of the heavy weight carried of all the memories of the difficult things of a life.

Then there are the fantastic things to tell the younger ones about opportunities. There is the wear and tear and the scars to show. Then excited one last time, helping them by their stories of what they found when they were there; youth's opportunity crowns the glory of elders of the tribe.

Show Don't Tell

Some mothers teach their daughters how to shop for shoes. Others show their daughter how beautiful are their own feet. Some fathers teach their sons how to fight with their fists. Others show their son the look in their eyes. Some mothers teach their daughters exactly what is best to buy. Others show their daughters what to walk by. Some fathers teach their sons all about cars. Others show their sons how to walk. Some mothers and fathers teach their children all they can about boys and girls. Others admit their own faults along the way, so their children can be free from teaching.

Stop Letting Go

What can't be held on to is let go because it lets go. We don't see it so easily. People, paths, religions, what we do can't be held on to and are let go because they let us go. Perhaps we should let go and more sensitively, allow others to let go of us. We don't let go of life; life lets go of us.

Revenge

No one can decide anything for you . . . anything because if they do, eventually you object and say no. It can be how you live, how you sleep or what you eat. If they decide how you will be disposed of, you will object by haunting them in their sleep.

Waiting Rooms

God's waiting room is not a place, it's when older people gather often on the coast, for the last days where at least the weather may be good. Some are happy with what they have done. Others regret what they have become. Some enjoy every day with no expectation. Others never happy with their situation.

Detachment

Detachment is compassion without any attachment, without any loss of love or lack of union or happiness.

Regardless Life Goes On

I had big problems as a child of chaos, but I didn't seem
to have the problems of competition with friends which
children have now. Maybe I was too pre-occupied with
dealing with chaos or maybe everyone else had too many
problems. Yes, we probably all had too much to deal with to
notice we were growing up, like sorting out bodily problems
whilst sitting learning about God.

Forever Now

I can still hear his individual voice, see her bright smiling
face, the twinkle in their eyes and hear them laughing. The
men and women who have been my companions, my mother
and father, grandparents, uncles and aunts, my friends and
colleagues. I hugged them all before they died and they
would not be disappointed if they knew I had cried. They are
together, with me now and with each other, all of us here in
stillness.

104. SILENCE

Silence's Sound

Silence starts all conversations and all talk ends in silence. If you are still, you can hear the silent pulse of the Universe inside you and everywhere, even in a busy market. Silence can answer any question and it can bring all action to stillness, most specially thought. Silence can let everything be listened to and heard in its receptive nature. Silence is the best barometer of inner stillness which thrives in silence. The effort of silence deepens stillness, whilst effortless stillness produces silence.

The loudest Sound

Absolute silence is not possible until you are dead, only when the sound of your heart beat has stopped. The silence we know but can't talk about is nothing to do with sound. It is only the noise of thinking. Thinking is the loudest sound; to man the most intrusive thing like a circling vulture endlessly waiting above us knowing we know they are there. We get attached to thoughts like emotional events instead of seeing them only like passing clouds.

We become so involved with them; we come to see them as us. Attachment to thinking can't be stopped but removing thinking's creation, the ego, by seeing it as just a collection of thoughts abolishes attachment to thinking. Then the ego is dead.

Knocking on Your Inner Door

There is nothing new to say which we haven't heard said before but there is a lot of silence knocking unheard on our inner door.

Listening

Not promoting, anyone, anything, any thought, not going anywhere, nothing to be gained, lost or found. Not having to talk, not having to listen, except for the inner sound, tuned into nothing else.

Before only the person speaking was to be understood but it's not the case anymore as the listener should be understood. The listener communicates the most, not concerned with transmitting anything other than silence, stillness, consciousness.

Our Best Friend

He was passionate about solitude, other people's right to be happy, to have the choice of a refuge from daily life. He gave what he could if you were genuine but was not interested if you weren't hungry. Most of his free time he spent working or with family, some in studying, writing and the rest in silent meditation. He left love on some hearts, some words, nothing material, like his own intangibility.

589

105. SOLITUDE

Solitude and Loneliness

Solitude is the joy of the self. Loneliness is no contact with the self. Solitude can exist in a market place. Loneliness in the company of those you know. Solitude is a union with the self. Loneliness is separation from others. Solitude is the self-connected to everything. Loneliness is an inner state of isolation. Solitude is desirable happiness. Loneliness is undesirable misery.

Solitude and the Things of Life

Solitude is an attitude of the mind detached from the things of life. It is living only in the self anywhere. Solitude is living in inner silence, surrendered to the self. You can be detached from the things of life but surrounded by people because solitude is an attitude of mind.

Solitude Seeing Where You Are

Like trying to look to the bottom of a muddy pond, in solitude, thinking settles and the past is seen clearly. In solitude, things before once missed are noticed and looked at for the first time. In solitude there is time to mourn, time to remember, salute and let go whilst looking at what is coming. Wonder is everywhere in the inner room of solitude.

The Most constant Friend

In solitude, the path seems less shaky, steadier, no looking out anymore. No more directions given or received and no one else left to be believed. My friend, my constant companion in solitude is stillness, in which silence lights the inner path.

The Stillness of solitude is the gift kings would want if it could be given. Solitude is the most priceless jewel the wealthy would desire if it could be bought. The stillness of solitude is free in exchange for the effort of looking inside.

Benefits of Solitude

The need for solitude begins when the world can't make you happy. You see that only through solitude can happiness be achieved with the world When no happiness can be got from outside, turning inwards, the curtains open on an inner life.

With others there is a confinement which can't be seen or expressed until solitude is experienced. Unlike those confined in the jungle or forest, those alone can grow deeper roots, wider branches and bear more fruit to nurture others

Solitude is the birthplace of man's best because only through struggling with oneself, one conquers all.

Practice and Effort

A mind which is not being controlled is attached to the things of life and can't get solitude. An uncontrolled mind needs tethering, and quiet to be in stillness.

Practice and effort eventually quiet the mind so there is solitude, detachment from the things of life.

I know because I don't have a choice over what I am anymore because I am lost to solitude, having been devoured.

Unswerving Solitude

Solitude seems at first a strange friend. Avoidance is the usual first greeting but you are welcomed next by sweet company. I think I will do this; I think I will do that are optional as anything goes.

A sense of urgency of enjoying the moment arrives quickly so as to savour the depth of self that only solitude can show. There are no critics; no one trying to be influential. There can be straight line inner achievement in unswerving stillness.

Detachment Inside is automatic

Detachment is not a thought or an idea which you can be because you want to. It is where you go inside when you have seen what the world is like and you are just automatically taken there by something inside.

Being in Solitude

I used to seem strange to me. At first it used to worry me but not any more. Yes, I don't feel so much part of the word as others seem to. They seem so involved, it almost makes me dizzy. I hide away, more happy on my own being quiet and still. Not so concerned with building things up for the future, I'm most my self getting on with the task at hand, especially if there isn't one.

106. STILLNESS

Happiness Inside

Happiness is what we all want. It is what we are, our nature, but we seem to have lost contact with it. It is just we cannot see it because it has become hidden inside us. Seeing it is inside, there is only one way of getting it. Going inside by turning inside.

No Final

Truth does not need confirmation. It has it already because it has everything. Truth does not need to be acknowledged or written about because it is complete. It is us who need to see truth, us who need to acknowledge it to confirm it. Then we have to follow it to be fully it, which means everything is secondary to it.

Being Still

Thinking is not being still. Being still is the conscious effort of stillness of no thoughts.

All We Can Ever Be

Not thinking about being still and just being still is the best we can be.

Active Stillness

Thoughts cannot make you happy no matter how good or
how long we have them because thinking must be replaced
with action as we have to be what we have seen. Only the
masterly inactively of being makes us happy.

Unity of truth

This is that. That is this is truth.

No One to Go to Except Inside

Deep inside, unaided, I stand before you, asking for help
and protection. Mercifully hear and answer me. Inside in the
stillness, the help, the protection, the kindness and love.

Eternal Stillness

Since seventeen, when for the first time I was able to
be conscious in the peace and bliss of stillness, nothing
has changed. The world with its people, buildings and
landscapes looks different on the outside but on the inside
everything is exactly the same in stillness.

Non Dual Duality

It is only by seeing there is self and not self and everything is
either self or not self that everything is seen as self.

Our Room

Our parents told us to keep our room clean and to keep it tidy. Nothing there we didn't need but plenty room for us to move around. Later we automatically applied this to know how to manage ourselves and to know the nature of our self which was left for us to decide.

No direct instructions, just an expectation of wanting the best for our self. Nothing we don't need except a simple room with light and shades, space and comfort silent and private. A place where all talk ends in silence all activities end in stillness.

The room our parents helped us with is the most private royal room, the inner sanctum. If we have lost our way, the treasure map to happiness is simply inside us in thoughtless stillness. It is subtle because just as there are no words for silence there are none for stillness.

The Task

Of all man's best thoughts the most important is not of saving himself by transporting himself to other planets or of prolonging his life by medicine. Of all man's best actions the most important is not saving himself by talks of peace to stop wars or ensuring the survival of the Earth.

Man's most important influence on his thinking and his actions is to stop both to reveal in himself stillness which is consciousness.

Incidentals

Incidental to being alive are prolonged physical ill health, being attacked by our thoughts, disturbances from within by frustration and disillusionment, loss of faith, hopelessness helplessness, bereavements.

The best about us is our sense of something permanent; our sense of that which always is, our ability to experience this in stillness as consciousness which eclipses everything we can think.

Actively still

Having more words does not improve us as more words don't help us understand ourselves or others. Only listening and looking do.

More words do not let us do things better. More activity does not help us understand what we or others are doing; only stillness does. Silence and Stillness speak louder than words or action.

More is achieved by being silent and still than words or activity.

Not Yet

Have you not seen what this life is like? Already you have let so many days go by without being still. Happiness is experienced when all he senses are overpowered by stillness.

Paradise Within

Contentment, the simple luxury of no pain, of idleness
within, with no shame or guilt only stillness . . . happiness.
Everything is sensed when all the senses are overpowered by
stillness.

The Ultimate State

Does what we are make any difference apart from being our
true self in stillness. Being the self that is in everything is
our greatest accomplishment. Nothing can be better because
being happy in our self cannot be compared. Celebrity
status, praise and recognition of intellectual eloquence are an
expression of external superficial happiness.

Assumed Reality

In meditation, stillness shows us as abstract without form
which we imagine, then draw and paint as the divine.
Then in meditation stillness shows us more, that there is
no difference between the self, the image and the divine.
Stillness unifies all.

Enough

What is next could be anything or anyone or somewhere
different but no more illusion to keep me fooled about the
truth. No more hallucination to trick my senses to invent
another reality. It needs to be simple, honest stillness.

The Refuge

How do we cope when we are turned upside down when we lose our bearings rudderless, unable to anchor ourselves to anything secure. Where our anchor lies most secure is in the stillness inside, not subject to winds of change. Central and still, not moved to the side. Who can take away from us what can only be seen by us, only known from where we have grown.

Self Absorbed

I have to leave this world frequently, well, most of the time because I have to be what I really am, disconnected, detached in solitude and stillness, my true self.

Serenity

In the stillness experienced just by sitting on your own with closed or open eyes, silence becomes a friend. In sitting on your own, everything about you and others can be fully seen and understood. There is no gossip on our own as all inner chatter is reduced to silence so that stillness allows serenity

Pushed and Pulled

The world pushes me away and I am drawn inside to stillness, consciousness . . . then I see the world.

107. WHO HAS HELPED SO FAR?

Unification

Religions point to seeing our inner self as our higher power inside as God. Most simply this is consciousness of 'I am.' This can be seen in the words from the east and the west over the last three thousand years.

Pre-Religion

The Pashupati Seal is a soapstone seal discovered at the Mohenjo-daro archaeological site of the Indus Valley Civilisation.

It is estimated to have been carved between 2350-2000 BCE and is thought to be the earliest prototype of the God Shiva.

The seal shows a seated cross-legged figure in the yogic 'padmasama' meditation posture with arms pointing downwards. It is important because it is one of the first communications from our ancient ancestors which reflects the stillness of silently looking inwards.

Hinduism

'Netti Netti' (Brihadaranyaka Upanishad 2.3.6 800-600 BC)
'Netti Netti' means, 'Neither this neither this,' which helps the mind to constantly disidentify with anything other than that which is everything.

Judaism

When Moses asked God for his name he answered, 'I Am That I Am. Thus shalt you say unto the children of Israel, I Am has sent me to you.'
(Exodus 3:14. 1400 BC)

Jehovah means I am, so knowing the self, God is known as they are taken to be the same.

Ancient Greeks

'Know the self.'
(Temple of Apollo, Delphi, Greece 500-300 BC)

Christianity

'Be still and know that I am God.' (Psalm 46)
'The kingdom of God is within you.' (Luke 17:20-21)

Adi Shankaracharya

Even after the Truth has been realised, there remains that strong, obstinate impression that one is still an ego - the agent and experiencer. This has to be carefully removed by living in a state of constant identification with the supreme non-dual Self. Full Awakening is the eventual ceasing of all the mental impressions of being an ego.

"The fool takes the reflection of the sun in the water of a pot to be the sun; the wise man eliminates pot, water, and reflection and knows the sun in the sky as it really is, single and unaffected, but illuminating all three. In the same way the fool through error and misperception, identifies himself with the ego and its reflected light experienced through the medium of the intellect. The wise and discriminating man eliminates body, intellect, and reflected light of consciousness and probes deeply into his real Self which illuminates all three while remaining uniform in the ether of the heart. Thereby he realises the eternal witness which is absolute knowledge, illuminating all three."

(Vivekachudamani. 700-750 AD)

William Shakespeare

'This above all-to thine own self be true.' (Hamlet, Act 1, Scene 111)

Ramana Maharshi

'Your duty is to be and not to be this or that. "I AM that I AM" sums up the whole truth. The method is summarised in "Be still." What does "stillness" mean? It means "destroy yourself." Because any form or shape is the cause of trouble. Give up the notion that "I am so and so." (Talks with Ramana Maharshi 363)

108. Introduction

Meditation Preamble

What am I here for? . . . To be happy inside.

Who am I? . . . I am not thoughts. I am not this bundle of thoughts, the ego.

I am that I am
Be still and know that I am God

My default state is I am ('I-I')

My consciousness of myself known to me as 'I' is the same as everything, which is also known as 'I'.
My consciousness of myself known to me as 'I' is the same as the Eternal, which is also known as 'I'.

The 'I' which is known to me is the same as the eternal 'I' which I am part of and is also me, so I am 'I' and I am also 'I'.

I am conscious of them being one and the same 'I-I'
Who I am is consciousness, which is 'I-I'

INDEX

∞

∞

∞

∞

∞

∞

∞

∞

Printed in Great Britain
by Amazon

63210478R00383